INDIAN: HEALTH SCENARIO
PERSPECTIVES AND DIMENSIONS

INDIAN: HEALTH SCENARIO

PERSPECTIVES AND DIMENSIONS

Edited by

G.R. KRISHNAMURTHY
AWADHESH KUMAR SINGH
SHAILENDRA KUMAR BAJPAI

In Association with
Ananya Institute for Development
Research and social Action, Lucknow

SERIALS PUBLICATIONS
NEW DELHI

First Published – 2008

ISBN: 978-81-8387-156-3

Published by

SERIALS PUBLICATIONS
4830/24, Prahlad Street, Ansari Road
Darya Ganj, New Delhi-110002 (India)
Phone : 23245225 Fax : 91-11-23272135
E-mail: serials@satyam.net.in

CONTENTS

Perface ix

Contributors xiii

PART-1—PERSPECTIVES

1. Emerging Health Perspective in Urban India 3
 • *P.S. Tripathi & Mukulika Hitkari*
2. Customers' Satisfaction in Hospitals 19
 • *Nishant Sinha & Tarun Gupta*
3. Health Communication: The Concept and Practices 28
 • *Shailendra Kumar*
4. Gender, Development and Women's Health in India 47
 • *Rekha K. Jadhav*
5. Disparities in Juvenile Sex Ratios in India: An Analysis 53
 • *D. Pulla Rao*
6. Trends of Sex Ratio in India: The Disappearing Girl Child 66
 • *Anand Bhaskar*
7. Fertility Issues for India 84
 • *R. Meenakshi*
8. Reproductive and Sexual Health Education: A Study of Adolescents in Lucknow 95
 • *Sanjay Pandey & Ajay Kumar Pandey*

PART-2—DIMENSIONS

9. Social and Ecological Aspects of Health–Anthropological Appraisal on Tribal Women of Wayand, Kerala 109
• *Bindu Ramachandran*

10. Demography, Socio-economic and Health Conditions of the Four Primitive Tribes in Nilgiri Hills of Tamilandu 121
• *T.S. Naidu & G. Palanisamy*

11. Anthropology and HIV/AIDS: Critical Issues and Challenges in A Vulnerable Region of North Bengal 145
• *Samar Kumar Biswas*

12. Household Level Impact of HIV and AIDS: A Study of High Prevalence States In India 172
• *Roli Misra*

13. Development of Primitive Tribal Groups in Karanataka: Some Preliminary Observations 183
• *Nanjunda D.C.*

14. Relevance of Traditional Healing Centers and Treatment of the Possessed 195
• *Shobha Devi R. Patil & G.R. Krishnamurthy*

PART-3—APPROACHES

15. Role of Shirisha–*Albizia lebbeck* (Linn.) Willd.) in the Management of Tamak Swasa (Bronchial Asthma) 219
• *Ramji Singh, S.K. Singh, O.P. Singh, Shriprakash, K.K. Rai, R.K. Tiwari & Aruna Devi*

16. "Clinical Trial on Guduchi Chitraka Yoga in the Management of Madhumeha (*Diabetes mellitus*)" 234
• *Ramji Singh, S.K. Singh, Shriprakash, R.K. Tiwari & Aruna Devi*

17. Coping Stress: The Mantra of Success 244
• *Anjali Ganesh & G.R. Krishanamoorthy*

18. Reviewing Organizational Stress and Climate: A Case Study of Government Doctors 254
• *Taruna & Archana Singh*

19. Why Does The Primary Health System Fail? 267
• *M.M. Verma*

20. Problems in Social Rehabilitation of Disabled 276
• *S.P. Pandey & A.K. Singh*

21. Need for Rehabilitation of Disabled 303
• *S.P. Pandey & O.P. Singh*

22. Equipping Dais for a Healtheir Tomorrow 319
• *Rameshwwari Pandya*

Index 339

PREFACE

Health in India is a complex subject. Sometimes, it is too bewildering and often staggering. A country with contradictions, India hardly spent 4.6% of G.N.P. on health during 1990's. The spending situation has not improved much even during the first decade of 21st century'. On the other, India has the latest and most sophisticated Information Technology in the world. However millions of people in rural India, still do not get the benefit of modern medicine specially in remote areas and tribal belts. Of course we have launched an ambitious network of Primary Health Care Centres (P.H.C's) throughout rural India. But unfortunately these have failed miserably due to various factors: lack of doctors, lack of medicines, lack of basic facilities etc. Still rural India suffers from chronic diseases like Asthma, T.B. etc. On the other, diabetes and other infection diseases pervade India, untreated and untackled.

Most of the health facilities and hospitals are located in urban India except in Kerala state. For instance about 60 % of the hospitals are in urban India, while 32 % are only in rural India. The national average population for one bed in 1993 was 1,412 people. Infact in states like Bihar and Madhya Pradesh there was only one bed for around 3,000 people. Coming to the selected diseases causing death, Asthma and Bronchitis account for roughly 60 to 70 % deaths, while heart attacks leading to 45 to 50% of deaths. Every 3rd person in the south reports to be diabetic. Coming to expenditure, both centre and state governments, spend roughly 30 %, while households have to bear 45 to 50 % of expenditure. However hospitalization cases per 1,000 populations are few in number, that is., 7 to 10 % (ranging from rural to urban India). Government hospitals including P.H.C's hardly cater to 20 % patients in rural India, while to 25 % population in urban India. Private practitioners treat around 60 to 75 % patients both in rural and urban India. Number of doctors per lakh population is hardly 48, while ratio of nurses is still low to be 45 per lakh of population. Compare these figures with 252 doctors and 742 nurses per lakh in developed countries. Then one really understands the Indian realities of health!! However these statistics do not fully scan the Indian health scenario in flesh and blood.

II

This book attempts to present a kaleidoscopic picture of health scenario in India and its important dimensions. Special focus was given to the fast emerging health perspectives in the first part of the book. First paper in the part one discusses the emerging health perspectives in urban India, while second dwells upon the concept of customer satisfaction in hospitals and the problems confronting the hospitals. The paper on health communication, focuses on this vital but missing link, in the health care scenario. Remaining papers in the part one concentrate on women's health, gender discrimination in health care and on the disappearing girl child due to the bias in sex ratio and also on the fertility issues essential to India. Last paper portrays the scenario of reproductive and sexual health education. Second part in the book, essentially concentrates on some of the important dimensions of health. First two papers discuss the aspects of health among tribals in Kerala and Tamil Nadu, the most neglected sections by health care system. Other two papers write about the tribal groups in Karnataka and the relevance of traditional healing centres in the treatment of the possessed. Two most important papers in this part, throw light on HIV/AIDS in highly prevalent states and including North Bengal, all as part of the frightening health scenario in India! As HIV/AIDS is spreading like wildfire in Indian subcontinent, we have chosen these papers to highlight on this disease and its impact on our over all health scenario and national expenditure on health.

Third part in the book spells out some of the approaches to tackle the mass-scale health problems. The first paper advocates tackling mal-nutrition as an essential component of women's health and empowerment programme. Two papers in this section, concentrate on the application and practice of alternative medicine, that is Ayurveda, for treating Asthma, (A killer disease in India) and diabetes which are rampent in most parts of India. As the modern medicine could not reach the most parts of rural India, for its lack of doctors, and prohibitive cost, the only alternative is to treat the mass-diseases like diabetes, Asthma and infections with alternative medical treatment. This is the only possible way to tackle India's mass scale health problems. Absence of health insurance in the country further aggravates the cost factor of modern medicine.

Other two papers in this part concentrate on stress-coping and stress treatment. As India is living in a post-industrial stage society, and as the life pace has increased enormously in present day India, the all fast-life professionals, executives, successful-people and rich-people are becoming stress prone. Hence the paper on stress coping, it spells out the success mantra without stress. The second paper discusses the organizational climate which contributes to the stress in organisations particularly to the government doctors and spells out some remedies for the same. The next paper raises fundamental question, "why does the primary health system fail"? As our P.H.C's could not serve the targeted population in rural India and as they could not fulfill the objectives for which they were created, this question is highly relevant. The paper also spells out some insights and measures to redeem the system of P.H.C's in India from its limitations. Two paper highlight the problems of disabled and focus on social rehabilitation of physically and mentally challenged persons. The last paper focuses on strengthening traditional system of healthcare.

Throughout this book we have followed the most comprehensive connotation for health. As per WHO "Health does not mean mere absence of disease/sickness; but the total well being of a person at physical/mental and social levels". This definition is the real criteria to judge the health of a nation particularly India.

This book is not a compendium on health. Neither it is comprehensive. However, it presents the fragraments of a total vision of health in India and its emerging perspectives and important dimensions. The book gives silhouette of the health scenario nay birds-eye-view on the subject. It is a book on health not on health care. It is the task of another volume to present scenario of health care in India.

25th December, 2007

G.R. Krashnamoorthy
A.K. Singh
S.K. Bajpai

CONTRIBUTORS

P.S. Tripathi; Reader, Department of Economics, DBS College, Kanpur.

Mukulika Hitkari; Reader, Department of Economics, DGPG College, Kanpur.

Nishant SinhaTarun Gupta; Jaipuria Institute of Management, Lucknow.

Shailendra Kumar; Ph.D. Scholar, Department of Sociology, University of Lucknow.

Rekha K. Jadhav; Lecturer, Department of Women Studies Karnataka University, Dharwad.

D. Pulla Rao; Associate Professor, Depatment of Co-operation and Applied Economics, Andhra University, Visakhapatnam, A.P.

Ananda Bhaskar; Senior Research Fellow, Department of Sociology, Lucknow University, Lucknow.

R. Meenakshi; Reader, Department of Economics, Sri Sarada College, Salem, T.N.

Sanjay PandeyAjay Kumar Pandey; Social Scientists, Pt. G.B. Pant Institute of Studies in Rural Development, Lucknow.

Bindu Ramachandran; Lecturer, Department of Anthropology, Kannur University, Thalasserry Campus, Kerala.

T.S. Naidu; Dean, School of Social Sciences and International Studies, Pondicherry University, Puducherry.

G. Palanisamys; Research Associate, Department of Anthropology, Pondicherry University, Puducherry.

Samar Kumar Biswas; Lecturer, Department of Anthropology, North Bengal University, Darjeeling, West Bengal.

Roli Misra; Department of Economics, DBS College, Kanpur.

Nanjunda D.C.; Director, M.N. Srinivas Centre for Tribal Research and Development, Kushalanagar Post, Coorg District, Karnataka.

Shobha Devi R. Patil; Head, Department of Social Work, Karnatak University, Dharwad.

G.R. Krishnamurthy; Director, TIME Business School, Mangalore, India.

Ramji Singh, S.K. Singha, O.P. Singh, Shri Prakash, K.K. Rai, R.K. Tiwari and Aruna Devi; Central Research Institute (Ayurveda), CCRAS, Lucknow.

Shri Prakash, R.K. Tiwari, Aruna Devi; Central Research Institute (Ayurveda), CCRAS, Lucknow.

Anjali Ganesh; Assistant Professor, TIME Business School, Mangalore.

G.R. Krishnamurthy; Director, TIME Business School, Mangalore.

Taruna; Birla Institute of Technology, Jaipur.

Archana Singh; Department of Social Work, Lucknow University, Lucknow.

M.M. Varma; Reader, Department of Social Work, Mahatma Gandhi Kashi Vidyapeeth, Varanasi, U.P.

S.P. Panday; Director G.B Pant Institute of Studies in Rural Development, Lucknow.

A.K. Singh; Director, Ananya Institute of Development Research and Social Action, Lucknow.

O.P. Singh; Associate Prof. Department of Community Medicine KG Medical University, Lucknow.

Rameshwari Pandya; Department of Home Science Extension and Communication, M.S. University, Baroda.

PART–I
PERSPECTIVES

1

EMERGING HEALTH PERSPECTIVE IN URBAN INDIA

P.S. Tripathi & Mukulika Hitkari

The Present Research Work-based specifically on State of Health among URBAN POOR–is an endeavour to draw special mention in pretext of the underlying fact that Urban Poverty much exceeds Rural Poverty, thereby adversely affecting manpower skills which could have been better streamlined into productive economic activities. The study is based on Eight Empowered Action Group (EAG) States viz.–UP, MP, Rajasthan, Bihar, Orissa, Jharkhand, Chhattisgarh and Uttaranchal-reflecting weak demographic trends.

For the first time, comparative study of UP, MP and Rajasthan forms an integral mention later in the Paper where Environmental conditions are, ascertainably, highly susceptible to disease and health of urban poor.

The NRHM (2005-2012)-acknowledging non-availability and substantial under utilisation of PHC (Public Health Care) Facilities in Urban Areas-has constituted a Task Force focussing specifically on EAG states which perform abysmally much below the National Averages on various Health Indicators (NSSO estimates, 2005). Requisitely, a proper functioning mechanism needs to be stringently developed for cause of Environmental Awareness; Lesser Risk Exposure to vulnerable conditions; and Facilitating preparation of Area Specific

Programmes prioritisingly emphasising on health status/care of UP, MP and Rajasthan.

The MoHFW (Ministry of Health and Family Welfare) has formulated guidelines for Development of City Level Urban Slum Health Projects in Overall Management Cities with population of 1 lakh and above. In lieu of pursuing the Cause of improving state of Urban Poverty and promoting Urban Health, the MoHFW has urged State Governments. to identify Priority Districts and initiate UHPs (Urban Health Programmes) so as to augment Infrastructural Development coupled with Community Linkages–mainly in EAG states.

HEALTH PARAMETERS IN EXISTING SCENARIO

Regarded as a foundational determinant of HDI (Human Development Index) and PQLI (Physical Quality of Life Index) – necessary for economic development and termed as a "MERIT GOOD" in Public Finance parlance, Health does not signify economic growth alone neither is directly proportional to Per Capita Income at all times. Not pertaining to any abstract condition, 'Health connotes a condition wherein human potential is fully utilised for the satisfaction of basic human needs'. Discernibly, analytical and survey-based studies on health scenario in India have reflected a strategic and a positive approach towards planning and facilitation of health care services. But 'Implementation' is gradually losing its stronghold. The National Health Policy (NHP) inclusively has parameters relating to (1) Medical Education; (2) Inter-sectoral Co-ordination; and (3) Interface between Indigenous and modern medicine.

Though Health Issue prioritisingly is dealt with concern by the Govt. in the competitive scenario, yet the state governments should, responsibly, accord greater measure of Attention plus Resource Mobilisation-more so for the Eight Empowered Action Group States (EAG) like UP, MP and Rajasthan (Dealt with in this Paper). In the above context, a major step treaded is adoption of a 'Project for orienting Parliamentarians on Population and Health Development Issue' launched in MP and Rajasthan. Laggingly, UP needs to focus on it largely for cost benefit results for which the project is eagerly awaiting green signal.

A multi-dimensional area of developmental planning, Health can not be measured in terms of Western Paradigm where economic growth is sufficient as an end in itself. Rather Health Status pertains to entailing access to publicly funded Social services to actually lend conceptual meaning to the term "Development"-focussing more on the "Enhancement of Human Capabilities". Thus Health Care/Status in its broader consensus implies not Income – Poverty Alleviation but Social Inputs and Standard of Living. The illustration below encompasses several socio-economic indicators in explaining strategies for developing widening parameters of Health.

Development Strategies in Health Sector

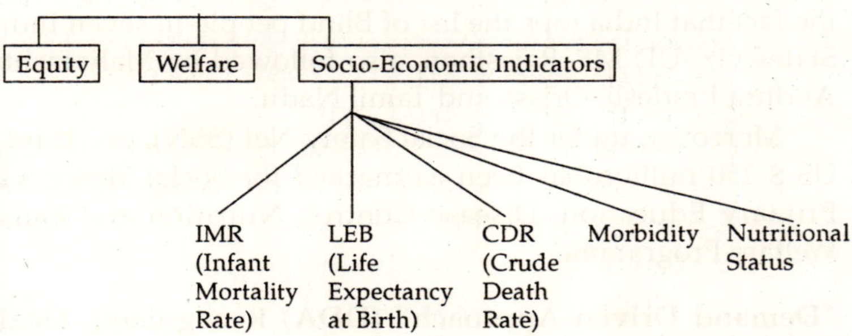

In a nutshell, Health parameters should have positive connectivity with 'Reprioritisation of Resources' with Cost Effective techniques and studied in conjunction with various quantitative and qualitative variables (Social Inputs) on which Heath Care depends, viz.- Nutrition, Per Capita Income, Water Supply, Sanitation, Housing Amenities, Community Health Services, Receptibility of people in availing health services, Education, Climate, PBPL (Percentage of People Below Poverty Line), Structure of the Economy, Number of Personnel and Household Characteristics and Environmental Conditions. Derailment of any of the above Social Input/Variable would question the efforts of the State Governments, especially in LISs (Low Income States) and EAG States.

Defining Role in External Assistance (WHO & World Bank)

WHO is the main UN Agency collaborating with countries like India in promoting and developing Health Care Facilities-the latter regularly contributing to the former. The Health Agency has categorically dictated the Governments to consider Health as not merely absence of disease or infirmity but a state of complete physical, mental and social well-being–so as to ensure optimal abilities, productive capacities and work performance.

World Bank (IBRD) has displayed considerable interest in aiding Health Projects for control of Leprosy, Blindness and Communicable diseases. Its implementation requires undergoing constant monitoring mechanism. Major Programme implementation is related to Blindness Control-keeping in mind the fact that India tops the list of Blind people-in seven Indian States viz.-UP, MP, Rajasthan, also followed by Maharashtra, Andhra Pradesh, Orissa and Tamil Nadu.

Moreover, under the Social Safety Net (SSN), one-third of US $ 250 million has been earmarked for Social Sector, viz.-Primary Education, Disease Control, Nutrition and Family Welfare Programme.

"Demand Driven Approach" (DDA) Recognising Health Care in U.P.

A commendable feature undertaken by Uttar Pradesh State-with lesser favourable demographic trends-in association with the MoHFW (Ministry of Health and Family Welfare) organised the first SWASTHYA MELA at Mathura from 17th to 20th September 2000. The success count can be manifested in the fact that over 30,000 persons underwent a complete health check-up coupled with Free Single Window Services for basic health care and Awareness through Indian System of Medicines being made accessible. Such Plan should be promotionally encouraged in EAG states specially and also strictly be held on an annual basis-a step towards strengthening socio-economic balances being driven by basic demand for health improvement.

Another significant stride taken by the State Government is the SWAJAL PROJECT. Natured by its paradigm shift in terms of delivery of sustainable water supply and environmental sanitation, the project investments are designed to test various policy options and to improve knowledge, attitude and practices about the linkages between health and hygiene providing high water supply service levels. With an expansionary approach, the 'Swajal Project derives its strength from being demand responsive and community driven'-taking into cognizance gender differences and catering to their needs accordingly.

Followingly, the State Governments of MP, Rajasthan and EAG states should extensively develop and Flag-off 'SAP' (Strategic Action Plan) for this Pilot Project towards Health Sector Reforms and ensuring :

- Quantity
- Quality
- Equity
- Reliability
- Coverage
- Accessibility of Services

The implementation would ensure participatory role of the community-mainly women folk-as well as NGOs in adequate Planning and improving water status on a Demand Driven Approach. Such a Programme could be aided by World Bank and UNDP at the initial stages.

OUTLAY DIVERSION TRENDS ON HEALTH

The Level of Public Expenditure on health in India is among the lowest in the world-more so it is observingly much less than the requisite norms count in low per capita income States of U.P., Madhya Pradesh and Rajasthan-where the case study for this Research Paper is being focussed. As per the UNDP Human Development Report 2004, India ranks 173 among 177 countries in terms of public outlay on health. Less fortunately at 0.9% of GDP, public expenditure on health in India is also the lowest among South Asian Countries. Viewing this, not only judicious qualitative spending but also increasing the need-based level of outlay on health should be a major policy statement in the present global scenario-which has created socio-economic divide alongwith regional disparities. In other words, 'Perfect Positive Correlation' is necessary between Expenditure Allocation and Expenditure Utilisation (EA∝EU)-so as to gradually overcome nutritional/productivity health deficits and cost liabilities. As a pilot programme, the 'National Health Policy' 2002; the Common Minimum Programme of the UPA Government; 2004; The 'National Rural Health Mission' 2005-have all endorsed the need to increase health expenditure imperatively to about 2 to 3% of GDP by 2010.

The following chart reflects the Statewise Requirement of resources for providing Basic Health Services by 2009-2010 (as percentage of GSDP) of EAG (Eight Empowered Action Group) States:

Chart-1

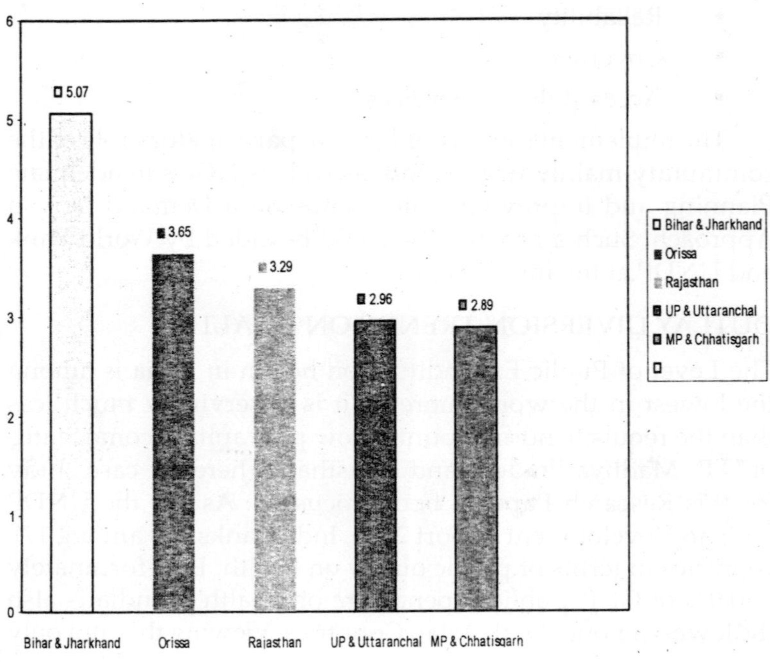

Estimates Suggest that in Low Income States (LISs) the requirement of resources for providing even the minimum health services is much more than 2 to 3% of their GSDP, Around 65% of the total shortfall in expenditure requirements to provide basic services in the health sector has been found to be in the States of U.P., Bihar, Madhya Pradesh, Orissa and Rajasthan.

Another feature which needs to be stressed upon is 'Additional Resource Requirements' (ARRs) for health sector. Very often the EAG States have limited capacity to generate additional resources for meeting health outlay requisites. The Chart below exhibits the Distribution of ARRs across the EAG States for meeting Basic Health Services by 2009-2010 :

Chart-2

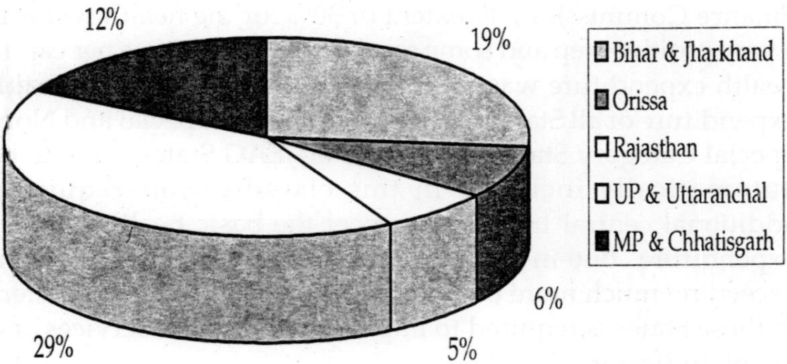

The above displayed states with additional health resource requirements are those which have the poorest health indicators in the country and, therefore, drag down the level of health achievement as well as standard of living. With the mid-term appraisal of the Tenth Five Year Plan highlighting that India is off-track in terms of attaining the MDGs (Millennium Development Goals) and Tenth Plan objectives, increasing the level of public outlay in these states has assumed indispensable significance. To be more specific in State estimations, most of the existing resources are used up in meeting their committed liabilities towards wages, salaries, interest payments and pensions. As per the alarming revelations for the 3 states on whom this case study is based, the trend shows that these are the maximum affected Regions with unplanned utilisation of resources.

Table 1
Revenue Use

State	*% of Revenue used up in Committed liabilities*
Rajasthan	95%
Uttar Pradesh	85%
Madhya Pradesh	75%

In a parlance, the writing is very clear on the wall i.e. These low income states should resort to re-prioritisation of expenditures, exigently, directed towards the health sector.

The "Equalisation grants" provided by the TFC (Twelfth Finance Commission)–to extent of 30% for the health sector is a very positive step and some respite for States whose per capita health expenditure was lower than average per capita health expenditure of all States viably applicable for Special and Non-Special Category States. Therefore, the EAG States come to be automatically included in this classification–requiring additional central transfers to meet the basic health services expenditure. But–in real sense of economic growth–amount exceeding much more than 30% pertaining to central transfers in these States is required to improve basic health services and health indicators.

It is to be noted that equally important is the 'Mode' of transfer of resources from Centre to the States-to be not "General" but in form of "Specific" purpose transfers targetted at the health sector only.

Health Care vis-a-vis Urban Poor Syndrome-A Tri-State Comparative Study.

This paper attempts Primary & Secondary data based Health Studies in the most wanted demographically unfavourable States of Uttar Pradesh, Madhya Pradesh and Rajasthan-specifically out of the Eight EAG States-and the requirements/policy programmes for 'Urban Poor' which stand out worsely more demand driven than the health state of the rural poor. Therefore, the analysis in this segment is factored by following Similarities and Dissimilarities (and State-Specific Highlights adopted to be discussed followingly). Health of the Urban Poor needs to be reiteratingly catered to owing to the following facts:

- Uttar Pradesh (UP) is the state with the largest population; Rajasthan is the state with the largest Area; and Madhya Pradesh (MP) is the state topping the Chart incredibly in Urban Poverty exceeding Rural Poverty to the maximum extent possible;
- Environmental Health is associated with deficient conditions and lack of awareness greatly in these States.
- Water Crisis (Supply, Quality, Accessibility) is the crucial demanding issue in these States defining urban destitution.
- UP, MP and Rajasthan-all have very weak and unfavourable demographic indicators as compared to other States in India-followed by immense socio-economic disparities;
- Lack of Educational Standards and less optimised implementation of Health Programmes.
- Health situation is extremely low/worse-off as compared to the National Average.

Urban Health Status in Rajasthan–Policy Highlights

In the state where 1/5th of Urban Populaton of 26.78 lakh live Below Poverty Line (BPL), the NFHS (National Family Health Survey) reveals extremely low health indicators. Formulating its own policy level mandate relating to LEB, Infant Mortality and Maternal Health issues, its significance was evidently recognised in policy strategies for urban poor being incorporated in State Population Policy. Policy highlights in context of Urban Poverty are:

- Prominent issue placements in policies include Housing, Land Tenure, Employment, Slum improvement, Women's Empowerment, Food Security and Drinking Water Supply-as these impinge on the health of the population.

- Strengthening services of 'PHCCs' (Primary Health Care Centres) and 'Community Linkages' for streamlining the developmental process-especially for Women and BPL Urbans recognized as "Vulnerable Groups".
- Special attention to Environmental Health conditions-characterised by problems relating to lack of availability of basic health services, unhygienic sanitation, Irregular Garbage Collection, Presence of Insects/Mosquitoes and Overcrowding making ailments prone to environment.
- Role of Private Sector towards Health Improvement is furthermore gaining support by the State-The initiative undertaken so as to comprehend the level of participation of this Sector for telling results in State of Urban poor.
- NRHM (National Rural Health Mission) provisions aim to bring health services closer to slum dwellers in urban areas.
- A major initiative is the establishment of "MRS" (Medicare Relief Society) in 1995-under whose umbrella latest Health Detection and Treatment Facilities are made available unhindranced. 25% of total Income acquired is utilised in providing Free Medicines to Urban BPL possessing MRS Card plus Health Services free of cost to Widows, Orphans, Senior Citizens above 70 yrs. and to prisoners.

Urban Health Status in Madhya Pradesh–Policy Highlights

The State where the proportion of population Below Poverty Line (BPL) is second highest in India as per NHDR (National Human Development Report 2001)-Urban Madhya Pradesh ranks as low as 28th among 32 States in HDI terms (much lower than UP and Rajasthan). Policy Highlights in context of Urban Poverty are:

- Separate Policy line up for Urban Poor is related not only with slum dwelling but also "Slum Clusters" e.g. in re-settlement and unauthorised colonies.
- Formulating its own policy mandate, the Govt. envisaged a dedicated 'PHI' (Primary Health Infrastructure) and a sustainable 'SDS' (Service Delivery System).
- Private Sector role still needs to be expanded in Health Care Services (which is currently underplayed).
- Government has been encouraging Environmental Health for greater demand and access to RCH (Reproductive and Child Health Care) Services for a specific health-oriented vision in the Low Income State to be achieved by 2011.
- The State Government has announced 11th May as the "Population Stabilisation Day."
- Policy for Installation of Sophisticated Medical Technology in Public Sector Hospitals by aid of Private Sector (in likes of Rajasthan and extensive need in U.P.).

Urban Health Status in Uttar Pradesh–Policy Highlights

The Single State housing largest number of Urban poor (almost 30% of Population in State would be residing in urban areas by 2016-an example in itself) and underserved by basic education, its health conditions are as Bad as those of Rural population. Alarmingly, nearly 3/4th of Urban low income and 2/3rd of medium income households still derive their drinking water from Public Taps/Hand Pumps. The programmes targetted definitely surpass their implementation-a serious concern. According to NFHS (National Family Health Survey), UP ranks 2nd only to Bihar in terms of incidence of Under Nutrition of children below 5 yrs-a dismal picture-that, too, more in Southern and Central Regions as shown in the Table.

Table 2
Proportion of Urban Poor in U.P.

Region	*% of Urban Population Below Poverty Line (BPL)*
Western	30
Central	33.4
Eastern	31.1
Southern	40.9

Policy Highlights in Context of Urban Poverty are:

- Special focus on reduction of regional urban disparities-mainly in Southern and Central regions of U.P–as part of awareness towards Environmental Health (Access to Safe Water and Sanitation are basic human rights and form indispensable components of Public Health Care).
- 'VAMBAY' (Valmiki Ambedkar Awas Yojana), 2001 and 'NSDP' (National Slum Development Programme) aim at planned programming for Slum Dwellers alongwith provision of physical infrastructural amenities.
- Govt. has formulated its own policy mandate pertaining to Mother and Child Health towards beneficial attainments till 2016 (long run target policy compared to MP and Rajasthan).
- Focus on 'UHPs' (Urban Health Posts) as a novel concept with adequate space, equipment and trained personnel for providing Door to Door health service in urban slums.
- Innovating methods of social marketing would be used for promotion and making health products in slums.
- By view of Tri-State Comparison, UP Govt. has emphasised the most on conducting surveys for revelation of Stark State of Urban poverty and improvements thereon. Also motivation is to ascertain the existing differences between Urban Poor and Rest of the Urban population.

- The NRHMs "Janani Suraksha Yojana "extends cash benefit of Rs. 600/- to urban poor women for delivering in health institutions.
- To effectively tackle malnutrition problem, Government has formulated the 'SPAN' (State Plan of Action on Nutrition) for 0-3 yrs. age group- aiming at Reducing:

Table 3
Degree of Malnutrition

Degree of Malnutrition	*% in 2000*	*% of targetted for 2010*
Moderate	52%	20%
Severe	5%	1%

- Major thrust on elimination of cases in vitamin A Deficiency.
- Finally, "Innovation Fund" and "Adolescent Girl Scheme" are also underway to focus on state of Urban Poor.

POLICY CONCLUSIONS ON HEALTH OF URBAN POOR

As inevitable from the study revelations about Urban Health, the subject of Urban Poverty surpassing even the problem of Rural Poverty in the global scenario is a crucially prevalent issue-needing perusal. Though the Government is aware of social equity and welfare existing in a non-judicious mode in most of the States even with justified per capita incomes, yet intensity of the problem of Urban Health Care Services is more evident in Eight EAG States including UP, MP and Rajasthan– which bear greater disadvantage in context of urban people living below poverty line owing to increasing Urbanization and Industrialization. Even the Pilot programmes undertaken by the NRHM, NHP, NPP and Tenth Five Year Plan have not made much headway both qualitatively and quantitatively.

Essential reinforcement of health care services have their manifestation in 3 factors to be considered:

(i) Though 3% of GDP is prescribed for health spending, the requirement is substantially higher in eight EAG states mainly UP, MP and Rajasthan.

(ii) Spending on Committed Liabilities be compulsorily mitigated and ARRs (Additional Resource Requirements) be augmented to meet health care services in urban areas.

(iii) Health Care–a fundamental ingredient of LICs (Low Income Countries)-should be made a policy imperative.

The social Inputs e.g. Education, Health, Water Supply, Environment, Medical facilities, Demographic trends, etc. need to be appropriately harmonised and co-coordinated for improved results in alleviation of Urban Poverty. Furthermore, more possibilities be explored for assembling urban health related data through Survey/Studies on District, State and Nation wide basis. It should also be remembered that mere augmentation of resources and allocation of funds would not serve the purpose/defined goal. Rather, "micro" level approach is the buzz call-i.e. Area-Specific priority programmes-to enable co-ordinated functioning mechanism.

Political involvement in Urban Health Sector would only be a squandering exercise. Need is for local level participatory role–undertaken as a Drive towards Health Awareness among Urban poor–in cooperation with District Authorities in the EAG states specially.

However, a Pilot step in EAG States pertains to Developing MMMHPs (Model Municipal Managed Health Programmes)-Rajasthan being a torch bearer in this regard. The programmes are taken up in selected cities with high density of population; and aim at ensuring access of Information devoid of any sort of complexities. MMMHPs intend to serve as "Learning Sites". Three segments need to be identified and considered for adequate functioning:

(i) Requisite capacity of Municipalities for improvement.

(ii) Adequate resource utilisation and proper channelisation.

(iii) Fund structure be allocated and maintained.

The above-mentioned Pilot Programme can be then Replicated in other Regions too with beneficial incorporations–strategically suited–greatly deduced from initial experiments.

Perceptibly, the Rajasthan Government commendably initiated series of Policy Measures comprehending level of participation of private sector for telling results in state of Urban Health Such Policy Dimensions relate to-

- Installation of Sophisticated Medical Technology in Public Sector Hospitals.
- Acceptance of donations and charities from private individuals or public bodies for medical purposes.
- Policy of Medical Colleges / Dental Colleges in Private Sector.
- Setting up nursing Institutions in Private Sector.
- Encouraging Private Investment in Medical Institutions, diagnostic centres and nursing homes.

To a great extent, such Policy Adoption responsibly by other EAG states like UP and MP intensively can lead to positive results in improving the health of urban poor.

REFERENCES

Economic Editors' Conference (2000), "Organised on 16th, 17th and 18th October, Backgrounder of Ministry of Health and Family Welfare", New Delhi.

Loughhead, S. (2001), "Urban Poverty and Vulnerability in India", Department for International Development (DID), New Delhi.

MoHFW (2004), "Guidelines for Development of City Level Urban Slum Health Project; Project Division, MoHFW; Govt. of India.

'National Health Policy' (2002), Ministry of Health and Family Welfare; Govt. of India.

National Human Development Reports, Planning Commission, Govt. of India, New Delhi.

Office of the Registrar General and Census Commissioner (2001), Slum Population of India Series; Census of India Report.

Report on (2003), "Health, Nutrition and Population" by Economic Census in India; USAID-EHP, New Delhi.

Rao, M. Govinda; Mita Choudhry and Mukesh Anand (2005), "Resource Devolution from Centre to States", in 'Financing and Delivery of Health Care Services in India : Background Papers'; National Commission on Macroeconomics and Health (NCMH); MoHFW; Govt. of India.

Reports of the Department of Women and Child Development: 'National Programme of Nutritional Support to Primary Education–Recent Initiatives'; Govt. of India.

Select Health Indicators by Standard of Living Index (SLI) (2002-04), Rajasthan, District Level Household Survey.

Select Health Indicators by Standard of Living Index (SLI) (2002-04), Uttar Pradesh, District Level Household Survey.

Select Health Indicators by Standard of Living Index (SLI) (2002-04), Madhya Pradesh, District Level Household Survey.

Tenth Five Year Plan (2002), Planning Commission, Govt. of India.

WHO Health Sector Reforms in India (2004), Initiatives from Nine States, A Report.

2

CUSTOMERS' SATISFACTION IN HOSPITALS

Nishant Sinha & Tarun Gupta

The idea of studying the facilities provided by Hospitals to the attendants (who accompany the patient) is generated from our and others experience of hospitals. The improper behaviour (lack of interest and enthusiasm) of hospital staff and lack of basic amenities made us to think over the concerns of attendants and visitors towards hospital facilities.

Providing good service quality is of great strategic importance in the management of any service organizations. Besides ensuring excellent clinical care, hospitals should also focus on providing quality service to their patients and visitors. The findings from this study could provide useful information as to how hospitals could better manage their services and harness information technologies to enhance their services. Healthcare service in this research is defined as all *medical support services,* such as; *nursing, food and beverage, ward service, counter service, and other ancillary services.*

A questionnaire survey was conducted on about 700 customers (attendants) who had previous experiences in one of the many private and semi-private hospitals of the healthcare system in Lucknow city. The method of survey was based on intercept interviews. Attendants' satisfaction levels were measured using a *Attendants Satisfaction Index [ASI] model.*

The study shows that there is still a lot of room for improvement in the healthcare industry. Specifically, the healthcare industry as a whole seems to be weak in factors such as; *Promptness, Attitude towards attendants, Communication, Consistency, and Knowledge.*

The hospital market has today changed from a sellers' market to a buyers' market, where the patient is all-important. Therefore to achieve customer satisfaction, the hospital has to develop itself technologically, as well as become more service-oriented.

A real customer from the hospital perspective is any individual who comes to hospital to avail its medical services but hospitals should also take care of those who accompany the patient as an attendant because the patient in most case does not have sense of what is happening during his treatment. The customer from the hospital is very different from the regular customer, the difference being *that he doesn't want to be a 'customer'* in the first place.

It is essential for a hospital to recognize this fact and reach out to its customers (attendants), if it wants to survive the competition. This can be achieved only by building a bridge of trust between the hospital and the community, so that the community can crossover to the hospital. One needs to understand the fact that patients do not flock to a hospital just because its services are cheap, but because of its good name and good image.

The major differentiating factor is that the customer of the hospital, unlike other industries, gets a close look at all the rungs of the hospital. He gets a chance to interact with practically everybody from the receptionists, admission staff, doctors, nurses, ward boys, ayahs, ambulance, personnel, billing staff, among others. The hospital therefore needs to take this difference into account while dealing with their patients.

The workings of the hospital are laid bare to the attendants and every interaction the attendant has with any staff member is a crucial factor in determining whether he would choose the same hospital again.

A hospital's primary objectives are usually humanitarian, philosophical or regulatory and based on some perceived need. However, a problem may arise when what the attendant 'needs' is different from what the attendant 'wants'. For instance, what a attendant needs from a hospital is reasonable good quality medical care for his patient, a clean waiting room, good clean civic amenities. Yet market research over the past few years has shown that hospitalized patients' attendants want a variety of amenities not associated with their need for reasonable services. They want smiling, empathetic nurses and staff, a wide selection of foods for their meals and a quick response to their calls.

To stay ahead of the competition, it is essential to keep the customer happy. Only satisfying the customer needs and wants and delighting the customer by exceeding his expectations with unanticipated benefits can achieve this.

Attendant satisfaction is a person's feeling of pleasure or disappointment resulting for comparing a product/service's perceived performance or outcome in relation to his or her expectations. As this definition makes clear, satisfaction is a function of perceived performance and expectations. If the performance falls short of expectations, the customer is dissatisfied. If the performance matches the expectations, the customer is satisfied. If the performance exceeds expectations, the customer is highly satisfied or delighted.

Customer satisfaction in a hospital is basically a state of mind of the attendant. It is the ability of the hospital service to meet the expectations of the attendant. Customer delight is all about exceeding the expectations of the attendants to make him highly satisfied with the hospital.

The hospital should aim for high customer satisfaction or customer delight because customers have no qualms in shifting when a better offer comes along from a different hospital. Those who are highly satisfied or delighted with the hospital are much less ready to shift. High satisfaction or delight creates an emotional bond with the hospital in the mind of the patient, not just rational preference. The result is high patient and attendant loyalty, which is what every hospital is looking at, to cut the competition.

In a hospital scenario, marketing is essential at all points. Every member of the hospital has to be an active agent in satisfying and delighting the attendant, which would translate into a source of strength for the community and the hospital.

Assume that a hospital sees some 10,000 OPD patients a year and each patient brings in an average revenue of Rs 1000 per year. This amounts to one crore in revenues annually, which is not a trifling amount. If the average profit margin is 10 per cent, the hospital would be making a gross profit of Rs.10, 00,000 per year. If you lose 20 per cent of your customers every year because of a poor relationship with them, you would lose Rs 20,00,000 worth of business every year which translates in terms of losing Rs 2,00,000 in terms of profit. Since we want patients and attendants to be loyal to the hospital over the coming years, there could be a staggering *'lifetime loss'.*

Most administrators do not factor the intangible assets of the hospital. In the intangible assets, we must surely include a loyal patient & attendants in addition to the highly skilled nurses, technicians and consultants. Actually the lifetime value of a loyal patient: *Customer Lifetime Value (CLV)* can be modeled on a mathematical basis. Since this subject is so important there has to be a customer relationship management officer who is recruited preferably from the hospitality industry. He should be on equal footing with the finance controller.

The story does not end here. Attendants also bring in their relatives and friends because they act as brand ambassadors.

OBJECTIVE OF STUDY

The study aiming at determineing the attendants' satisfaction index for private and semi private hospital in Lucknow and to determine the attributes that affect the satisfaction level of Attendants (Customer for hospitals).

METHODOLOGY

The research methodology includes data collection through questionnaires prepared for attendants (specific type of customers). The data collected through the questionnaires has been analyzed with the help of statistical techniques by using the SPSS software.

The major aspects of our study were to analyse the different facilities provided by hospitals to the attendants in the form of common room, water, vigil, canteen and on spot room services. We have considered some of the emergency service attributes like Quality of treatment, ambulance quality, knowledge and professionalism of emergency staff and doctors to make our study more comprehensive. We have also given a look to price related factors how they affect patients and attendants in opting a particular hospital with respect to the services provided. The findings of our study has shown us the relationships between different variables, which are supposed to affect the attendants' satisfaction and comfort level. It also helped us in finding major factors influencing the attendants' choice for hospital. With all these findings and information, we have tried to suggest some key areas where the improvements could be done and more intensive and specific strategies could be prepared. The questionnaire consists of close-ended questions only ; this is to avoid the complexity of analyzing huge subjective data. At first we had designed the questionnaire from general point of view. Then we went for a pilot survey which is done to find out whether our questionnaire is fulfilling our study objectives. The study covers people of all age groups who are getting treatment for their patients from private and semi private hospitals only. We have taken a sample of 700.

ASI CALCULATION

The total mean of healthcare Industry is calculated by taking discriminant score into consideration. The individual ASI scores for hospitals are obtained by dividing total mean for a hospital with the total mean of Industry.

FINDINGS

The quality of facilities (Common room ,Water, Vigil, Canteen, On spot room service) available for attendants is different with respect to different hospitals.

The characteristics of doctors (Knowledge of the subject, Courteousness, Willingness to help, Efficiency, Ability to complete the treatment) attending the patients vary with the hospitals.

The study shows that the *Quality of service* (Process of problem resolution, Hospital staff courteousness, Doctors' attitude, Doctors' handle the call quickly, Knowledgeable doctors, Reference to another hospital) has very strong association with the recommendation given by attendants to others.

The study reveals that the *Quality of service* (Process of problem resolution, Hospital staff courteousness, Doctors' attitude, Doctors' handle the call quickly, Knowledgeable doctors, Reference to another hospital) has very strong association with the satisfaction of attendants.

The study reveals that the variables under Quality of service are important for attendants' overall satisfaction with hospital services in the following order. This result has been derived by applying *discriminant analysis* on data. This statistical tool is applied to know which attribute is most important discriminator for satisfaction of attendants' satisfaction. The *discriminant function* that we have got is

$$Y = -8.412 + .984x_1 + .274x_2 + .357x_3 + .103x_4 + .039x_5 + .324x_6 + .326x_7$$

- Quality of Service (x_1)
- Process of Problem Resolution (x_2)
- Hospital Staffs Courteousness (x_3)
- knowledgeable doctors (x_6)
- Doctors' attitude (x_4)
- Doctors' handle the call quickly (x_5)
- Reference to another hospital (x_7)

Y = Overall satisfaction with hospital/hospital services (yes/no).

The study shows that the following variables regarding Expectations and Experiences are important for attendants' overall satisfaction with hospital services in following order.

Discriminant function for this result is mentioned below which will be used to classify new observation as satisfied or dissatisfied on the basis of mentioned attributes.

$$Y = -5.999 + .436x_1 - .049x_2 + .482x_3 + .298x_4 + .072x_5 - .166x_6 + .582x_7 + .204x_8 - .074x_9 - .038x_{10}$$

- Quality of treatment performed (x_1)
- Made you feel comfortable (x_3)
- Ease of obtaining appointment (x_7)
- Willingness to go out of the way to satisfy (x_4)
- Efficiency in handling treatment (x_8)
- Convenience of contact hours (x_6)
- On spot help (x_{10})
- Helpfulness of staff (x_5)
- Avoiding inconvenience to you (x_2)
- Clean comfortable waiting area (x_9)

Y = Overall satisfaction with hospital/hospital services (yes/no).

The study shows that there is very high association between the emergency services and recommendation of attendants for a particular hospital.

The study reveals that the following variables regarding emergency services are important for attendants' overall satisfaction with hospital services in following order.

Discriminant function for the result

$$Y = -7.205 + .279x_1 + .243x_2 + .037x_3 + .240x_4 - .029x_5 - .123x_6 + .537x_7 + .507x_8 - .391x_9 + .678x_{10}$$

- Time required to solve the problem (x_7)
- Quality of treatment (x_8)
- Telephonic support (x_1)
- On spot support (x_2)
- Quality of ambulance (x_{10})
- Ambulance services (x_9)
- Knowledge and professionalism of emergency doctors (x_4)
- Knowledge and professionalism of emergency staff (x_3)
- Ability of emergency staff to diagnose the problem (x_5)
- Ability of emergency staff to diagnose the problem (x_6)

Y = Overall satisfaction with hospital/hospital services (yes/no)

Chart 1: Shows the mapping of means of different variables considered for studying Hospitals (Semi private and private) & Nursing homes in and around lucknow. This chart reveals that Hospitals are performing better than the Nursing Homes but they require an overall improvement taking into fact whatever facilities they are providing to the attendants of the patients as the perception map shows that hospitals and nursing homes both are performing below industry average.

Perception Mapping for Hospitals

Variable names

Quality of treatment performed

Avoiding inconvenience to you

Chart -1

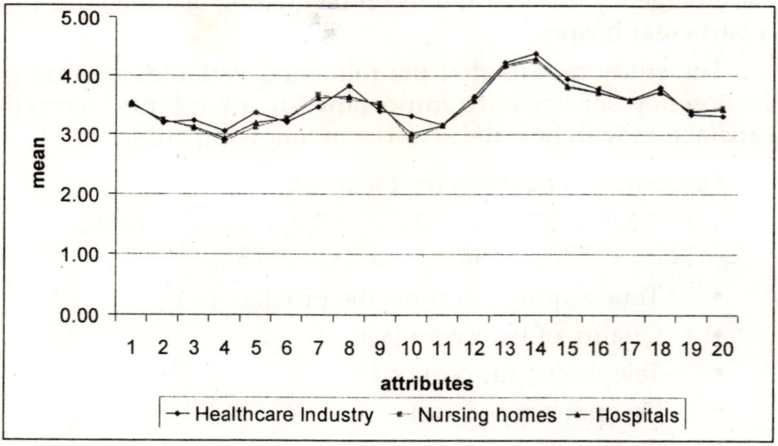

Made you feel comfortable

Willingness to go out of the way to satisfy

Helpfulness of staff

Convenience of contact hours

Ease of obtaining appointment

Efficiency in handling treatment

Clean comfortable waiting area

On spot help

Telephonic support
On spot support
Knowledge and professionalism of emergency staff
Knowledge and professionalism of emergency doctors
Ability of emergency staff to diagnose the problem
Ability of emergency staff to diagnose the problem
Time required to solve the problem
Quality of treatment
Ambulance services
Quality of ambulance

Limitations of the Study

- The sampling covers some areas of Lucknow only. So, there is possibility that the report doesn't reflect the situation of hospitals other than those present in Lucknow.
- The answers given by the respondents are based on their understanding of the questions.
- Limited Time for getting information from attendants

REFERENCES

Benchmarking for Success, Freeman, James M, Healthcare ExecutiveMar/Apr98, Vol. 13 Issue 2, p. 51, 1p, 1bw.

A Model For Achieving Quality in Hospital Hotel Services, Randall, Lyn, Senior, Martin, International Journal of Contemporary Hospitality Management; 1994, Vol. 6 Issue 1/2, p. 68, 7 p.

Utility Customer Satisfaction on the Rise, Electric Light & Power; Sep/Oct 2005, Vol. 83 Issue 5, pp. 55-55, 1 p.

Problem Solvers. Pollock, Ted, Supervision; Mar 2004, Vol. 65 Issue 3, pp. 13-15, 3 p.

Why Do *Customer* Relationship Management Applications Affect *Customer Satisfaction*?Mithas, Sunil,Krishnan, M. S.·Fornell, Claes, Journal of Marketing; Oct 2005, Vol. 69 Issue 4, pp. 201-209, 9 p.

3

HEALTH COMMUNICATION: THE CONCEPT AND PRACTICES

Shailendra Kumar

Even after fifty- nine year of attaining independence India is still struggling to identify the goals to be achieved through the process of development. The dilemma of choosing the alternative between the path of erosion of values of attaining material development or face stagnation and allow the age-old and time-tested social values to flourish is becoming sharper and sharper with the passage of time. The dilemma has become complex because the nature and structural character of Indian society is gradually drifting towards heterogeneity. Indian inhabits around 100 crore people of whom around 75 percent are rural based having different ethnic, linguistic, religious and socio-cultural background. Politically, the democratic forces have directed India and her economic structure has been chronically ill with evils of poverty, inequality and ignorance. These socio- structural dimensions have given rise to a series of inadequacies such as increase in number of poor people who are socially powerless. This attribute has made a huge proportion of Indian population dependent on the government owned welfare bureaucracies who claim to have political, financial and even professional monopoly of setting standards of what is valuable and what is feasible for this over whelming powerless majority.

This main bias has over shadowed the people for whom most social welfare programs including medical health and family welfare are drafted and subsequently implemented. It is known that adoption of such approaches has increased the yawning gap between the people and the government. Visibly, even well intentioned developmental programs have only been able to develop tame compliance and greater psychological dependence of people on government with almost no effort at raising self-motivation among them. Our development communication strategies have broadly failed to bring the downtrodden and unprivileged sections of the society to the main stream of development. In other words the development communication of Indian society has seldom been with the people rather it has been directed to them. Further, most of the development communication inputs in welfare oriented programs have been overplayed for those who need them least. In short, the development communication contents and messages are not yet clear about the goals of development. Apparently, present developmental communication programs seem only apt to address the symptoms rather than the causes and such programs usually operate through points in the system, which have little leverage to change.

The task before the developing countries is not merely to get better results within the existing framework of economic and social institutions but to mould and refashion them in such a way that they effectively contribute to the realization of wider and deeper social values. Adoption of an approach would imply that instead of making mechanistic and deterministic messages, the focus shifted to treat them more humanistic in nature and form. It would thus be necessary that development communication is only support to development. This process has to be continuous and consistent to aim at raising aspirations of people so as to help them to develop copying behavior appropriate to developmental initiatives. Basically development communication has to raise the level of social consciousness among people that can help them to word transformation.

THE CONCEPT AND ISSUES

No doubt that health and family welfare program is an integral part of over all development program of the country. Fortunately development communication has been playing vital role throughout the various developmental phases of the program by using massively different communication media and methods. In spite of the large-scale efforts of educating and motivating people for accepting small family norms, changing the health practices of people, introducing spacing methods the achievements of program have always fallen short of the resource being put in it. Mostly a moot question being asked as to why development communication efforts have being absolutely incidental to actual adoption. Some research studies have shown that factors such as paucity of resource the vastness of Indian traditional ethos low education and literacy profile, diversity of language and dialects, lake of coordination between IEC and Policy planners and the overall resistance to change, are important for this imbalance. The deeper analysis however, shows that development program in any field where formal resource have been deployed to promote communication, socio-structural factors play a vital role in reception of new ideas in any community. In other words, factor within the universe of the socio-cultural set up have largely been responsible for preventing innovative ideas from being functional and operational at community level.

These contradictions are visible at grass root level where on the one hand multipurpose workers are expected to promote extension education and on the other hand, they are handed over targets to fulfill failure to achieve these targets invite punitive measures. Most administrators view motivational and educational technique as magic which when applied anywhere on anybody can yield results in the form of acceptance and adoption of family planning measures. It needs to be recognized that implementing educational and motivational efforts in the community not only requires patience but also capabilities of the health workers for effective development communication such contradictions in philosophy and implementation need a serious consideration.

In order to back the wider audience and prepare simple educational tools the IEC development communication activities in health and family welfare are gradually losing their educational components and are becoming propaganda.

Than Another issue that needs to be attend by communication scientists and policy makers is that the present development communication efforts in health and family welfare programs seldom use the knowledge and the talent available at the local levels. It is becoming more evident that expensive mass media technology is receiving higher emphasis at the cost of the traditional media usage of traditional media is not only acceptable creative but affordable also. The urgency of containing the population did not allow the planners of development communication policy and programs to pay due affection to the needs of different regions of the country This instead of mass media covering areas like health, sanitation mother and child health in even simple massage such as small family as happy family become a contradiction in itself.

The challenge that are at the fore front a family planning communication policy can be briefly subsumed under massage content, media mix and organization of media. The newer challenges are more in making the media decentralized. Choice of suitable media and developing integrated approach giving due recognition to the socio-economics environment of country is another one. The focus and emphasis of the future development communication strategy in health and family welfare programme has to be rural based and addressed to the rural poor and urban poor as its target audience. For a country like India where red of literacy and level of purchasing power is low, the choice of media assumes an importance for ant meaning full strategy. The purpose of development communication in health and family welfare has been more information oriented which needs to be supplemented by development messages through which functional and purposeful relationship between people could be developed. This is important because family planning involves subjective motivation and the questions relating to it are very carefully considered. The present message content has been greatly influenced by the urban alienating culture which has infused among people a sense of social isolation powerlessness and frustration. Unless the massages do not provide information regarding the economic advantages of family welfare programme, the real aspirations of rural and urban masses will not get attracted towards adoption.

Further the most important issue which merits attention is to provide linkage between the development communication strategies of different welfare programme as part and parcel of the large whole. In philosophy and in principle this approach has been accepted. But it has always lagged in its implementation for various seasons. The isolated development communication approach has brought in contradictions within the developmental programmes. Health and family welfare programmes has come to a stage where rural people appear to be aware of the benefits of the family welfare but the socio-economic pressures operate against it. In this case, the development communication strategy should attack the socio-economic pressures that confront the rural and urban poor rather than planning strategies vertically for programme acceptance. Any development communication strategy be it health or education should be such that the development communication treat rural people as intelligent, conscious and capable of learning new things. This naturally implies that unless media original in and relate themselves to the world of values and environment of the community there is bound to be irrelevant and ineffective. In brief, development communication strategy in health and family welfare programme has to be such that it not only empowers but enables the rural an urban poor to take informed decisions in relation to his personal and delicate question on health and family welfare.

HEALTH AND FAMILY WELFARE AS A KEY FACTOR IN DEVELOPMENT

Development implies progressive improvement in the living conditions and quality of life of the individual, community and society. Development in one sphere of life leads to development in other spheres. Thus no distinction can be drawn between economics, sociology and health and family welfare development. Economics development is an instrument to achieve social development which in turn is necessary to achieve economics development. The purpose of development is to prepare people to lead economically productive and socially satisfying lives. How ever social faction and economics productivity is perceived in different ways in different societies. Every where people strive to increase in purchasing power which enables them to get them and there children better and sufficient food and housing, better education, better opportunities of leisure and most important, better health. Unless the people have healthful living, they can not enjoy the other benefits of life. There fore, health development is essential for social and economics development. This is the reason that any activity attempted to improve health and socio-economic situation should be regarded as mutually complimentary to each other rather then competitive. It is an academic debate whether health and family welfare development only consumes resources or whether it is an economically productive factor contributing in over all development. Health and family welfare development contributes to action and organization in support of the development process.

For instance the control of certain communicable diseases often helps to promote development in general. Proper nutrition and reduction of sickness increases work productivity. Breaking the vicious circle of malnutrition and infection leads to improvement of physical and mental development of the child. Vaccinating entire child population against vaccine-prevented diseases brings reduction in child mortality which can induce a feeling to have small family further, by drawing on untapped sources-man, finance and material for Health and Family Welfare development, one can contribute to the awakening of social interest which is very important for mobilizing people's efforts for development in social and economic field.

No sector, be social, economic, or health and family welfare can function independent of each other in the process of development. Activities in one field impinge of the goals of another. There fore, there is a need to have Co-operation between social and economic sectors to bring development and to promote health and family welfare development as a part of it. The primary health care and family welfare approach, which aims at achieving health and family welfare for all essentially based on this principle.

Health and family welfare of an individual and of the society, when we consider as an indicator of social and economic development of the nation, needs to be seen in its entirety and not in independent of other aspects of life that contribute to the overall development. In the post-independence period, the country has a freedom to decide her policies and priorities for development in all spheres of life including health and family welfare, but we still observe vertical approach even in the planning and implementation. As a result, we notice uneven development in some fields. Over-riding priorities assigned to non-health sectors in the five year plans are hardly disputed; but at the same time the priority assigned to health and family welfare does not appear to synchronize with requirements of health and medical needs of the people. It is indeed paradoxical that in spite of extensive advancement in literacy and education as well as improved methods of development communication, there still exists a gap between existing medical and health protective knowledge and people's acceptance and its use.

Further, there are different arguments, not to justify the priority assigned to health and family welfare sector but to justify slow development in health and family welfare field. Some attribute availability of meager resources as contributory factor: some say unprecedented population explosion that continues to maintain widening gap between demand and supply of health and family welfare services; while some blame the health and medical professionals for their attitudes to wards health and family welfare services.

The long history of health and family welfare service development in this country shows an unattributable trend towards medical and family welfare services through institutionalized approach whose ultimate aim is to cure the individual from the ailment. There is a change in the concept of medical care which was once limited to treatment as it now covers prevention and rehabilitation. New type of therapy and preventive medicine is observed to be shifting the methods from infectious to degenerative chromic diseases. Further more, associated with medical ham, often an integral part of it is the group of trained Para–medical personnel who have demonstrated the contribution that trained Para- medicals can make in medical setting. Another development which is observed is the change in the functioning of practicing physician. The traditional attitude held by some that a clinician is not a social scientist and, therefore, should have no concern with the social problems of his patients, is rapidly undergoing change. It is a fact that most medical schools and medical educators realize that a traditional concept of physician is no longer compatible with the complex life of modern community. As a result of this change, a new type of physician seems to have developed, a man who considers himself something more than a mere guardian of health, one who must feel concerned himself with non-medical problems of his patients, relatives and family members.

In the process of development, communication is necessary for both understanding and what can be called mind-management. Communication is integral to cultural and social existence. It is not merely conveys to the various entities in a society, its cultural attributes and patterns of interaction in different social groups, but it even creates new facets which attain the forms of symbols as well as elements of culture. In its totality of functions, development communication is an instrument to promote social, cultural, economical, political and health and family welfare actions for change. It is the articulation of social relations between human beings. It is central to the creation and development of society in terms of satisfaction of physical needs collectively, as also of intellectual and emotional needs as social relations develop and become more complex. Development communication is thus the product of society as well as molder of society. It is therefore, necessary to establish structural links between different development communication channels and the actor of change.

HEALTH COMMUNICATION STRUCTURE IN INDIA

Realizing the complexity of health and family welfare behaviour which, in the case of Indian society, is largely guided by informal but deep-rooted socio-cultural values, the country has adopted such measures which the people voluntarily accept to keep them healthy. Thus, the process of motivation of the people is attempted through mass media and interpersonal communication. The health and family welfare communication structure in the country that exists at the national and state level varies marginally. However, the development communication infrastructure is controlled by both, government and private sectors. The government has the absolute control over mass media ; while the private sector controls newspapers, film industry and advertising. The boundary of powers and roles of central and State government in the matters of development communication policy and planning are defined under the constitution of the country. In the matter of health and family welfare communication, the Ministry of health and family welfare at the central and state level is primarily responsible for policy planning and implementation, of course, through the Ministry of information and Broadcasting at the national level; and through the directorate of information and publicity at the state level.

The government with this Infrastructure uses mainly three Channels of Communication:

(i) Electronic Media which includes All India Radio, Doordarshan and Films;

(ii) Print Media which includes news papers; advertisements and other printed materials; and

(iii) Interpersonal contact through a band of health and family welfare workers and the people at various levels. Although, health and family welfare communication policy is basically directed to disseminate health and family welfare information to educate and to change health and family welfare behaviour of the people, but only first two goals seem have received more emphasis, as these have demonstrability character, this can easily be measured.

Chart-1

Broad Framework of Health and Family Welfare Communication in India

Level	*Implementing*	*Policy Planning Agency*
i. Central	Ministry of Health and Family Welfare.	Mass Media Unit. Directorate General of Health Services (Central Health Education Bureau)
	Ministry of Information & Broadcasting	All India Radio, Doordarshan, Films Division, Directorate of Audio Visual Publicity Song and Drama Division
ii. State	Ministry of Health	Directorate of Health Services (State Health Education Bureau, Family Planning Bureau).
	Directorate of Information and Publicity	Directorate of Information and Publicity
iii. District	District Health Office	District Health Education Unit (District Mass Media and Education Officer)
	District Publicity Office	District Publicity officer.
iv. Primary Health Central/ Peripheral Level	District Health office	Block Extension Educator Auxiliary Nurse Midwife Multipurpose Health Worker/Family Welfare Social Worker Community Health and Family Welfare Volunteer.

With a rapid expensive of development communication network in India, more means are used to educate the messes and make them self reliant in the matter of health and family welfare. The broadcasting system has increased enormously during the fast few years. It covers at present 90 per sent by population and 86 percent by area. So also the television network that increased expensively covers new 83 per sent by population and 67 per sent by area. These two networks have undoubtedly replaced the traditional way of face-to-face or interpersonal communication welfare the members of the community. The impact of modern means of development communication on social, cultural and political behaviour of the individual and community at large has well been documented which suggest that mass communication process is proved to be a very powerful instrument of social change. However, in a democratic country like India mass media cannot be used in a coercion style. Therefore operational process of the mass media has to take into account country: socio-cultural structure which has influence over individual and community health and family welfare behaviour.

ROLE OF DEVELOPMENT AGENCIES IN HEALTH AND POPULATION COMMUNICATION

The National Population Policy (NPP) has set three types of objectives. These are:

(a) The immediate objective for fulfilling the unmet Needs in respect of Birth control and allied health

(b) facilities including provisioning Of reproductive and child health care;

(c) the medium term objective of printing the total fertility rate to the replacement level by the year 2010 and the long term objective to achieve a stable population by 2045.

In pursuance of these objectives, the NPP 2000 formulated certain national socio demographic goals to be achieved by 2010. Within the list of 14 goals included there, six goals can be identified where the panchayat bodies and other development agencies can directly play some effective role. These goals are as follows:

(a) to achieve universal immunization of children against all vaccine preventable diseases,

(b) to promote delayed marriage for girls not earlier than 18 and preferable after 20 years of age.

(c) to achieve universal access to information counseling and providing services for fertility regulation and contraception without any coercive methods,

(d) to achieve 100 per cent registration of births, deaths, marriage and pregnancy;

(e) to promote vigorously the small family norm so that by 2010 TFR will be equivalent to the replacement levels; and

(f) to ensure convergence of social sector programmes for making family welfare and health programme people centered.

With the passage of the seventy Third and seventy fourth amendment to the constitution of India the Panchayatiraj institutions are entrusted with the responsibility for making socio-economic plans and implementing the programmes In the social sector development specifically in health family welfare and education (in particular primary education) the panchayats became the principal means for action. Being the peoples institution it can influence the masses. Again any step towards restraining population increase therefore should be done through counseling of the campus but not through any coercive methods. Here lies the scope of the Panchayats, Non Government Organizations (NGOs) and other development agencies. They can play a very positive role to act as monitor for reducing very causes of population growth and in implementing of the health and family welfare social workers and development. Communicators can deliver certain services related to health and family welfare easily and more effectively and they have strong linkages with the common people. In members of these development agencies have the capacity to reach the mind of the people in significant ways because of their easy acceptance by the local people.

Then the propagation of the message of small family norm and its contributory benefits will help to create awareness among the poor people and may try to motivate them. In this concerned the village panchayats and other development agencies can organize and lead a mass movement at each and every corner of India villages for putting a check on the rising population.

At the last the problem of population growth in our country cannot be tackled by the government alone. The governmental system due to its inadequate flexibility cannot reach out to each any ever household–thus whatever action be taken its sustainability is mostly not ensured. Towards this and the governmental mechanism may encourage collaborative arrangements with the local bodies' non-governmental organizations, civil society or any other persons having interest in the matter. For ensuring horizontal linkage among the functioning departments it is necessary that a co-coordinating body should be evolved for ensuring convergent action. By virtue of it status the Panchayats and other development bodies can play the role of coordinator. But one weak point in this chain is that the Panchayats and other developments bodies are suffering from certain limitations. For example, most of the development bodies have very limited financial resources and inadequate personnel support. To overcome the financial weakness it is required that both the centre and the state governments should ensure a regular flow of fund in the form of grant in aid to the Panchayats and other development institutions (from the village to the district level). For taking up jobs related with the measures of population control and health improvements. As regards the manpower support to the Panchayats and other development agencies proper devolution of power is necessary so that they can have functional control over the officials of the government department. NGO collaboration may ease the stringency provided both the NGO and the Panchayats come forward and join hands together. As NGOs generally have the rural base and expertise along with their built in flexibility it is expected that instead of sporadic action NGO- Panchayats collaborative action would help to achieve the target in reality. The whole task is multi-dimensional on one hand and urgent on the other hand because the time span is very limited for achieving the target.

THE LIMITATIONS

The mass media have many limitations to influence individual behaviour. The impact of mass media depends on the kind of audience. Information disseminated through the channels commonly used by the public health and family welfare agencies is fairly easy for most potential audience to avoid, since these audiences are not more captive. Moreover, even if they are exposed to any channel of development communication, there is no certainty that their exposure will lead to learning and more so to action or acceptance meaning thereby to change the behaviour. An example of statutory warning on the cigarette packet "Cigarette smoking is injurious to health" proves this point.

According to New York Academy of Medicine, it is easy to sell symptomatic relief from illness or the promise of cure rather than to sell health and prevention of disease.

The knowledge that is acquired alone does not lead to an achievement; it is the extent to which the knowledge is put to practice and action is important. Every individual has his own likes and dislikes and also his ideological frame of mind in accepting the message from the development communication channels. The reader of the newspaper and other printed material, viewer of television, cinema etc; and listener of radio or audio material does not select every single item out of the vast output of development communication. Ideas that do not fit in their belief system lead to psychologically unbalanced state. Different people have different perception to interpret and to adopt. Hence, the results of development communication efforts would not be the same as expected. Further mass media also indirect way contribute to ill health.

If the consumer products advertised in mass media are bad for health, then the mass media contribute to ill health" – says how it. He again argues that the obvious example of bad effects of mass media can be seen in the advertising of cigarettes, sweets, cakes, chocolates, wine etc. Mass media, thus act as a two-edged weapon. Then, there are a variety of ways in which mass media can promote ill-health.

There are:

(i) Through advertising products which affect health.

(ii) Through publishing information which demonstrates health risks attached to certain products.

(iii) Through decrying warnings of danger, and

(iv) Through encouraging inadvertently the use of products by actively supporting similar but less dangerous substances.

Research in the risk of smoking has suggested that smoking has suggested that smokers of cigarettes have fifty times greater risk of lung cancer. Everyone knows the health risk of use of tobacco either through smoking or chewing ; but there is a little crusade to arouse public opinion to combat the persuasive power of cigarette commercials. The media excepting those governments- controlled seems to have indirectly joined with the tobacco industry in promoting use of tobacco. Although there is no adequate evidence that drugs of different kinds promote ill health. But media play a role to make the situation worse. That's why, Young(1973) says that "the greater the public health risk caused by psychotropic substance, the less amount of information is critical of its effect".

There is another fallacy to presume in the process of the development communication that "stimulus- response process" is as effective in changing health behaviour as in mind that effect of new ideas and practice spread gradually and unevenly in society through various combinations of mass media and interpersonal network. Mass media on a free and open society can be efficient in creating opinions among people not previously inclined to one way or another on a given issue. According to Kuppuswamy, eminent communication scientist of India "changes in values and health behaviour effected by mass media cannot be used with any effect to bring about a change in the attitudes of people towards any problem".

Then, it is a common phenomenon on one hand, we observe that a farmer is quick in his decision to adopt improved methods in agriculture which demonstrate high yield; but he does not appear to respond with the same speed to action involving health and family welfare behaviour. But there are no sufficient efforts to explain this phenomenon. Any action that demonstrates its benefit or returns in a more tangible form and in a short run is more likely to be adopted than the action that does not demonstrate. This is how the individual, basically tries to justify his action in different situations. It means that the individual acts differently in different situations and also acts selectively. Social change takes place in stages, with the material aspect coming first. The values come later; technical and impersonal changes come before primary group relation changes. Whenever the individual has no equivalent substitute for the things to adopt, he does not accept the innovation quickly. There are many areas in health and family welfare field where the individual has little substitutes with which he can adopt these and change his behaviour.

Most of the studies suggest that the mass media essentially tend to serve as reinforcing agent rather than producers of massive change in attitude. In India a democratic country, where people have freedom of being exposed to various mass media, they like to read and view or hear the issues that are in consonance with their beliefs and values. Even they are exposed to various channels of mass communication, they can exercise selective perception operates as a limitation on the influence of mass media in respect of opinion and perception change communication, resulting, in a limited influence on individuals or community's health and family welfare behaviour. Bearing in mind these limitations of development communication can bring miraculous results in health and family welfare behaviour. It can bring some change in lightly held attitudes but not in deeply entrenched ones. This vividly suggests that one has to distinguish individual behaviour that is akin to change and that is not akin to change.

Besides these, the development communication is subjected to have limited effect due to operational factors at various levels, more particularly in use of electronic media. In India, where the print media cannot have a maximum reach because of high illiteracy, the radio is a significant medium of development communication. Radio, being under the control of the government, has to cater to the needs of every sector, in addition to board casting commercial programmes to generate revenue. This result in allocation of little time to a few programme broadcast on radio.

Kakar (1987) reports that out of total hour of broad casting in a particular year, health and family welfare programmes get only 5 percent time which is inadequate.

Then, television network covering about 83 percent by population is the most powerful channel of development communication. However, its limitations, due to operational factors do not vary much from that of radio. Then programmes telecasted on health and family welfare points out a kind of variation at different television centers. Both in quantity of and time given to these programmes. It is suggestive of the fact that low priority assigned to health and family welfare on television is unlikely to make much impact howsoever the channel is powerful.

Looking in to the limited role of development communication in changing health and family welfare behaviour, one can think of interpersonal communication, which in the context of complexity of health and family welfare behaviour assumes greater significance. However, interpersonal communication cannot be considered as substitute for mass media. Interpersonal communication can be between the physician and his community ; between family members; between the educator and his pupils; between elite group such as educated youths and their community; etc. In this communication, word of mouth and personal communication from a trusted source is significantly more effective than mass communication from a remote source, however, prestigious that source may be. Innumerable studies, have established more credibility of interpersonal communication than mass communication. Promotion of interpersonal communication at institutional, family and community level for health and family welfare is reflected in development communication strategy of government, by way of integrating it in the training Curricula of mainly Para- medical and family welfare workers. However their role seems to be more as an informer of health and family welfare information than a development communicator per se.

CONCLUSION

Health and family welfare development and development communication are closely interlinked and mutually interdependent. In the country like India the development communication strategy needs to be developed in a manner that can cater to the needs of diverse groups based on social and cultural background. Merely by transferring health and welfare information to the people. Through various channel of development communication, especially mass media, alone will not bring health and family welfare development. The goal of achieving health and family welfare behaviour change should be a central point of development communication strategy which needs to be operated in the spirit. Health and family welfare communicator, therefore, should have the following components of activities if it is directed to achieve behavioural change.

1. Assess the needs of the community; different target groups.
2. Assess the local resource available to meet these needs.
3. Assess the areas of likes and dislikes of the people to wards types of development communication.
4. Generate need of the programme i.e. development programme.
5. Provide scientific, specific and basic information.
6. Build up attitudinal change and assess its extent.
7. Create atmosphere to act for decision.
8. Confirm the extent of action.
9. Provide support to sustain action.

"In the new situations where the role of development communicator is not as transmitters of knowledge, he has to widen the boundaries of his roles thus performing a role of social activist or the change agent. Although development communication is a specialized science it can be enriched by integrating fundamental elements of social science which can offer development communicator realm of knowledge than may make him sensitive to social values, social needs and social dynamics of the community. The development communicator for the health and family welfare field has to work with and for the people. Therefore, he(development communicator) cannot afford to ignore the forces that integrate or disintegrate the community. "

REFERENCES

Cool, John, "Communication and Family Planning" in Satellite Communication Series Publication, ISRO, Ahmedabad.

Ghosh, D.K. (2001), "Population Policy : Role of Panchayats", Yojana, Vol. 45, July, pp. 36-39.

Hiramani, A. B. and Neelam Sharma (1992), "Health Communication in India: A Policy Perspective" in S.R. Mehta (Ed.) Communication and Development: Issues and Perspectives. Jaipur: Rawat Publications, pp. 262-263.

Howitt, Dennis (1982), Mass Media and Social Problems. Oxford: Oxford University Press, pp. 62-87.

Kakar, V.N. (1987), Communication in Family Planning–India's Experience. National Institute of Health and Family Welfare Publication, New Delhi, pp. 23-59.

Kuppuswami, B. (1976), Communication and Social Development in India. Sterling Publishers, New Delhi, pp. 41-59.

National Population Policy (2000).

New York Academy of Medicine Report (2005), New York.

Pant, K.C. (2000), Planning Commission Report. Government of India.

Trakroo, P.L. and Lalitendu Jagatdeb (1992), "Some Issues of Development Communication in Health and Welfare" in S. R. Mehta (Ed.) Communication and Development: Issues and Perspectives. Jaipur: Rawat Publications, pp. 243-44.

Young, J. (1973), " The Amplification of Drug Use" in Cohen and Young (Ed.) The Manufacture of News. London : British Press, pp. 33-48.

4

GENDER, DEVELOPMENT AND WOMEN'S HEALTH IN INDIA

Rekha K. Jadhav

This paper discusses the gender dimension of poverty levels and health inequalities in India. Alleviation of poverty in the developing world is the primary factor for the development of agencies and resources that are being diverted for the same purpose. There is need for the effective management and utilization of resources by the target groups that are essential to poverty alleviation strategies. Besides, gender bias in poverty studies indicate that women are particularly disadvantaged with respect to building tangible assets, access to resources such as the health care, education and labour force participation. This paper focuses more towards poverty, since poverty is increasing rapidly in the developing world and it remains a formidable challenge.

GENDER AND DEVELOPMENT

Development has been a global issue that has become prominent of the World War II, a time when the United States began to extend its role in emphasizing the benefits of modernization towards development. The success of the Marshal Plan in Europe convinced the developed world to undertake similar strategies in order to industrialize the third world. Development is purely a biological metaphor involving the natural processes of growth towards a full-fledged form at one level and when checked at the another level, it consists of conscious planning and intervention by which the resources, techniques, experts are assembled and are invested in the developing countries so as to improve the rates of economic growth and development. The notions of developed and underdeveloped were effectively created after 1945. Development within society needs to satisfy certain conditions pertaining to the capacity to obtain physical necessities particularly food, employment, equalization of income, education, political participation and societal independence. Hence promotion in economic growth will benefit developing countries and eventually the developed nations as well. By 1970's it was traced that the real development was taking place wherin at the same time voices were calling for the inclusion of women in the development process as there were negative impacts in various development projects. The ideas about how to effectively include women in development have shifted considerably. This focus shifts through various phases from women in development, women and development to gender and development which further indicates the need to envisage the relationship of women and men and the resulting inequalities as well as recognizing the multiple roles played by women in reproductive, productive and community work. Each of these perspectives, state the form of social changes that have influenced these perspectives.

In 1980's more holistic perspectives emerged. Gender and Development (GAD), steered away from the limitations posed by women in development (WID) and women and development (WAD) perspectives that focused upon social relations between men and women. So, development here is a complex process subjected to the social and economic factors, category of analysis is not restricted to women only but rather upon the social relations between men and women, where men are viewed as potential supporters of women. Focus in gender and development is on diverse relationship that men and women share as part of their everyday lives, the interaction of relationships within the existing social structures whether at the household or workplace gains importance in analysis. The individual position in the household and in the society, the effect of specific regional and broader global forces of social, economic and political factors shaping the interaction of these relationships are considered. Women are actually perceived as active participants in the overall process of decision making and not more recipients of development. Further, it is easier to examine the integration of social, economic, political and other factors into the domestic and reproductive lives of individuals as members of a society. The real emphasis is on the functioning of these various parts as an integrated whole, which can then lead to the betterment of individuals and the society itself by mating the basic physical, emotional and creative needs of the population. An interesting dimension here is that even the state should come forward to take part in the development process particularly in promoting women's emancipation. For this, involvement is urged at the all levels of the state, local, regional and central such that the welfare and the maintenance of the future generation is a shared concern and not just an individual responsibility.

Poverty remains a daunting challenge for the developing countries and there is an urgent need to reveal such conditions and create such conditions particularly made suitable for women to overcome poverty. There is need for change and development because gender dimensions of poverty and health do truly affect women folk.

POVERTY AND WOMEN'S HEALTH

Poor, particularly women and children who suffer for more inequalities than men are the underprivileged groups in the developing as well as in the developed countries. The causes of morbidity and mortality indicate poverty as the most basic cause for ill health and early death of the poor people. Health problems are direct manifestation of their social, physical environment and many health problems may be traced to malnutrition, workplace dangers, environmental pollution, stress etc., poverty is combined with the current social, political, economic condition that largely contributes to the deterioration of health status and provision of health care in developing nations, since poor women often lack to àccess medical facilities because of her critical household conditions. Women's health and the health of their households will improve significantly and lead to better participation of women in the developmental process, if the political, economic and ideological barriers stopped. The health of Indian women is intrinsically linked to their status in society and poor health has repercussions not only for women but also their families. Women in poor health are more likely to give birth to low-weight infants. They also are les likely to be able to provide food and adequate care for their children. Many of the health problems of Indian women are related to or exacerbated by high levels of fertility. India is one of the few countries in the world where women and men have nearly the same life expectancy at birth. The fact that the typical female advantage in life expectancy is not seen in India suggests there are systematic problems with women's health. Indian women have high mortality rates, particularly during childhood and in their reproductive years. According to the reports of International Institute for Population Science (IIPS), fertility has been declining in India, by 1992-93 the total fertility rate was 3.4. However, there are large differences in fertility levels by state, education, religion, caste and place of residence. Kerala, which has high levels of female education and autonomy, has a total fertility rate under two whereas Uttar Pradesh, relatively the most populous state in India, has a total fertility rate of over five children per woman.

Unwanted pregnancies terminated by unsafe abortions also have negative consequences for women's health. Reducing fertility is an important elements in improving the overall health of Indian women. Maternal mortality is most likely related to differences in the socio-economic status of women and access to health care services among the states. The high levels of maternal mortality are especially distressing because the majority of these deaths could be prevented if women had adequate health services. Most women do not receive health care during pregnancy because some women think it to be unnecessary. Hence, there is a definite need to educate women about the importance of health care for ensuring healthy pregnancies and safe childbirth. Besides, another reason for the low level of prenatal care is lack of adequate health care centres in rural India.

Majority of births in India still take place at home in non-hygienic conditions or births that are not attended by trained medical personnel are more likely to have negative outcomes for both mother and child. The number of infants who die in their first year is an important indicator of infant and maternal health. Infant mortality is commonly a result of low birth weight, poor nutrition, inadequate prenatal care, the mother's level of education, and her overall health, due to poor diet, stress, smoking, drinking and drug use or HIV/AIDS. It appears that poverty, combined with low female literacy under nutrition, poor environmental sanitation, the attitudes and perceptions of women and expectant mothers, traditions and taboos observed during pregnancy as far as infant feeling practices, provide a backdrop for high infant mortality and often maternal mortality for example the overall state for maternal mortality in India is 572.3 per 100,000 births, showing regional variations.

CONCLUSION

Health requires clear water, air and food, adequate housing, safety and security, healthy working conditions and emotional and material supports. The poorer segments of Indian society are disadvantaged with respect to women's health care facilities and nutrition compared to men particularly during the early years of her life as well as during their reproductive years. The high mortality rates of females during childhood not only reflects in general the cultural preferences given towards male child care and the will of having male children. Besides, it also indicates the problem of female literacy in India. Hence later age of marriage, smaller families as well as knowledge of contraception and better earning capacity can certainly alleviate poverty and improve the economic status of poor women.

NGOs are particularly important in the area of poverty alleviation at the community level. Although it appears that a significant number of studies deal with the conceptual understanding and ways of measuring poverty, poverty alleviation in India still remains a top priority with the policy makers. However, there are some grass-root initiatives taken by NGOs and other organizations to include the poor particularly women in poverty reduction strategies. For example, the Self Employed Women's Association (SEWA) has grown to encompass over 200,000 members in five Indian states. Many associations NGO's are on their way to measure poverty and are struggling hard to support towards poverty alleviation strategies. It would be interesting to examine the constraints and challenges faced by these organizations in working with the poor. Health is a function, not only of medical care, but of the overall integrated development of society. Therefore to raise the health status and quality of life of people particularly women, a focused approach integrating the development of social, cultural, economical and educational needs to emerge to bring about the overall transformation of a safe, healthy society.

REFERENCES

Chatterjee, Meera (1990), "Indian Women : Their Health and Economic Productivity", World Bank Discussion Papers 109, Washington DC.

Clinskaya, Elena and A. Thomas Mroz (2000), "The Gender Gap in Wages in Russia from 1992 to 1995", *Journal of Population Economics*, No. 13.

Charulatha Mitra (2002), "Women's Development Goals : Reshaping Globalisation", Authors Press Publications, New Delhi.

Gwynkirk, Margo Okazawa, Rey (2000), "Women's Lives", Mayfield Publishers, Toronto.

R.N. Pati (2003), "Socio-Cultural Dimensions of Reproductive Child Health", A.P.H. Publishings, New Delhi.

Health for the Millions (2000), July-August, Vol. 26, No. 4.

5

DISPARITIES IN JUVENILE SEX RATIOS IN INDIA: AN ANALYSIS

D. Pulla Rao

INTRODUCTION

The term 'Sex' describes the biological differences between men and women which are universal and determined at birth. The term 'Gender' is used to describe a set of qualities and behaviour expected from men and women by the society. The main differences between sex and gender are (i) Sex is a biological and physiological in nature, whereas gender is a sociological in nature. (ii) Sex is determined by birth but gender is determined by the society. (iii) Sex cannot be changed but gender can be changed. (iv) Sex is universal but gender contexts specific i.e., varies according to place, time, culture etc.

The typical Indian woman is best portrayed on the celluloid as the eternal tear-jerking image. The indefatigable 'Gruhini' adorns the status of a doormat. Her 'pathi' is the real God on the earth to her. He could be wayward; he could be dipsomania; he could be half Witter; he could be moron; yet she submits herself even to his unjust demands as in mythological stories where 'Anusuya' carrying her husband on her head to a prostitute house. This hackneyed image is obviously a reflection of womanhood in Indian society. Nevertheless, for centuries she has been subjected to eternal exploitation by men folk. The male domination, perpetuated either by economic necessity or social compulsions, has taken a heavy toll on the half of the global Homo sapiens. The problem is not, of course, unique to India, but it is particularly serious in this country, and certainly deserves public attention as a matter of major priority. The focal areas, where gender disparities are deliberately sustained and meticulously fostered from time immemorial are: (a) Overall sex ratio or female-male ratio (FMR) including juvenile sex ratio (JSR), (b) literacy and education, (c) food and nutrition, (d) health care system, (e) work participation rate and opportunity to employment, (f) access to economic resources particularly income and property, and (g) political participation. An attempt is made in this paper to ponder over first major issue i.e., sex ratio. An attempt is made to highlight the available factual information at international, national and state levels.

CONSTITUTIONAL AND LEGISLATIVE PROVISIONS RELATING TO WOMEN IN INDIA

Before analysing the gender disparities in India in a comparative perspective, it would be appropriate to briefly review the constitutional provisions and legislative measures relating to women in India. The Constitution of India not only grants equality to women but also empowers the state to adopt measures of positive discrimination in favour of women for neutralising the cumulative socio-economic, educational, political disadvantages faced by them. To be more precise, Article 14 confers on men and women equal rights and opportunities in the political, economic and social spheres. Article 15 prohibits discrimination against any citizen on the grounds of religion, race, caste and *sex*. Article 15(3) makes a special provision enabling the state to make *affirmative discrimination in favour of women*. Article 16 provides for equality of opportunities in matter of public appointments for all citizens irrespective of sex. Besides the above Fundamental Rights, the Constitution also enshrines the following Directive Principles of State Policy, which, though non-enforceable by court of law, provide guidelines for framing government policies. Article 39(a) mentions that the state shall direct its policy towards securing all citizens, men and women equally the right to means of livelihood, while Article 39(c) ensures equal pay for equal work for both men and women. Article 42 directs the state to make provision for ensuring just and humane conditions of work and maternity relief for women. Above all the Constitution imposes a fundamental duty on every citizen through Article 15(a) and (e) to renounce the practices adversely affecting the dignity of women.

In addition to these constitutional provisions, special legislations have also been enacted to make the de jure equality into de facto one. The state has enacted the following women specific and women related legislations to protect women against social discrimination, violence, atrocities and also to prevent social evils like child marriage, dowry, rape, practice of sati etc. The Child Marriage Restraint Act of 1976 raises the age for marriage of a girl from 15 years to 18 years and makes offences under this Act cognizable. An amendment brought in 1984 to the Dowry Prohibitions Act of 1961 made subjection of women to cruelty a cognizable offence. The second amendment brought in 1986 makes the husband or in-laws punishable if a woman commits suicide within 7 years of her marriage. Also a new criminal offence of dowry death has been incorporated in the Indian Penal Code. The Medical Termination of Pregnancy Act of 1971 legalises abortion by qualified professionals on humanitarian or medical grounds. Amendments to criminal law 1983 provide for a punishment of 7 years in ordinary cases of rape and 10 years for custodial rape cases. The maximum punishment may go up to life imprisonment. A new enactment of Indecent Representation of women (Prohibition) Act of 1986 and the Commission of Sati (Prevention) Act 1987 have also been passed to protect the dignity of women and prevent violence against them as well as their exploitation. The Immoral Traffic (Prevention) Act of 1956 as amended and renamed in 1986 makes the sexual exploitation of male or female a cognizable offence. Hindu Succession Act 1956 enables Hindu Women to inherit or bequeath the property of their fathers along with their brothers. The Factories Act 1948 (Amended up to

1976) provides for establishment of creche where 30 women are employed (including casual and contract labourers). The Maternity Benefit Act 1961 makes the extension of maternity benefits mandatory on the part of factories. The Equal Remuneration of Act of 1976 provides for equal pay for equal work for both men and women.

SEX RATIOS OR FEMALE-MALE RATIO (FMR)

Sex ratio is one of the existing crucial manifestations of the wide spread disparities between the female and male. Sex ratio is defined as number of females per 1000 males. Sex ratio is a useful indicator to understand women's health and position in any society. There are remarkable variations in the FMR in different regions of the world. In Europe and North America, even though males outnumber females at birth, women tend to outnumber men substantially later with an average ratio around 1.05. In contrast to this, in many parts of third world countries, FMR tends to be substantially below unity. In India, the FMR averaged around 933, which is one of the lowest in the world. India has distinction along with China and few other South Asian countries having a deficit of females for a long period. This is largely interpreted as the symptom of low status of women and discrimination of females existing in the county. Unusually high mortality Indian women faced relative to males until recently confirmed this fact. The female mortality registered significantly high rates than males at the younger ages, through it reverted recently.

OVERALL SEX RATIOS IN INDIA

Ashish Bose and Agnihotri stated that 2001 census has revealed a shocking truth namely, sharply declining female-male ratio in several states. They further stated that migration cannot explain this phenomenon, which must be the consequence of female foeticide on a massive scale, if not female infanticide and higher female child mortality rates. Sex ratio is a useful indicator to understand women's health and position in any society. India has distinction along with China and few other South Asian countries having a deficit of females for a long period. This is largely interpreted as the symptom of low status of women and discrimination of females existing in the county. The female mortality registered significantly high rates than males at the younger ages, though it reverted recently. This is revealed through a study of the sex ratios existing in our country from 1901 onwards. Strangely enough, in spite of the advances in medical sciences, the drop in death rate from 42.6 per cent in 1901–1911 to 8.4 per cent in 2001, the tremendous advances made in eradication of malaria and control of infectious diseases like tuberculosis, as well as, an increase in life expectancy for women from 23.3 years in 190 – 1910 to 64.2 in 1996–2001, the sex ratios of our population continue to be adverse for women. In 1901, the sex ratio was 972 females per 1000 men. This ratio has been continuously declining from 1901 onwards except in 1951, 1981 and 2001. It is 933 in 2001 (Table 1).

Table 1
Population and Overall Sex Ratios in India: 1901-2001

Census year	*Total population (in millions)*	*Sex ratios (females per 1,000 males)*
1901	238.10	972
1911	252.09	964
1921	252.32	955
1931	278.98	950
1941	318.66	945
1951	361.09	946
1961	439.24	941
1971	548.16	930
1981	685.18	933
1991	844.33	927
2001	1027.02	933

Source: Census of India, 2001.

CHILD SEX RATIO (CSR)

The age distribution of population in the Indian census follows five yearly groupings like 0- 4, 5-9, 10-14 and so on. In 1991, it was decided to calculate literacy rates for the population seven years and over. Therefore, a new category of 0-6 age group was introduced in the primary census abstract, and literacy data for the age group seven and above were sorted out. Besides 0-

6 age group, was convenient to study the import of the Integrated Child Development Services etc. In keeping with this practice, the 2001 census tables give data on literacy after excluding 0-6 age groups. In this process separate figures are available for the sex composition of the 0-6 age group which is also called the juvenile group.

Child Sex Ratio (CSR) in Global Perspective

Data on declining child sex ratio in the developed world have been published in the "World Population Prospects: The 2002 Revision, Volume II, Sex and Age Distribution of Population, United Nations, New York, 2003 (U.N. Secretariate, Department of Economic and Social Affairs, Population Division)". The period under study covers the 50 years from 1950 to 2000. If there was a culture of silence and denial in the Third World, then it was very much there in the First World too, where the technologies for sex selection originated and the notion of individual choice got vulgarized to unimaginable extents.

The average CSR (0-4 age group) in the developed regions comprising Europe, North America, Australia, New Zealand and Japan showed a steady decline in the 50-year period from 957 female children (per 1,000 male children) in 1950 to 949 in 2000. In contrast, the CSR for this age group in the least developed countries (49 in all-34 in Africa, nine in Asia, one in Latin America and the Caribbean and five in Oceania) stood at 998 in 1950, much higher than that in the developed block, and in 2000 it was 976.

Similarly, the CSR for the 5-9 age group was 1,002 girl children in 1950 and 977 in 2000. Though the decline is sharp, the figure remains much higher than the corresponding figure for this age group in the more developed regions. Even in South-East Asia, where in 1950 the CSR stood at 1,003, the figure came down to 963 in 2000, and the reasons for the decline were not entirely cultural. If they were so, then in the absence of sex-selection technology, female children would still have been eliminated by mass foeticide. As in Africa, the CSR decline in Islamic countries between 1950 and 2000 was not permanent. In fact, Afghanistan showed a marginal improvement. And,

Iraq, reeling under the weight of U.N. sanctions, showed a dramatic improvement in the survival of the girl child in the 0-4 age group. In 2000, its CSR stood at 964, higher than the world average of 949 (Table 2).

Table 2
Global Child Sex Ratio

Country	*0-4 Age Group*		*5-9 Age Group*	
	1950	*2000*	*1950*	*2000*
North America	977	951	957	952
Latin America & Caribbean	977	962	982	964
Northern Europe	953	949	960	952
Iraq	945	964	954	965
Saudi Arabia	968	055	968	955
Iran	986	951	980	949
Afghanistan	948	947	933	939
Pakistan	968	944	999	939
Asia	944	936	956	932
China	892	898	903	897
Nepal	992	943	979	934
Bangladesh	1014	954	1003	950
Sri Lanka	758	966	868	970
India	976	941	982	934
South-East Asia	1003	963	1013	967

Source: World Population Prospects: The 2002 Revision, Vol. II. Sex and Age Distribution of Population, United Nations.

Juvenile Sex Ratio: An All India Perspective

The data in Table 3 shows a sharp decline in the sex ratio of the under 0-6-age population in the last 40 years, i.e., 976 in 1961, 964 in 1971, 962 in 1981, 945 in 1991 and 927 in 2001, a decline of 18 points in this last decade.

Juvenile Sex Ratios: State Wise Break up

The data in Table 4 we present data for two groups: 0-6 age group and 7+ age group. It will be seen that in most of the States and Union Territories the child sex ratio has gone down in 2001. The decline is most prounced in Punjab where the sex ratio in the age group 0-6 years fall from 875 to 793 (a decrease of 82 points), in Haryana (59 points), in Himachal Pradesh and Chandigarh (54 points each) and Gujarat (50 points). These declines are in areas which had already been flagged as showing

Table 3
Sex Ratio in 0-6 Age Group

Year	*Sex ratio in 0-6 age group*	*Variation*
1961	976	–
1971	964	–12
1981	962	–2
1991	945	–17
2001	927	–18

Source: Census of India, 2001.

low sex ratio among children and as regions which were seeing a rapid growth of sex determination clinics (pre–natal Diagnostic Techniques, PNDT) and questionable abortions, with a high likelihood of female foeticides. Surprisingly even Maharastra, the first state who have been passed the pre–natal Diagnostic Techniques (regulation and prevention) act (PNDT act) also registered a decline in the under – 6 sex-ratio, from 946 to 917 (29 points). In fact all states except Kerala, Mizoram and Tripura who had impact of Christian Missionaries have reported fewer girls than boys under six years.

Juvenile Sex Ratio in Andhra Pradesh

Juvenile sex ratio is very low as compared to overall sex ratio in Andhra Pradesh as per the 2001 census. Juvenile sex ratio is decreased from 975 in 1991 to 964 in 2001 in the state. Of the four plausible reasons for a change in sex ratio (differential mortality, differential undercount, change in sex ratio at birth and sex-specific migration), differential infant and child mortality is often considered as the main reasons for decline in sex ratio at younger ages.

District-Wise Juvenile Sex Ratios In Andhra Pradesh

To a great surprise and dismay, however, a decline in sex ratio is observed in the age group 0-6 between 1991 and 2001 in the state. The decline is to the tune of 11 points from 975 in 1991 to 964 in 2001. Considering census year 1981-2001, the decline amount to around 28 points. The all India pattern also portrays nearly the same picture as far as juvenile sex ratio is concerned. The 0-6 age group sex ratio for 1991 and 2001 census years is

Table 4
Juvenile Sex Ratio By States/Uts in India Ranked According to Decline in Sex Ratio of 0-6 Population

Rank	India/States/UT	Sex ratio (0-6 age group) 1991	2001	Difference points
	India	*945*	*927*	*–18*
1.	Punjab	875	793	–82
2.	Haryana	879	820	–59
3.	Himachal Pradesh	951	897	–54
4.	Chandigarh UT	899	845	–54
5.	Gujarat	928	878	–50
6.	Delhi	915	865	–50
7.	Uttaranchal	948	906	–42
8.	Dadra & Nagar Haveli UT	1,013	973	–40
9.	Daman & Diu UT	958	925	–33
10.	Goa	964	933	–31
11.	Maharashtra	946	917	–29
12.	Arunachal Pradesh	982	961	–21
13.	Nagaland	993	975	–18
14.	Orissa	967	950	–17
15.	Bihar	953	938	–15
16.	Manipur	974	961	–13
17.	Jharkhand	979	966	–13
18.	Madhya Pradesh	941	929	–12
19.	Meghalaya	986	975	–11
20.	Uttar Pradesh	927	916	–11
21.	Assam	975	964	–11
22.	Karnataka	960	949	–11
23.	Andhra Pradesh	975	964	–11
24.	Chhatisgarh	984	975	–9
25.	TamilNadu	948	939	–9
26.	Andaman& NicobarIsland UT	973	965	–8
27.	Rajasthan	916	909	–7
28.	Pondicherry UT	963	958	–5
29.	West Bengal	967	963	–4
30.	Mizoram	969	971	2
31.	Kerala	958	963	5
32.	Tripura	967	975	8
33.	Sikkim	965	986	21
34.	Lakshadweep UT	941	974	33
35.	Jammu & Kashmir	NA	937	–

Source: Compiled from population of India 2001, Census Results and Methodology by Ashish Bose.

presented in Table 5. The decline is observed in almost all the districts except Nellore and Anantapur. The sharpest decline is observed in the districts of Mahabubnagar, Adilabad and

Warangal. Interestingly, Mahabubnagar and Adilabad are some of the poorest districts in the state. As the decline is observed in almost all the districts covering all regions, it does not likely to follow any particular economic or social pattering.

Table 5
Juvenile Sex Ratio by Districts, Andhra Pradesh

District	*1991*	*2001*	*2001-1991*
Srikakulam	986	976	–11
Vizianagaram	996	981	–15
Visakhapatnam	985	973	–12
East Godavari	994	978	–16
West Godavari	984	977	–7
Krishna	964	959	–5
Guntur	970	955	–14
Prakasam	969	966	–4
Nellore	937	955	19
Cuddapah	968	952	–16
Kurnool	955	944	–11
Anantpur	962	963	1
Chittoor	970	959	–10
Adilabad	986	964	–22
Nizamabad	979	966	–14
Karimnagar	981	977	–3
Medak	981	964	–17
Hyderabad	963	950	–13
Rangareddy	972	970	–2
Mahabubnagar	981	957	–24
Nalgonda	981	962	–19
Warangal	977	955	–22
Khammam	981	968	–12
Andhra Pradesh	975	964	–11

Source: Computed from Census of India (2001) Andhra Pradesh, Provisional Population Totals, Paper 1 of 2001 Series, 29.

District-Wise Rural Urban Variations in Juvenile Sex Ratios in Andhra Pradesh

We have also presented at the juvenile sex ratio for rural and urban areas in Table 6. It is thought that sex determination tests, if widely practiced, should be concentrated more in urban areas where such facilities are easily available and should reflect in the decline in urban sex ratio more than rural. The data, however, shows no such indication, both rural and urban areas experienced decline in juvenile sex ratio without much exception.

Table 6
District-Wise Rural Urban Variations in Juvenile Sex Ratios in Andhra Pradesh

District	*1991*		*2001*		*2001–1991*	
	Rural	*Urban*	*Rural*	*Urban*	*Rural*	*Urban*
Srikakulam	988	976	976	975	-12	-1
Vizianagaram	999	977	986	956	-13	-21
Visakhapataam	994	969	978	963	-16	-6
East Godavari	991	1003	974	993	-17	-10
West Godavari	989	959	976	981	-13	22
Krishna	968	956	968	942	0	-14
Guntur	970	969	953	961	-17	-8
Prakasam	969	969	967	959	-2	-10
Nellore	971	828	955	955	-16	127
Chittoor	972	959	963	946	-9	-13
Cuddapah	969	963	949	952	-20	-11
Anantapur	960	971	961	971	1	0
Kurnool	952	967	941	956	-11	-11
Mahabubnagar	983	958	957	959	-26	1
Rangareddy	980	962	994	945	14	-17
Hyderabad		963		950	0	-13
Medak	982	974	965	956	-17	-18
Nizamabad	984	960	965	972	-19	12
Adilabad	991	969	968	951	-23	-18
Karinmagar	991	944	982	957	-9	13
Warangal	982	953	954	960	-28	7
Khammam	982	974	968	971	-14	-3
Nalgonda	982	977	960	981	-22	4
Andhra Pradesh	979	962	965	958	-14	-4

Source: Computed from Census of India (2001) Andhra Pradesh, Provisional Population.

CONCLUSIONS

Gender discrimination or inequality from womb to tomb is a patent fact in the traditional cultures of the developing countries. In India too, discrimination on the basis of sex often starts at the earliest stages of life. The development processes of independent India, at a pace never achieved before, have also not succeeded in stopping the decline of sex ratios. A large number of migrant males who come to work in some cities may be responsible for the adverse female sex ratio. The other reasons for decline in sex ratio are differential mortality between males and females, differential undercount of females than males and drop in the female births leading to adverse sex ratio at birth.

The child sex ratio for the 5-9 age group was 1,002 girl child in 1950 and 977 in 2000. Though decline is sharp, the figure remains much higher than the corresponding figure for this age group in the more developed regions in the world.

There is a sharp decline in the child sex ratio of the under 0-6 age population in the last 40 years in India. In most of the States and Union Territories the juvenile sex ratio (0-6 age group) has gone down in 2001. Maharashtra, the first state which has been passed the PNDT act also registered a decline in the under–6 sex–ratio, from 946 in 1991 to 917 in 2001 (29 points). Juvenile sex ratio is very low as compared to overall sex ratio in Andhra Pradesh as per 2001 census. Juvenile sex ratio is decreased from 975 in 1991 to 964 in 2001 in the state. There is no doubt that increasing use of pre-natal sex determination tests and female foeticide must have contributed significantly to the significant decline in the juvenile sex ratio in the last two decades.

REFERENCES

Agnihotri, S.B. (2001), "Rising Sons and Setting Daughters Provisional Results of the 2001 Census", in Vina Mazumdar and M. Krishnaji (eds.) Enduring Conundrum: India's Sex Ratio, Centre for Women's Development Studies, Rainbow Publishers, Delhi.

Ashish Bose (2001), Population of India, 2001 Census Results and Methodology, B.R. Publishing Corporation, Delhi.

Ashish Bose. (2001), "Fighting Female Foeticide: Grouping greed and Shrinking Child Sex Ratio", *Economic and Political Weekly*, Sept. 8, pp. 3427-29.

Coale, A. (1991), "Excess Female Mortality and the Balance of the Sexes: An Estimate of the Number of Missing Females," Publication and Development Review, 17, pp. 517-23.

Government of India (2001), SRS Bulletin, Vol. 35, No. 1 Registrar General, New Delhi.

Harriss, B. (1989), "Differential Child Mortality and Health Care in South Asia" *Journal of Social Studies*, 44, pp. 21-23.

Mahendra K. Premi. (2001), "The Missing Girl Child", *Economic and Political Weekly*, May 26, pp. 1875-80.

The Annual Reports of the Department of Women and Child Development, Ministry of Human Resource Development, Government of India, New Delhi, 1985-86, 1997-98.

The Annual Reports of the Ministry of Health and Family Welfare, Government of India, New Delhi, 1985-86, 1997-98.

Visaria, Pravin (1961), The Sex Ratio of the Population of India, Census of India, 1961, Monograph No. 10, New Delhi: Registrar General of India.

6

TRENDS OF SEX RATIO IN INDIA: THE DISAPPEARING GIRL CHILD

Anand Bhaskar

Any society is characterized by its population and basically its population structure. The mstudy of the structure and characteristic of population, which is also known as the study of the composition of population, covers many aspect of population studies, which embraces the following basic personal, social and economic characteristics or attributes of any population: age, sex, race, nationality, religion, language, marital status, household and family composition, literacy and educational attainment, employment status, occupation, income, etc.

Sex and age are the basic characteristics or the biological attributes, of any demographic group and affect not only its demographic but also its social, economic and political structure, for they influence birth and death rate, internal and international migration, marital status composition. Sex and age are also very important because they are the "visible, indisputable and convenient indicators of social status". Each individual is ascribed a certain status in society on the basis of sex and age. It is well known, for instance, that in the traditional Hindu family, status is accorded on the basis of sex and age; men are more important than women and older persons are more important than younger persons. So culture and tradition is responsible for the status and role of individual in a society and this also affect the demographic composition.

Sex Structure: According to Bhende and Kanitkar (1978) for the study of the sex-structure of any population, the following two measures are generally adopted: (1) the percentage of males in the population, and (2) the sex ratio. Of these two measures, the later is more frequently used in the study of population. The sex ratio of a population may either be expressed as the number of males per 100 female or as the number females per 100 males. But Indian census defines *sex ratio as "the number of females per 1,000 males"*. According to the 2001 census in India, the sex ratio is 933; it means 933 females per 1,000 males.

Indian society is a plural and multidimensional society; where the sex ratio varies from region to region and community to community. According to the census 2001, women make up 48. 2% of India's population. The female population grew at a slower pace of 23. 27% during the decade 1981-91. The sex ratio which was 972 females per 1,000 males in 1901 declined to 927 in 1991, and went up only slightly to 933 in 2001. India is among the very few countries with an adverse sex ratio which is attributed to higher mortality among women in all age groups right from childhood through child-bearing ages, high maternal mortality and female infanticide. The districts with the worst child sex ratio were all in Punjab and Haryana, two of India's wealthiest states. While the ratio of males to females at birth is about 52:48, there is a sharp decline over the years. While the sex ratio of infants is 861 female to 1,000 males the ratio plummeted to 849 by age fourteen.

The 'First Report on Religion Data, 2001' collected during census 2001 and released by the Registrar General and Census Commissioner of India, brings to light the persistent bias among communities against the girl child and clarifies that region plays a greater role than religion in overall development indicators. Although the population growth rate among both Hindus and Muslims fell significantly between 1991 and 2001, the most alarming revelation of census 2001 was the declining child sex ratio within the age-group 0-6 years. More distorting is the continuing bias shown by prosperous communities towards the

Table 1
Statewise Sex Ratio (Female per 1,000 Males) in India

State/UT code	India/State/Union territory*	Census Year 1901	1911	1921	1931	1941	1951	1961	1971	1981	1991	2001
	INDIA[1,2,3]	*972*	*964*	*955*	*950*	*945*	*946*	*941*	*930*	*934*	*927*	*933*
30.	Jammu & Kashmir[2]	882	876	870	865	869	873	878	878	892	896	900
2.	Himachal Pradesh[3]	884	889	890	897	890	912	938	958	973	976	970
3.	Punjab	832	780	799	815	836	844	854	865	879	882	874
4.	Chandigarh*	771	720	743	751	763	781	652	749	769	790	773
5.	Uttaranchal	918	907	916	913	907	940	947	940	936	936	964
6.	Haryana	867	835	844	844	869	871	868	867	870	865	861
7.	Delhi*	862	793	733	722	715	768	785	801	808	827	821
8.	Rajasthan	905	908	896	907	906	921	908	911	919	910	922
9.	Uttar Pradesh	938	916	908	903	907	908	907	876	882	876	898
10.	Bihar	1,061	1,051	1,020	995	1,002	1,000	1,005	957	948	907	921
11.	Sikkim	916	951	970	967	920	907	904	863	835	878	875
12.	Arunachal Pradesh*	NA	NA	NA	NA	NA	NA	894	861	862	859	901
13.	Nagaland	973	993	992	997	1,021	999	933	871	863	886	909
14.	Manipur	1,037	1,029	1,041	1,065	1,055	1,036	1,015	980	971	958	978
15.	Mizoram	1,113	1,120	1,109	1,102	1,069	1,041	1,009	946	919	921	938
16.	Tripura	874	885	885	885	886	904	932	943	946	945	950
17.	Meghalaya	1,036	1,013	1,000	971	966	949	937	942	954	955	975
18.	Assam	919	915	896	874	875	868	869	896	910	923	932
19.	West Bengal	945	925	905	890	852	865	878	891	911	917	934
20.	Jharkhand	1,032	1,021	1,002	989	978	961	960	945	940	922	941
21.	Orissa	1,037	1,056	1,086	1,067	1,053	1,024	1,001	988	981	971	972

Contd...

State/India/State/ UT code	Union territory*	Census Year 1901	1911	1921	1931	1941	1951	1961	1971	1981	1991	2001
	INDIA[1,2,3]	*972*	*964*	*955*	*950*	*945*	*946*	*941*	*930*	*934*	*927*	*933*
22.	Chhatisgarh	1,046	1,039	1,041	1,043	1,032	1,024	1,008	998	996	985	990
23.	Madhya Pradesh	972	967	949	947	946	945	932	920	921	912	920
24.	Gujarat[3]	954	946	944	945	941	952	940	934	942	934	921
25.	Daman & Diu*	995	1,040	1,143	1,088	1,080	1,125	1,169	1,099	1,062	969	709
26.	Dadra & Nagar Haveli*	960	967	940	911	925	946	963	1,007	974	952	811
27.	Maharashtra	978	966	950	947	949	941	936	930	937	934	922
28.	Andhra Pradesh	985	992	993	987	980	986	981	977	975	972	978
29.	Karnataka	983	983	969	965	960	966	959	957	963	960	964
30.	Goa	1,091	1,108	1,120	1,088	1,084	1,128	1,066	981	975	967	960
31.	Lakshadweep*	1,063	987	1,027	994	1,018	1,043	1,020	978	975	943	947
32.	Kerala	1,004	1,008	1,011	1,022	1,027	1,028	1,022	1,016	1,032	1,036	1,058
33.	Tamil Nadu	1,044	1,042	1,029	1,027	1,012	1,007	992	978	977	974	986
34.	Pondicherry*	NA	1,058	1,053	NA	NA	1,030	1,013	989	985	979	1,001
35.	Andaman & Nicobar Is*	318	352	303	495	574	625	617	644	760	818	846

Note:1. For working out the sex ratio of India and Assam for 1981, interpolated figures for Assam have not been used.

2. For working out the sex ratio of India and Jammu and Kashmir for 1991, interpolated figures for Jammu and Kashmir have been used.

3. For working out the sex ratio of India, Gujarat and Himachal Pradesh for 2001, estimated figures for affected areas of Gujarat and Himachal Pradesh have been used.

4. The sex ratio for Arunachal Pradesh is not available for the years 1901-1951 and for Pondicherry it is not available for the years 1901, 1931 and 1941.

Table 2
States and UT are Arranged in the Descending Order of Sex Ratio: (Census 2001)

Rank	*State/UT*	*Sex ratio*
1.	Kerala	1,058
2.	Pondicherry	1,001
3.	Chhatisgarh	990
4.	Tamil Nadu	986
5.	Manipur	978
6.	Andhra Pradesh	978
7.	Meghalaya	975
8.	Orissa	972
9.	Himachal Pradesh	970
10.	Uttaranchal	964
11.	Karnataka	964
12.	Goa	960
13.	Tripura	950
14.	Lakshadweep	947
15.	Jharkhand	941
16.	Mizoram	938
17.	West Bengal	934
	INDIA	933
18.	Assam	932
19.	Maharashtra	922
20.	Rajasthan	922
21.	Gujarat	921
22.	Bihar	921
23.	Madhya Pradesh	920
24.	Nagaland	909
25.	Arunachal Pradesh	901
26.	Jammu & Kashmir	900
27.	Uttar Pradesh	898
28.	Sikkim	875
29.	Punjab	874
30.	Haryana	861
31.	Andaman & Nicobar Island	846
32.	Delhi	821
33.	Dadra & Nagar Haveli	811
34.	Chandigarh	773
35.	Daman & Diu	709

girl-child. The report mentions that Sikhs and Jains – two of the more prosperous communities in the country record the lowest child sex ratio. The Sikh community, with 786 girls for every 1,000 boys, has the lowest child sex ratio followed by the Jains (870/1000).

According to the report, the overall sex ratio, although better than the child sex ratio, is dismal too. The data discloses some disquieting figures among the various religious groups. There are 931 Hindu women for every 1,000 Hindu men, which is less than the national average of 933 women for every 1,000 men. The figure among Muslims is slightly better, at 936/1000. Christians have the highest sex ratio: 1,009 females per 1,000 males, Sikhs record the lowest overall sex ratio: 893/1,000.

Table 3

Sex Ratio and Other Indicators Among Different Communities in India***

	Overall Sex ratio	*Child sex ratio (0-6 years)*	*Proportion in India's total population***	*Overall literacy rate***	*Female literacy rate***	*Female work participation rate***
Hindus	931	925	81.4	65.1	53.2	27.5
Muslims	936	950	12.4	59.1	50.1	14.1
Jains	940	870	0.4	94.1	90.6	9.2
Sikhs	893	786	1.9	69.4	63.1	20.2
Christians	1,009	964	2.3	80.3	76.2	31.7
Buddhists	953	942	0.8	72.7	61.7	31.7
Others	992	976	0.7	47.0	33.2	44.2

Note: *As number of females per 1,000 males; **as per cent; ***based on census 2001.

SOME INTERESTING FACTS:

- Female literacy among Sikhs and Jains is encouraging as compared to other religions. Despite this, the two communities have the lowest child sex ratio.
- The Jain community has the highest female literacy rate at 90.6. But female work participation is the lowest in this community at 9.2%.
- Buddhists, with a female literacy rate (61.7%) lower than that of Sikhs (63.1%) has a higher child sex ratio (942/1,000) than both Sikhs and Jains.
- The child sex ratio of Muslims (950/1,000) is better than that of Hindus (925/1,000).
- In Punjab, the child sex ratio is lower than 900/1,000 amongst all religious groups.

- In Gujarat, Muslims face much better than Hindus on almost all counts. Female literacy among Muslims (63. 5%) is better than that among Hindus (56. 7%). The overall literacy rate among Muslims (73. 5%) is better than that among Hindus (68. 3%). Among Muslims the child sex ratio is 913/1,000; among Hindus its 880/ 1,000.

The report questions the popular belief that literacy rates have a direct bearing on population and that literate people are less prone to gender bias. Although this may be true in some other cases as with Muslims having one of the lowest literacy rates (59. 1%) and the highest population growth rates, the same logic does not hold true among the Jain community that has the highest literacy rate (94. 1%) but a low child sex ratio. The report is quick to point out that Tamil Nadu, despite its literacy rate, has been able to keep a check on its fertility rate.

RELIGION VERSUS REGION

There are regions in the country where all religions have either a high literacy rate or a low literacy rate. Therefore it would appear that the effects of religion are weak in several parts of the country and that overall regional factors and low or high development among the states contribute to the improvement or lack of progress in literacy.

The southern states report Muslim population growth rates lower than the national average, because population growth rates in general are lower here. The same holds true for Christians – although the community has the highest child sex ratio across the country its child sex ratio is down to 870/1,000 in Punjab. States such as Punjab, Haryana and Gujarat depict a distinct bias against the girl-child regardless of religious affiliation.

The report echoes India's north-south divide that is clearly reflected in a number of key development indicators. The child sex ratio makes it clear, that the southern states are less biased towards girl-children than their northern counterparts (Table 4).

Table 4
The North-South Divide

North		South	
Punjab	788	Kerala	960
Haryana	819	Tamil Nadu	942
Delhi	868	Karnataka	946
Chandigarh	845	Andhra Pradesh	961

Child sex ratio (0-6) as number of girls per 1,000 boys.

Economists have long discussed how social services function much better in south Indian villages compared to those in the north. The report argues that one of the reasons for this is the poor status of women in the north. Historically, Punjab has always reported good economic indicators but is poor on social indicators, whilst in Kerala the reverse is true.

The 'First Report on Religion Data 2001' concludes that regional disparities remain the biggest challenge to overall development in the country.

This regional disparity can also be seen at the state level. U.P. has the biggest populace in the country and its population is much more than Pakistan. There are only four countries which have more population than U.P. These are China, U.S.A., Indonesia and Brazil. But any one can realize that the regional disparities in U.P. are not only in the demographic account but also in other areas, such as socio-economic development, modernization, literacy, etc. Often, U.P. is divided in East and West and it is argued that Western U.P. is more developed than Eastern U.P. But an interesting fact is that where highest sex ratio districts are in Eastern U.P. the lowest sex ratio districts are in Western U.P. Table 5 shows that all 23 districts of Western U.P. are the below on average sex ratio of U.P. so this is an important figure which represents the regional disparities prevailing in U.P.

SEX AND GENDER BIASEDNESS

Sex is simply a biological distinction between male and female. It is basically a difference in chromosome and its primary relevance is to reproduction. But the concept of gender is a cultural phenomenon with its corresponding emphasis on

Table 5
The East-West Divide in Uttar Pradesh

Rank	East		West	
1.	Azamgarh*	1020	Bijnor	896
2.	Jaunpur*	1014	Jyotiba Fule Nagar	885
3.	Pratapgarh*	1004	Bulandshahr	879
4.	Deoria*	1002	Rampur	879
5.	Mau*	986	Moradabad	875
6.	Sultanpur	980	Meerut	872
7.	Ambedkar Nagar	978	Bareilly	871
8.	Ghazipur	976	Muzaffarnagar	871
9.	Sant Kabir Nagar	974	Saharanpur	865
10.	Kushinagar	963	Aligarh	862
11.	Gorakhpur	960	Ghaziabad	860
12.	Ballia	953	Hathras	858
13.	Siddharath Nagar	948	Mainpuri	957
14.	Faizabad	939	Firozabad	852
15.	Basti	938	Etah	849
16.	Mahrajganj	934	Farrukhabad	848
17.	Chandauli	922	Bagpat	847
18.	Bhadohi	917	Agra	846
19.	Varanasi	903	Hardoi**	844
20.	Sonbhadra	898	Badaun**	842
21.	Mirzapur	897	Shahjahanpur**	842
22.	Kaushambi	895	Gautam Buddh Nagar**	841
23.	Allahabad	879	Mathura**	840

Sex ratio as number of females per 1,000 males is based on Census 2001.

Note: 1. Sex ratio of India is 933 and U.P. is 898 according to Census 2001.
2. The bold data represents that they are below the average level.
3. * is the highest sex ratio in U.P. while ** is the lowest.

attitudes and behaviour. In other words, gender is a cultural bag which determines that each sex must be socially and culturally different. According to cultural differences, every society expects men and women to perform their gender roles.

Sexism is an ideology and a universal phenomenon which exaggerates the differences between men and women and rationalizes the superiority of men. Biologically the differences between men and women are not unequal and both are treated as human beings but this is culture which creates differences between them and transforms sex into gender and ultimately gender biased-ness takes place. As M. Haralambos quotes in his book (1980):

> Original sin in the Gerden of Edam was women. She tasted the forbidden fruit, tempted Adam and has been paying for it ever since. In Genesis, the Lord said, 'I will greatly multiply thy sorrow and thy conception; in sorrow thou shall bring forth children; and thy desire shall be to thy husband, and he shall rule over thee'.

Sociologists would regard the above quotation as a mythological justification for the position of women in society.

During the past three decades, there have been rapid changes in South Asia, not only in the socio-economic and political sector, but also in the demographic sector. In most of the countries of this region, the population growth has declined as a result of fertility decline. In most cases, it has been belief that lower fertility should increase the value of human capital, help to accelerate the socio-economic development and bring about greater gender equity. However, in some countries lower fertility helping towards the gender bias, for example gender preference, especially for male children, and India is one of them. The evidences show that the prevailing gender discrimination is one of the major problems in the Indian society. The preference of male child and discrimination against the female child is causing the rapid disappearance of female child in India.

On every index of welfare and development, Indian women are at the bottom, be it literacy, medical attention, nutrition, infant mortality, poverty, death rate or wages. Several peculiar Indian customs such as Sati, child marriage, dowry, ban on widow remarriage, in the absence of civil registration of marriages, female infanticide, and the institution of Devadasi made the position of women precarious and indefensible. Now every attempt is being made to restrict even nature's own sex selection process. There is widespread use of sex determination tests which invariably lead to female foeticides. The law regulating the sex detection process has simply sent the business underground. As Kalpana Sharma wrote in the Hindu Magazine (August 29, 2005):

> Sex-detection and sex selective abortions are today spreading like an infectious disease, from the rich to the poor, from the upper castes to the SC's and even to the ST's ... while in 1971,

the child sex ratio for ST's was 985 (against a national average of 945), in 2001 it had fallen to 973. And among SC's, the figures were 946 in 1991 and 938 in 2001.

According to Sharma, surveys in Haryana and Punjab have revealed that some women genuinely believed that if their numbers declines, their value would increase because men will not find brides. Instead, men are buying brides from other states for as little as Rs. 5,000 (in Haryana a buffalo costs Rs. 40,000). These women are available to all the men in family. Instead of being valued, women are now becoming targets of violence in districts with the lowest sex ratios.

Amartya Sen(1990), highlights, taking gender balance in industrialized countries on his point of reference, and he found the evidence of female deficit in Asia and Africa. He concludes that about 11% women are missing in these both continents.

The common indices of gender preference used in various aspects are sex ratio at birth, sex differentiation in infant mortality. In India, sex preference is mainly manifested in the form of excessive mortality of female children. The excessive mortality of female children relatively to males is found to be due to the discrimination against females in the allocation of food and health care within the household. The daughter mortality differentials between northern and southern India were attributed to variations in women's status and the strength of sex preference. Dyson and Moore (1983) also found that sex differentials in child mortality are much higher in the northern then the southern states of India. They established that the main reason for the relatively high sex ratios in the northern part of the country is higher female mortality; they attributed this phenomenon to the discrimination against females in access to food and medical care. They also related the differentials observed in the northern and south to variations in kinship system and female autonomy.

According to the Census of India the number of males in the 2001 census was 531,277,029 and that of females, 495,738,169. This actually indicates that there are over 35 million fewer females are missing as compared to male population (Table 6). During the last decade, the absolute deficit of females increased by about three million. More significant is the report on the sex ratio for children below six years of age. The Registrar General reports that the sex ratio for this age group has gone down from 945 in 1991 to 927 in 2001–a large decadal difference.

Table 6
Sex Ratio and Total Number of Missing Female in India

Year	*Total number of female per 1000 male*	*Total population (million)*		*Missing female (million)*
		Male	*Female*	
1961	941	226. 3	212. 9	13. 4
1971	930	280. 4	264. 1	19. 9
1981	934	343. 9	321. 4	22. 9
1991	927	435. 2	403. 4	31. 8
2001	933	531. 2	495. 7	35. 5

Source: Census of India 2001.

CAUSES OF THE GENDER PREFERENCES AND DECREASING SEX RATIO IN INDIA

Gender preferences for children of a certain sex can have an impact not only on fertility but also on mortality and sex ratio. A preference for children of one sex, i.e. males, may lead to problems, a 'marriage squeeze', deterioration of the family system and have effects on the future fertility of countries; it may even interrupt the advance towards sustainable social and economic development in countries where such a preference exists. However, in India the process has taken a skewed turn, fertility levels have dropped accompanied by economic development, but entirely without the social enlighten that must come within the outcome is small family with its 'one boy and one girl', which contributed the low child sex ratio.

The low sex ratio is an important indicator of the inferior position of women in the Indian society. Many authors have tried to know the reasons behind the low sex ratio in India. Pranab Barthan (1982) mentions that there are four causes, the historical, cultural, ecological and sociological, responsible for low sex ratio in India. The committee on status of women in India (1975) concluded that 'an increase in the neglect of female lines as an expendable asset' is the only reason for the declination of the females in the Indian society. But if we study Indian society then we find that there are many factors or causes which play major role in the process of declining sex ratio and these are: Demographic factors, economical, social, cultural, psychological and technological, institutional, etc. But all these factors are not independent. They are interrelated and play a cumulative effect on Indian society, so to trace the exact cause is very complex and difficult. Indian society is an enigma so these causes are also enigmatic in nature.

These factors can be classified into micro and macro level. Micro level factors include the individual characteristics of parents, especially the mother. The improving socio-economic and educational status of parents could affect preferences for the sex children, particularly because the increasing autonomy of the mother would lead to a girl preference. In the macro level factors, the fertility decline and population policies, cultural setting and socio-economic factors are main causes behind this. Goodkind (1994) focuses that in India fertility decline has been an achievement of population policy. Such policies usually concentrate on reducing the total fertility rate or the number of children per woman, so it has increased concern among couples who, if they are going to have fewer children, would want to make sure they bear some sons. India's family planning programme with its 'one boy and one girl' norm contributed to the low sex ratio. In the two children norm family, if the first birth is female, then the pressure to produce a boy is much more. As a result, the parents` targets elimination of all subsequent female foetuses till male child is finally conceived.

Since 1980, ultrasound clinics have mushroomed all over the country. The illegal practice of using ultrasound scans to identify female foetuses and then aborting them is an important cause of drop out of females. In 1994, the Pre-Natal Diagnostic Technologies (PNDT) Act banned the practice, but it has proved toothless. The states like Punjab and Gujarat were first to ban the use of sex determination tests–point to the PNDT failure. In Punjab not even one clinic of the approximately 3,000 clinics with ultrasound facilities has been registered. These clinics openly advise their foetal sex determination techniques and if the foetus is female, doctors or midwives conduct an illegal abortion and charging some fee. The Punjab-Haryana-Himachal Pradesh belt in the north is known by some researchers as 'India's Bermuda Triangle', where girls vanish without a trace.

The gender bias in India is so entrenched in the country's cultural heritage that right from conception and birth to womanhood and death, the female suffers discrimination at all levels. In a patriarchal society that idolizes sons, a female child is usually considered as a burden and given less of the family's affection and resources. She is socialized to accept an inferior and subservient status– less opportunity, less authority, less property and less attention.

In the Indian society, it is culturally accepted that Indian women should work only in household, not the outside of household, so that they become an economic burden for the family. On the other hand men go outside for work and bring money for the family, so the boys become '*Kamaoo poot*' for the family. That is why people prefer a male child besides female child. Dowry is another important factor. Parents' reluctance to raise large amounts of money for a girl's down is often cited as the reason for decline in the sex ratio. Girls and women routinely suffer from poorer health and nutrition, infanticide and high rates of death from pregnancy and child birth.

The roots of the problem can be traced to deep-rooted patriarchy and anti-women attitudes in the country. In Hindu tradition, it is believed that son is the ultimate source of 'Moksh' and only son can pray for the release of the souls of dead parents, and only males can perform last rites. The cultural factors such as kinship systems tend to value males more highly than females. For example traditional patrilineal kinship system requires a woman to marry out of her family of origin and after marriage she can not support to parents like a son. Sons are expected to provide economic support to their parents in old age and in contrast, daughters are treated as burden in every respect since their parents are compelled to arrange for dowry.

Because of this women have no economic independence and not inherit property. In north India, a folk-lore is– "a son for us and daughter for others". In the south the suffix for a boy is *chiranjeevi* (one who lives long), but for a girl it is *sowbhagyavati* (lucky), meaning she is lucky if her husband lives long. This is in a country where women represent the most important powerful goddesses who are worshipped by all men: Saraswathy, Lakshmi, Sakti, Annapoorna and Kali. In spite of the fact that independent India has passed several constitutional and legal safe-guards to protect the interests of women, many of these are continually transgressed by the concentric circles of powerful Indian patriarchy.

Bhende and Kanitkar (1978) mentioned that demographic factors are also important in such direction. They argued that male predominance at birth is primarily a biological phenomenon and does not vary much from country to country. Studies in India indicate that the Indian sex ratios at birth are in keeping with this biological pattern. Ramchandran and Desphande (1972), who studied the sex ratio of births in maternity homes in India, found that the ratio was 106(106 males per 100 females), and that there was not much regional variation. According to the finding of the Sample Registration Scheme, the sex ratio of births in rural India was 107. 8 (107. 8 male per 100 females) in 1969. The authors also argue that the male foetus is known to be biologically weaker than the female foetus, and thus biological disadvantage is reflected in the higher male mortality rate on the first day, in the first week, the first month and the first year of life.

An evaluation of Table 7, which presents infant mortality rates by age and sex for selected countries provide ample evidence that in all other countries except in India, male mortality is invariable higher than female mortality for all age groups, while in India this situation provides only for those who are less than one month old. When it is realized that after the first month of life, social rather than biological factors start playing a more important role in determining mortality, the reasons for the exceptional picture that India presents become clear.

Table 7
Infant Mortality Rates by Age and Sex for Selected Countries

Country	*Year*	*Sex*	*Under 1 day*	*1-6 days*	*7-25 days*	*25-36 days*	*Under 1 Year*
USA	1993	M	3.5	1.3	1.0	3.5	9.3
		F	3.0	1.0	0.8	2.6	7.4
Japan	1994	M	1.1	0.8	0.7	2.1	4.7
		F	0.8	0.7	0.6	1.7	3.8
UK	1994	M	0.2	3.5	0.9	2.3	6.9
		F	0.2	2.5	0.9	1.8	5.4
Sri Lanka	1989	M	11.	–	3.1	5.7	19.9
		F	8.6	–	2.9	5.1	16.7
Pakistan	1992	M	3.5	31.7	15.5	47.2	97.8
		F	5.0	25.0	14.3	59.7	104.0
India	1992-93	M	–	57.0	–	31.7	88.6
		F	–	48.1	–	35.8	83.9

Source: 1. United Nation, Demographic Year Book, 1995, New York, 1997, pp. 390-96.
2. For India, National Family Health Survey, 1992-93, p. 218.

FINAL CONSIDERATIONS

On the basis of above discussion, we can conclude that the decline in the sex ratio is not only for the children but also overall sex ratio are reported from all over India, but the most striking regions are Punjab, Haryana, Delhi, Gujarat, Andhra Pradesh and Western U.P. , where abortions of female foetuses after sex determination test are widely practiced. Greater neglect of female babies in terms of provision of food and medical attention also decreases their chances of survival. According to UNICEF, about 402 districts of India where the number of deaths of females up to age five is higher than males, though biologically female babies have better chances of survival than male babies. So we can conclude that among the others, the main reason behind the sex ratio in India is gender biasness, lower status of women in Indian society and other socio-cultural practices. The important causes of sharp decline of sex ratio are:

1. Unregulated use of pre-natal diagnostic technologies in whole country.

2. The existing state laws, policies and programmes fail to comprehensively address issues of girls and women's survival.
3. Demand of more sons for the old age security and escape from the dowry problem.
4. Culturally supported gender discrimination and low status of women in society.

SUGGESTIONS AND POLICY IMPLICATIONS

From the foregoing discussion, it is evident that missing girl child and gender discrimination have emerged as a big problem in Indian society and it is very necessary to get rid of this problem. However, it may contribute degradation of society. So, it is necessary to improve the children's chance of survival, and also for raising women's status, guaranteeing better access to opportunities for their work outside the home and education. This all will result in the reduction of sex preference. In this context, it is very important that a number of measures should be necessary to implement to reduce the infant and child mortality, such as, comprehensive health and nutrition programme, especially focusing on women and children providing for safe motherhood, universal immunization of pre school children, and the wider availability of drinking water and sanitation; including provisions for supplementary food and vitamins for children.

This is the duty of the government that it should not only make policies and programme for girl child welfare but also implement them properly. It is also pertinent that PNDT Act should be implemented strictly. In this context, NGO's and voluntary organizations should come to play vital role and state should take help for participation of these association in such programmes and lastly, the most important is to bring change the mind-set of the people without which all the measures taken will be futile. And if we succeed in this direction then Amartya Sen's argument will become true that "If the women are not being discriminated, then nation sex ratio is about 105 women per 100 men".

REFERENCES

Abraham, F. M. (2006), "Contemporary *Sociology*", Oxford University Press, New Delhi.

Action Aid India (2001), *Tackling Gender Issues, www. actionmaidindia.org.*

Bandhan, Pranab (1992), "Little Girls and Death in India", *EPW,* 17 (36).

Bhende, A. and Kanitkar, T. (1978), *"Principles of Population Studies,"* Mumbai, Himalaya Publishing House.

Committee on Status of Women in India (1975), "Towards Equality: Report of the Committee on the Status of Women in India, GOI, Ministry of Education and Social Welfare, New Delhi.

Dyson, T. and Moore, M. (1983), *"On Kinship Structure Female Autonomy and Demographic Behaviour in India"*, Popualtion and Development Review, 9 (1).

Goodkind, D. (1994), *"Sex Preference for Children in Vietnam"*, Paper Presented on Issues Related to Sex Preference for Children in the Rapidly Changing Demographic Dynamics in Asia, Seoul Republic Korea, November.

Haralambose, M. (1980), *"Sociology: Themes and Perspectives"*, Oxford University Press, New Delhi.

Jain, Devaki (ed.), (1975), *"Indian Women"*, Publications Division, New Delhi.

Lahiri, Subrata (1974), "Preference for Sons and Ideal Family in Urban India,' *Indian Journal of Social Work,* vol. 4, no. 1.

Ramachandran, K. V. and Deshpande, Vinayak (1972), *"The Sex-ratio At Birth in India by Regions",* The Milbank Memorial Fund Quarterly, vol. 42, No. 2, Part I, April 1964, pp. 84-85.

Ramachandran, S. (2001), *"Concern Over India's Vanishing Girls"*, Deutsche (DSE), Frankfurt, Germany.

Registrat General of India (2001), *"Census of India", www. censusindia.net.*

Sen, A. (1990), "More Than 100 Million Women are Missing', Review of Books, New York.

Viraria, Pravin M. (1969), *"The Sex Ratio of the Pof India'*, Census of India, 1961, Vol. 1, Monograph, No. 10.

Warren Thompson (1953), *"Population Problems"*, McGraw Hills, New York.

7

FERTILITY ISSUES FOR INDIA

R. Meenakshi

INTRODUCTION

Both developed and developing countries face the challenge of sustained economic development in the wake of demographic changes because population growth is not simply a problem of numbers but it is a problem of human welfare and development. An important demographic dimension which has a bearing on the number of growing population as well as their welfare is fertility. Although mortality rates differ widely among countries, differences in population growth are mainly the result of differences in fertility rates. There are fast growing economies in the midst of full-blown socio economic transformation which are in a vicious circle of growth, development, poverty alleviation and fertility transition. In contrast, there are countries which seem to be sinking deeper into economic decay and trapped in a vicious circle of economic stagnation, social unrest and increasing fertility.

WORLD POPULATION SITUATION

Over the last 35 years the population of the Earth has doubled. The United Nations estimated recently that the world's population is now growing by about 78 million a year. At the current pace, world population is increasing by about 1 billion every 13 years. At this rate, the world's population, which surpassed 6 billion in 1999, is projected to rise to over 8 billion by 2025 and reach a 10.9 billion mark by 2050. During 2025 to 2050, eight countries are expected to account for half of the world's projected population increase: India, Pakistan, Nigeria, the Democratic Republic of the Congo, Bangladesh, Uganda, the United States, Ethiopia and China, listed according to the size of their contribution to population growth Comparing the *centennial* growth of developed and developing countries reveals a dramatic divergence. Developing countries in Africa and Asia will account for about 90 percent of the increase in world population projected by 2050, while the population of most developed countries will decrease. The population of the developed countries as a group will have increased by less than 350 million between 1950 and 2050. The developing countries, on the other hand, will have an estimated 6.8 billion people more, thus almost quintupling their 1950 population.

Hence developing countries will far outpace developed countries in population growth because of a young age structure as well as higher birth rates. High birth rates in the past, and falling but continued high birth rates for many developing countries, guarantee several decades of growth. In the more developed countries, very low proportions of youth and high proportions of older people are significant factors in the ensuing population decline.

COUNTRYWISE POPULATION SCENARIO

More than 75% of the world population lives in the 'poor' countries. The 1991 census reported a total population of 846.3 million indicating an increase of nearly 24 percent from that of 1981. This implies an average annual population growth of 2.11 percent, based on roughly 27 million births a year. At this rate, India will overtake China early in the next century, becoming the most populous country in the world. The United Nations has recently projected that India's population will swell to 1363 million in 2025 and 1628 million in 2050, while China's will be contained at 1392 million. The Indian population has already acquired a sizeable growth momentum. In spite of a vigorous family planning programme, the population size will grow. It is also likely that the size of the population below the poverty line will grow. The needs of the population in future in respect of food, housing, sanitation, employment, education and nutrition may be tremendously high. At the national level, the birth rate was 22.8 births per thousand in 2004 with a death rate of 8.38 per thousand. This birth rate has to decline by about seven points in the next six years.

FERTILITY AND FERTILTY RATES

Fertility, i.e. the basic ability to reproduce is at the root of reproductive health. Both infertility as well as high levels of fertility are bad for health. High prevalence of infertility has important psychological and sociological impact on the community. At the same time very high levels of fertility means that women are devoting greater part of their lives to child bearing leading to high exposure of maternal complications. In the contemporary Indian context, high levels of fertility are a major problem. Hence reduction in fertility levels is viewed as an indicator of improvements in reproductive health. The three common measures of fertility are; (a) Crude Birth Rate (CBR), (b) Age-specific fertility rates (ASFR), and (c) Total Fertility Rate (TFR). Crude birth rate (CBR) is the simplest of all and is defined as the number of births per annum per 1000 population. However, crude birth rate is influenced by the age-sex structure of the population apart from its true fertility experience. ASFR or age specific birth rate for a given age group is defined as the number of children born to women in the said age group per 1000 women in the same age group. TFR is the average number of children a woman would bear throughout her reproductive life. Total Fertility Rate is of two types. The Desired Total Fertility Rate (DTFR) calculates a desired TFR from desired family sizes by subtracting from the number of actual births namely those births that exceed each woman's reported desired family size. Wanted Total Fertility Rate (WTFR) reflects women's future desire for children to classify births as wanted or unwanted.

Population growth rate is decreasing more swiftly than expected because of faster fertility decline. It is estimated that Fertility peaked in the 20-24 year age group and declined sharply after age 30. Women in their 20s were responsible for almost 60 percent of total fertility. For instance when the TFR = 2, each pair of parents just replaces itself. Actually it takes a TFR of 2. 1 or 2.2 to replace each generation which is called the replacement rate because some children will die before they grow up to have their own two children. In countries with low life expectancies, the replacement rate is even higher (2.2–3). Women in rural areas had on average one more child (TFR 3.7) than women in the cities (TFR 2.7), and there were wide variations among regions and states. Changes in fertility can be ascertained by studying trends in the levels of a summary measure of fertility such as CBR and TFR as well as in birth order distribution and age pattern of fertility, as the latter provides more information about the age and order of birth at which changes are occurring.

GLOBAL FERTILITY TRANSITION

Fertility rates have begun to decline in most countries. World development reports point out a decline in the total fertility rate for high income counties from 1. 9 to 1.7. Italy, Spain and Germany report a low fertility level of 1.2. Thailand, Singapore and the two Koreas are the Asiatic countries which have reported a very low level of fertility. In some countries of Africa and the Middle East, women average about six to eight births in their lifetimes. In Europe, the average falls far short of two children. Such low rates will ensure population decline and, in many European countries, the annual number of births is less than the number of deaths. The United States has one of the highest birth rates among developed countries, with a total fertility rate of 2.0. Other developed countries have fertility rates lower or much lower than 2.0. Fertility has reached below-replacement levels in 23 developing countries accounting for 25 per cent of the world population. This group includes China whose fertility during 2000-2005 is estimated at 1.7 children per woman. Since 1990-1995, fertility decline has been the rule among most developed countries. The few increases recorded, such as those in Belgium, France, Germany, the Netherlands and the U.S., "have been small."

FERTILITY TRANSITION IN INDIA

The rapid, but very uneven fertility decline observed in India over the last three decades have left demographers, economists and other social scientists wondering at the exact determinants of this demographic revolution that has now brought fertility in parts of the country, such as in Southern states, to European levels. Economic, social and regional explanations were put forth but have usually failed to offer a global explanatory framework accounting for the variety of fertility transitions across regions and social groups.

The United Nations Development studies point out that India and China, the two most populous countries in the World along with other 86 countries will reach a dramatic reduction in their fertility levels within the next ten to fifteen years. By that time India's fertility rate would have reached 2.10 nearer to the replacement level of fertility. Replacement level of fertility ensures replacement of one generation by another. China's rate of fertility is expected to be slightly low at 1.94. India has attained by now the second stage of fertility transition after a drop in the CBR from a level of 40 plus to a moderate level of around 23. By the year 2010 however at current rates India's population would have climbed to 1.21 billion and China's to 1.41 billion while the global population would have aggravated to 7.29 billion from the present 5. 85 billion. The Chinese demography experts were striving to stabilize its fertility rates at 1. 7 which meant one child per family and two in some cases. China's average fertility level, which has reached 1.70 today, would begin to stabilise at 1.85 from 2015 to 2050, while India's would begin the decline to 1.85 only from 2030. One need not be surprised if India turns out to be the most populous country in another quarter decade. Thus fall in fertility becomes the only way to contain population growth in India.

STATEWISE FERTILITY SCENARIO IN INDIA

In India some states have done better in reducing fertility and some others have not done well. In states like Andhra Pradesh, Gujarat, Kerala, Goa, Maharashtra, Orissa, Karnataka, Punjab, West Bengal and Tamil Nadu, the level of fertility is considerably low as against those in Madhya Pradesh, Uttar Pradesh, Bihar, Rajasthan, Assam and Haryana where birth rates are quite high. The urban population of states like Bihar, Gujarat, Haryana, Madhya Pradesh, Punjab, Rajasthan and Uttar Pradesh has a higher fertility level than the national fertility level. It is clear that different states in India are in different stages of fertility transition and they exhibit vast socio-economic and demographic diversity across the regions. States like Kerala and Goa have done remarkably well and have nearly achieved Net Reproduction Rate (NRR) of unity i.e. a mother is replaced by one daughter. Kerala and Goa had achieved below-replacement levels, and fertility was close to replacement level in Tamil Nadu. In Kerala, the major reason is high female literacy. The inference, it draws, is that education of women is very important. Kerala has other advantage too because of its matriarchal system. Therefore, women enjoy higher autonomy which helps reduce fertility. Of course Kerala's overall socio-economic development has also been quite good with emphasis on education.

It has been found that Family Planning programme has been strong where socio-economic development preceded it. Higher is the rate of overall growth, greater is the likelihood of fertility rate to come down. Other southern states namely Tamil Nadu and Andhra Pradesh too are fast approaching the replacement level of one. However, in north India, the fertility rates-though are going down- are still very unfavourable. The north Indian states UP, Bihar, MP and Rajasthan that account for 40 per cent of India's population still have high fertility rates. In these states, women do not have much of a say in the family and society. There is a distinct north-south divide on female autonomy. Punjab, Maharashtra, Gujarat have been economically well developed but social development has not been as high as Kerala. Nevertheless, fertility rates have been high due to strong son preference which cuts across all socio-economic strata and even rich with high social status and education wait for a son after two or more daughters. A population survey reveals that couples in Kerala with two sons or two daughters said no to any more children. But in other states, couples with two daughters preferred to take further chances for a son while those with two sons wished to close the chapter. It is because of the son preference, sex ratio is declining except Kerala where there are more number of women than men.

It may however, be mentioned that Kerala, Karnataka, Maharashtra, Gujarat, Punjab and Tamil Nadu are the states where the levels of socio-economic development are also higher than those in Bihar, Madhya Pradesh, Rajasthan and Uttar Pradesh. These are also the states where the family planning programme has been more successful. This implies family planning efforts coupled with the socio-economic improvements seem to hold a greater promise for the decline in fertility in India. In general the level of fertility is considerably below the national average in South India. This could be attributed to higher levels of female literacy and education, higher level of female labor force participation. Intense efforts by these states to implement family planning programs, to increase the couple protection rates in these southern states. Demographers and sociologists now find Tamil Nadu as a model for all round qualitative improvement of Demographic indicators with its stress on welfare schemes like nutrition meal programmes etc., The experience of Kerala and Tamil Nadu could be replicated in other states to diffuse the population bomb.

FUTURE PERSPECTIVE FOR FERTILITY TRANSITION

Under the family planning programme more than 44 percent couples are said to be protected now. In some states, this figure is still higher. No doubt, the success of the family planning programme after more than 42 years of service is not very satisfactory specially in arresting and cutting down the growth rate of the population, but a measurable improvement in the quality of life of the people seems to have begun. What is, therefore needed at present is to generate a wave of social change in favour of the small family and to create a demand for different family planning methods because the decline in fertility through contraception seems to determine the economic prospects of the country. More serious efforts are required to generate confidence among the couples that their children are going to survive and their economic lot is going to improve with a small family. But to wait for development to promote the family planning practices and adoption of the small family norm would lead to an unduly burden of the population, which can frustrate all efforts of development in the country. Therefore, the state and society both have to compromise their respective expectations from each other and the family planning programme has to be recognised as an integral part of the overall socio-economic development plans. The involvement of the Panchayats and the empowerment of women to handle health and family planning activities will be the most desirable step. The NGO's might play a significant role in educating people to take new roles in this regard. It is clear that the behaviour of the couples in respect of their childbearing would largely depend on the family and community in which they live. The favourable attitude for family limitation would be largely determined by their aspirations about their children and their life in future, conditioned by their present perception of their social and economic factors.

Population experts appear to be reaching a consensus that there has been a perceptible decline in the fertility rates in many countries of the world. The decline is accounted for by the "new demographic transition" in the less developed countries (LDCs). The decline in fertility rates began in the 1950s in some LDCs and became more widespread during the current period. However the process has not yet begun in many of the LDCs. There is a most striking paradox in global population trends. On one hand we have had a rapid *decline in fertility* for over two decades in many developing countries-not to mention the already very low fertility in most of the highly developed nations and on the other hand we will almost certainly experience a *further massive increase of the world population.*

A UN report points out that the future population growth is highly dependent on the path that future fertility takes. Because of its low and declining rate of population growth, the population of developed countries as a whole is expected to remain virtually unchanged between 2005 and 2050. In contrast, the population of the 50 least developed countries is projected to more than double, passing from 0. 8 billion in 2005 to 1.7 billion in 2050. The key question is whether the recent downward trend in fertility in LDCs will continue, stabilize at the current level, or rise again. A primary concern about the future is that the poorer and less developed countries will end up with an increasing share of the world's population, with the share of the developed countries which declined from 34% to 22% over the 1950-2000 period. Considerable difference exists in demographic growth patterns among various regions. The 12 largest LDCs (China, India, Indonesia, Brazil, Bangladesh, Pakistan, Nigeria, Mexico, Vietnam, Philippines, Thailand, Turkey) contain 55% of the current world population and the fertility decline of these nations is expected to have the maximum impact. Seven of these countries have had fertility decline of 14-35%. The force of the "population momentum" must also be considered. Most developing countries' population have a young age distribution with considerable potential for population growth even after the fertility level reaches a replacement level and the net reproduction rate equals one. India's future population size will largely depend on its prospects for continued fertility decline, linked to the success of its reproductive and child health programmes. Higher female literacy and higher autonomy to women and educating and empowering women is what could achieve drop in fertility in other states. Detailed information on fertility and family planning practices will help family welfare organizations and the Indian government target their program efforts in the years ahead.

CONCLUSION

It is essential that the development programme have to be made increasingly population oriented, especially in the rural areas. Moreover, the family planning programme has to emphasize more on the spacing methods so that the younger couples could be protected against conception and the programme gets more credibility. In fact, the decline in the fertility of younger couples will depend on the level of social and economic development.

It has been observed that the fertility rate is high among adolescents. This should be curtailed since it has high risk and both the mother and the child are exposed to high mortality and morbidity. An increase in marriageable age is desired but not possible given our peculiar social customs. At the most we can persuade them not to have children early. But even this too seems uphill task considering the social pressure to prove fertility and virility. So these are the areas which need to be addressed and message should be spread to marry late or postpone giving birth to a child.

There is every reason to hope that Government population policies and improved technology impact will substantially reduce the cost of fertility control to poor families. The remarkable increase in the female labour force participation rate has also reduced the incentive to have larger families. There is no need to debate whether the fertility transition is due to family planning or to economic development. What is noteworthy in China's case is that both the fertility transition and economic transformation were products of a command system, which had effects on both the timing and the strength of the fertility transition. India's TFR is expected to fall to 2.1 only in 2010 compared to 3. 2 in 1995 while China and Thailand have already gone below replacement level of fertility.

The question is what prospects are there for India to meet the challenge of growing population, whether it would be overwhelmed by the burden of more than a billion people or would be able to feed, house and cloth this billion in comfort in 2010 AD will depend upon the intensified efforts for family planning. The extent to which the present and future generations adopt the policy 'a small family is a happy family' will determine the size of India in 2020 AD. These require massive efforts to contain population. It can be done only if different states take efforts towards this goal. This broad scenario at the aggregate level may not reveal the totality of the situation as large variations persist between different regions and states in the country. Demographic problems at the macro level can be solved only with a proper perception of the position in each individual state. A strong political commitment to social objectives, the dedicated involvement of successive governments in intensified family planning programs for another thirty years join efforts of the top administrative level of various departments the dedicated cooperation of regional level staff can contribute to its success. The desire for providing higher education to children, the rising cost of education and standard of living along with aspirations of good life for their children are sure to act as better motivating factors to have lesser children on the part of present generation. If only government could intensify its efforts to increase this awareness coupled with a higher outlay for population control programs on the one hand and child development schemes on the other, India need not worry about its population being a detrimental factor in achieving sustained development.

REFERNCES

Pathak. K.B., Singh, B.S., (1995), "Fertility Transition in India: Problems and Prospects", The Family Welfare Programme in India. Edited by Hari Mohan Mathur, Vikas Publishing.

Zaman. W, (1980), "Third World Q", The World Population Situation. Jul; 2(3), pp. 546-54.

Rele J.R. (1992), "Fertility Levels and Trends in South Asia: An Assessment and Prospects", Jan-Jun; 48(1-2), pp. 133-54.

Bhagat. R.B, (2002), "Integration of Demographic Issues in Sustainable Development: Reflections on India's Population Policies", Population Geography, Volume 24, Numbers 1 & 2 June-December 2002.

Christophe Z. Guilmoto and S. Irudaya Rajan, (2005), "Fertility Transition in South India" SAGE Publications.

John C. Caldwell, Pat Caldwell and Peter McDonald, (2002), *"Policy Responses to Low Fertility and its Consequences: A Global Survey"*, *Journal of Population Research*, May, 2002-2004 World Population Data Sheet of the Populations Reference Bureau.

8

REPRODUCTIVE AND SEXUAL HEALTH EDUCATION: A STUDY OF ADOLESCENTS IN LUCKNOW

Sanjay Pandey & Ajay Kumar Pandey

The socio-demographic, sexual and reproductive health situation of adolescents in India is pathetic since they are ignored in most of the health programmes run by the government and non-government organizations. The adolescents face more risks and vulnerability of chronic diseases since their knowledge level regarding sexual and reproductive health is found to be poor. Most of the adolescents get such knowledge and information through unauthentic and non-scientific literature. They also hesitate to share their experience with their parents and guardians. And thus, they are becoming more prone to vulnerability of sexually transmitted diseases because the proportion of pre-marital sex is growing rapidly particularly in the urban areas. The problem of married adolescent girls is growing rapidly since their access to reproductive health care is found to be inadequate and poor. Thus, interventions are required for providing health education and life skill development to the adolescents.

Present paper is based on a major study conducted under a multi-centric action oriented programme for imparting reproductive and sexual health education among school going adolescents in selected schools of Lucknow city. The findings of research also highlight the contribution of action programme on the understanding and perception of adolescents regarding reproductive and sexual health issues. The paper purports to review the needs, knowledge, practices, perception, attitude and behavior towards reproductive and sexual health issues.

ADOLESCENT'S NEEDS TO KNOW AND PRACTICE

Boys largely have no specific need to know on activities related with either of the following: recreation, outing, play/exercises, friends/peers, bath/genital, privacy, being inhibition free, seeking information/guidance, nutrition, reproductive health, sexuality/ sexual act, and gender issues. Girls specifically need to know about activities on recreation, nutrition, reproductive health, sexuality and sexual act.

ADOLESCENTS' SOURCES OF INFORMATION GUIDANCE

On studies, boys consult teachers or parents; on general health they consult doctor and parents; on nutrition parents are consulted; about reproductive health boys consult friends and counselors; on sexual health boys consult friends, parents and others; on friendship they consult parents and relations; and on all other matters boys consult doctors or any other sources. On studies girls consult teachers and parents; on nutrition they consult parents and doctors; on reproductive health they consult doctors and parents; on sexual health they consult parent and doctors; on issues related with friendship girls consult friends and parents.

ADOLESCENTS' KNOWLEDGE AND PRACTICES

Most boys know that pulses have protein; fruits have vitamins; However, boys largely do not know as to what nutrients (viz. Carbohydrates, fat, protein, iron, calcium, vitamins), bread or roti, rice, milk, egg, butter, green vegetables, peanuts, Gurh (Jaggery), fish, chicken/meat have in them. Hence, boys' knowledge about nutrients in food items they take is considered poor. Most of the girls do not know as to what nutrients (viz. Carbohydrates, fat, protein, iron, calcium, vitamins) are present in pulses, bread or roti, rice, milk, egg, butter, green vegetables, peanuts, Gurh (Jaggery), fish, chicken/meat they take in their daily meal. Hence, girls' knowledge about nutrients in food items they take is considered poor.

PHYSIOLOGICAL CHANGES IN ADOLESCENTS

During the adolescence period, adolescents observe following physiological/bodily changes: rapid gain in weight, growth of hair in genital area and in armpits, white discharge, change of voice, development of breasts, onset of menstrual cycle, nocturnal emission. On seeing these bodily changes in them, a few girls feel worried, and most boys feel a sense of maturity. On the whole they feel mature. Most share these changes with their friends.

PERSONAL AND GENITAL HYGIENE

Most adolescents wash/clean body (parts like face, hands, hair, etc) with soap/shampoo and water. They clean their genital/sexual parts. Most change their undergarments daily.

REPRODUCTIVE HEALTH

Most boys and girls are able to correctly identify reproductive organs in male or female body charts. Most of them are able to figure out as to how a woman becomes pregnant. Most adolescents hold both the mother and father responsible for determining the gender (sex) of the child. Most talk out issues like boy/girl friend, marriage, adult movies, etc., with friends and classmates. Most adolescents don't read romance/love/sex/related magazines or see pornographic album/blue movie or visit internet sites. Out of those that ever did read/see such material most read magazines. Most don't read any educational material on reproductive/sexual/health/bodily changes. Out of those that do read, most read resources related to bodily changes, or about HIV/AIDS or on sexual health.

About one fourth adolescents think "sex" means intercourse. For any sexual/reproductive health related problems, most adolescents consult doctors (allopathic), friends (boy or girl) or mothers. Most feel that a girl should have her first baby at the age ranging from 19 to 25 years, but most of the remaining feel that this should happen below 18 years of age. Most of them are aware that pregnancy can be avoided by use of family planning methods. They know that information/ guidance in this regard can be got from government clinics/ hospitals. Most know that care to pregnant and new born and family planning/contraception facilities are available in these centres.

Most of the adolescents are aware of the various family planning methods available for male as also for female. They want to know more about family welfare methods. Most of the adolescents want to know more about who, how and why of family welfare methods. To gather such information, adolescents mostly prefer doctors, counselors, television, booklets, and lectures to be prominent sources of information disseminating such knowledge.

Most adolescents are aware of what is "abortion". They know it should be performed by a qualified doctor/nurse. But, most adolescents don't know as to when be it safe to have an abortion. Most adolescents know that an unsafe abortion can cause death. Most girls know as to what is 'menstruation'. They can largely explain as to what it is. Most believe that a woman can become pregnant if she has intercourse during menstruation. Most girls see the onset of their first bleeding (menses) from eleven to fourteen years of age. Most girls are never told that they would bleed one day, and start menstruating. Most or the remaining are told about it by their mothers and sisters. After the onset of periods most girls consult some one or the other. Most consult mothers or sisters. Most think that a girl should use napkins/sanitary pads or clean cloth only during their menses; they feel that used cloth and pads should be thrown out after single use. Most feel that girls should change cloth/napkins/pads once or twice a day.

Most girls feel problems with their menstruation. Most have stomach ache/cramps. Headache, body ache, tiredness/ weakness, and pain in legs, during menstruation periods. Gynecological problems most girls face are: discharge with foul, pain during bleeding, excessive bleeding. Psychological problems girls face are: feel messy, anxiety, embarrassment, weakness, irritation, bad mood, and low self esteem. Some girls feel like rubbing their sex organs to derive pleasurable sensation. About one fifth do that. Most girls feel it's natural, shameful and abnormal.

Seminal Discharge/masturbation is seen by most boys as a natural process that contains sperms, which is a sign of vitality. Most think that only some boys do masturbation, its natural process that weakens body. Wet dreams are seen by most as loss of semen, but a natural process of watery discharge. Most boys have nocturnal emission/wet dream. They don't feel anything special about it. Most boys didn't discuss about it with anyone. Most of the remaining discuss with friends/peers, doctors, brother.

SEXUALITY

During adolescence adolescent boys and girls develop certain lovely/tender desires or wishes. Most of the boys and girls feel lonely, want to be friendly with opposite sex, want to meet the dream girl/boy, and wish to marry her/him. The qualities most of the boys/girls like in their life partners are: qualifications, intelligence, friendliness, submissiveness, good family status. What do the adolescents like to do with their dream boys/girls. Most want to hold hands together, go to picnic/restaurant, and not do anything that goes against the norms of society/wishes of parents. Neither most of the boys nor most of the girls seem aware of the legal age of marriage. Most favour first sexual act only after marriage. Most perceive pre-marital sex to be bad/ immoral and risky. Less than 10% of boys/girls have any intimate (sexual) relationships. About one fourth of adolescents tend to be homosexual/lesbian. Few are also subjected to sexual abuse or harassment against their wishes. Most of abused adolescents are being sexually abused by their own relative/ intimate or by a person whom they liked. Most are sexually forced by people of opposite sex.

INTERPERSONAL RELATIONS

Most adolescents have friendly relations with their parents. They share personal feelings mostly with mother and friends, and personal problems with mother-father and friends. Most aspire to be teachers, engineers or anything depending upon situations then. Role models of most adolescents are their parents. Most feel stressed out on account of studies career, and poor academic performance, whereas about one fourth feel no stress.

UNDERSTANDING RTIS, STDS AND HIV/AIDS

Most adolescents have heard of Sexually Transmitted Diseases (STDs). Most get informed about the disease from television, newspapers, and from social workers. Most of them know symptoms of STDs. According to most of them the symptoms are: discharge from genital, burning sensation, bleeding from private parts.

Most have heard of HIV/AIDS. Most of them know that HIV/AIDS is transmitted through sexual relations, transfusion of blood and by sharing of needle. However, plenty of others need to know about it. Most adolescents know that HIV/AIDS can be prevented by practice of safe sex, having only one sex partner, not sharing needle, and by taking tested/safe blood. Most know that HIV/AIDS is not curable. Most want to know more about treatment, methods of preventions, mode of spread, window period. Only a few respondents feel that people living with HIV/AIDS face discrimination in the society. Most adolescents feel that they are isolated and don't get proper treatment.

LIFE SKILL DEVELOPMENT, RISK TAKING BEHAVIOUR AND SUBSTANCE ABUSE

Few adolescents (including girls) smoke cigarettes. Few also have ever taken narcotic drugs or alcohol. Few are drug/ alcohol dependent also, mostly for the last six months. About one fourth faced serious crisis situations in life. Most adolescents out of them faced financial crisis, failure in academic life, accidents/ injuries or prolonged diseases. For coping up with the crisis/ stress most talk it out or go for counseling.

ABOUT THE PROGRAMME

According to boys and girls included for programme, topics covered in classroom discussions were: physiological changes, reproductive organs, nutrition, self, RTI/STI, HIV/AIDS. These topics were taught to most two or three times. Activities undertaken in programme were: class room, question and answer, exhibition, teen clubs, question box, distribution and educational material. Largely, the programme did benefit adolescents and they found information given understandable. They largely needed more information, found that topic was given appropriate time. Enough time was given to clarify their doubts. Questions were also asked during classroom discussions. Most of the respondents dropped questions in question box. All discussed classroom discussion with classmates, friends and parents. Most received educational material. Majority of them found it useful. Participation of adolescents in programme brought about good change in their knowledge. It brought about good change in behaviour of respondent boys and girls.

RECOMMENDATIONS

- Reproductive and sexual health education should be provided to school going adolescents through developing course curriculum in ninth, tenth, eleventh and twelfth standards of education in schools. However, teachers for providing such education need orientation in order to deal such issues effectively and efficiently without creating any problem and tension. Such course curriculums are to be developed carefully keeping in view of important and vital issues for education and methods of education and knowledge. If possible separate classes with the use of audio-visuals may be held by the experts and concerned teachers to adolescent boys and girls.
- There is a need to hold government accountable for enforcing the legal age of marriage for both boys and girls. The child marriage prevention Act should be effectively enforced to prevent early marriages.

- Adolescent girls need specific policies to address specific sectors like education, health, family welfare, nutrition, HIV/AIDS, sports, etc. An integrated and holistic development programmes for empowerment of adolescent girls are needed. Adolescents in different circumstances like adolescent with disabilities learning disorders, adolescent sex workers, children of sex workers and street children need more visibility in policies.
- Effective and efficient administration of Kishori Shakti Yojana, Balika Samridhi Yojana, Kasturba Gandhi Balika Shiksha Scheme and other schemes oriented for empowerment of adolescent girls should be ensured while the coverage of such schemes be extended.
- Educational, nutritional, health, livelihood and recreational programmes need to be designed keeping in view of the socio-cultural expectations and economic pressures on adolescent girls.
- Reproductive and sexual health programmes are to be designed keeping in view of rights to health care services, right to information about prevention, reproduction, right to healthy life, nutrition, education, creation and freedom from violence and abuse. More emphasis is required for counseling sensitization, education, and improving the health care services to meet out the emerging needs of reproductive and sexual health to the adolescent girls.
- The change of mindset of administrators, policymakers, political leaders and service providers towards adolescent girls need to be changed and they should recognize that the needs and desires of adolescent girls are different from the needs and desires of adolescent boys.
- Health and nutrition education is very important for adolescent girls in under to create awareness regarding sexual and reproductive health as well as to help parents in understanding the importance of marriage and child bearing at matured age.

- Services are needed that reach out beyond the clinic to enable young women to seek prenatal visits and adequate obstetric care and to obtain counseling or services relating to coercion and violence as well as STI symptoms.
- Better understanding of the causes of the sexual and reproductive health needs of married adolescents who remain unmet why informed choice continues to abide them and how services should be structured to overcome the social, cultural and economic constraints that married adolescents face has to be understood in right perspective.
- Tele-health services may be strengthened and through opening more information kiosks, connecting health centres on line, involving community based organization, particularly NGO's and district level Panchayats and urban local bodies, or Autonomous Development Councils.
- There is a need to improve constant and quality of on going family planning services, evolving appropriate indicators for monitoring quality of services as well as coverage levels.
- A massive awareness campaign involving the community, religious traders and opinion makers at all levels is necessary to counter demographic imbalances along with effective policies and programmes in favour of girl child.
- A completely new strategy based on a holistic approach of awareness, incentives, education, nutrition and enforcement need to be worked out to protect the rights of the girl children, women should have access o comprehensive, affordable and quality health care, which should go beyond the reproductive health to take into account their vulnerability to various endemic, infections and communicable diseases. The social and health consequences of HIV/AIDS and sexually transmitted diseases also needed to be tackled from a gender perspective.

- Community participation should be promoted by encouraging and organizing orientation and training programmes for members of Mahila Swasthya Sanghs, SHG's, NGO's, Panchayats, local bodies, youth clubs etc. These community based organizations may be RCH services as well as monitoring other health care services.
- A mass awareness programme for malaria, tuberculosis, HIV/AIDS, cancer, etc. should be held at fairs, and haats in rural areas and be increased interaction of health workers with local population.
- There is a strong need of local IEC efforts, effective community utilization and social marketing of health programmes, services as well as contraceptives.
- Marriage cum pregnancy counseling may be promoted through improving community participation, integrated schemes of child development, immunization and nutrition.
- Special programmes for adolescents should combine intervention from different areas such as health, education, life education development, micro credit, small business development and safe environment for entertainment.
- Young people need more supportive environment within their families, schools and communities and thus specific packages of their education, training and knowledge sharing should be designed and implemented. Those adolescents who are not attending schools, non-formal education including special package on their emergent needs of education should be provided to them.
- Confidential counseling services should be provided to the adolescents through established resource centers at government and non-government levels. The resource centres should be made well equipped with appropriate technology, literature and other resources in order to cater the needs of the adolescents.

- Adolescents need to be provided with better information and services to help them understand their sexuality and protect them from unwanted pregnancy. Greater awareness of the ability of reproductive health services could reduce the numbers of young women who resort to unsafe abortion.
- School teachers, college teachers and NGO workers need to be involved from the planning stage to ensure that adequate knowledge and information on reproductive and sexual health is being imparted to the young population through their various other developmental programmes.
- In the designing and implementation of intervention programs for providing reproductive and sexual health to adolescents, involvement of young people is imperative. Similarly, consultation of adolescents during the development of IEC materials and training manuals is required in order to field test them for feasibility and acceptability. There is need to enhance young people's awareness, self efficacy and autonomy to enable informed decision making and reduce unsafe and unwanted sexual activity.

PART–II

DIMENSIONS

9

SOCIAL AND ECOLOGICAL ASPECTS OF HEALTH–ANTHROPOLOGICAL APPRAISAL ON TRIBAL WOMEN OF WAYAND, KERALA

Bindu Ramachandran

Hon. Former President of India APJ Abdul Khalam once said" empowering women are a prerequisite for creating a good nation. When women are empowered, society with stability is assured. Empowerment of women is essential as their thoughts and value systems lead to the development of a good family, good society and ultimately a good nation. The term empowerment generally used nowadays by administrators, planners, policy makers, researchers and social workers. The dictionary meaning of empowerment range from' give power to' and 'give capacity to perform some mental or physical activity', 'to delegate authority'...etc. But it is important to look at the context in which discussions over empowerment and indeed women's empowerment have arisen. Betellie (1999:590) argues, empowerment is largely about 'ordinary, common people, rather than politicians, experts and other socially or culturally advantaged persons, an improvement in the quality of life is integral to understanding the term. But whether this perceptions and meanings are shared by the grass root women especially the tribal is still in debate.

Demographic trends indicate a comparative better status of women in Kerala. According to 2001 census, out of the total population of 31841374, 15468614 were males and 16372760 were females, showing a sex ratio of 1,058 females to 1000 males. Female population of Kerala is 16.5 million, which constitute 51.8% of the total Kerala population. Sex ratio is favorable to women among all religions (Hindus: 1,041; Muslims: 1,048 and Christians: 1,013;-Census of India. 1991).

Table 1

District Wise Population, Sex Ratio and Density of Population in Kerala, (2001)

District	*Area in Sq. km*	*Population total*	*Female*	*Percentage of female to total population*	*Sex ratio*	*population density*
Thiruvananthapuram	2192	3234707	1663283	51.42	1058	71476
Kollam	2491	2584118	1335502	51.68	1070	1038
Pathanam thitta	*2637	1231577	643542	52.25	1094	574
Alappuzha	1414	2105349	1092777	51.9	1079	1496
Kottayam	*2208	1952901	988468	50.62	1025	722
Idukki	*4476	1128605	562200	49.81	999	252
Eranakulam	2950	3098378	1562497	50.43	1017	1050
Thrissur	3032	2975440	1553393	52.21	1092	981
Palakkad	4480	2617072	1351278	51.63	1068	584
Malappuram	3550	3629640	1870161	51.52	1063	1022
Kozhikode	2344	2878498	1479824	51.41	1058	1228
Wayanad	2131	786627	393230	49.99	1000	369
Kannur	2966	2412365	1258221	51.16	1090	813
Kasaragod	1992	1203342	615579	51.16	1047	604
State	38863	31841374	16372760	51.42	1058	819

*Changes in area from 1991 census due to shifting of area to and fro

Source: Provisional population totals 2001.

As in other parts of the country, the Tribes of Kerala constitute a weaker section of the population constituting 1.14 per cent of the state population, and ST population of India is 8.20% of the total population. There are 35 communities recognized as Scheduled Tribes distributed in all most all districts of Kerala. Among this five are (Cholanaicken, Kattunaicken, Kadar, Kurumbar and Koragar) classified as the primitive tribes constituting nearly 4.8 per cent of the total Scheduled Tribe population of Kerala.

Table 2
District- Wise Population of Scheduled Tribes in Kerala and Overall Sex Ratio

District	*Per cent*	*Scheduled Tribe share to state*	*Sex ratio(F/M)*
Thiruvananthapuram	0.6	5.7	1113
Kollam	0.2	1.4	1121
Pathanamthitta	0.5	1.8	1057
Alappuzha	0.1	0.9	1001
Kottayam	0.9	5	1044
Idukki	4.5	14	998
Ernakulam	0.3	2.8	978
Thrissur	0.2	1.3	1105
Palakkad	1.5	10.9	984
Malappuram	0.3	3.4	1046
Kozhikode	0.2	1.6	1031
Wayanad	17.3	37.4	1019
Kannur	0.8	5.5	1039
Kasaragod	2.5	8.3	1005
Kerala	1.1	100	1027

Source: Census of India 2001.

Among the scheduled tribes of Kerala, in 1981, there were 992 women per 1000 men and in 1991, the sex ratio is 996. While the national figures showed a down ward trend-from 983 in 1981 to 972 in 1991. Among all Indian states Kerala stands first in the sex ratio favorable to women for Scheduled tribe population. More over an important factor of women's health is their life expectancy at birth. It has been increasing steadily in Kerala and in India. In Kerala, female life expectancy increased from 50 years in 1960 to 73.6 years in 2000(Meera Bai 2006).

II

The tribal communities of Kerala are distributed under different economic categories such as food gatherers, agricultural and other daily wage workers, and settled agriculturists. whatever the development programme be, it is difficult to bring them under one roof due to their heterogeneous nature of culture. More over there are other factors also influencing their development such as education, culture contact, and exposure to mass Media and development programmes of the government.

In Kerala, Wayanad district experience predominant tribal population with a share of 35.8% in 1991 and 37.4 in 2001 to the total population of the district. Tribal population of Wayanad constitutes 17% of the total population of the district. Infant Mortality rate (per 1000 births) is 22 in 2001 with a crude birth rate of 19.5 (per 1000pop) and total fertility rate of 2.0 (Human Development Report Kerala 2005). It was found that the general and reproductive health situation of the tribal women in Kerala was very poor. Women had high abortion ratio and infant mortality rates. (Socio-economic survey of Primitive Tribes-1996-97). Studies conducted by Attappady Hill Area Development Society highlighted that tribal people of Kerala suffered from a number of illnesses such as sickle cell anaemia, thyroid disorder, cancers, and addiction related disorders. Contagious diseases such as cholera, viral fever, jaundice and TB were also common among tribes. In addition to all, ecological changes have seriously affected the traditional practices.

Among Kattunaicken, a food gathering tribe of Kerala, women are mostly engaged in gathering items such as roots, tubers, fruits and other edibles from the forest. Introduction of new forest policies and prohibition of hunting has stopped their frequent entry into the forest for collection. The disappearance of wild edibles from their diet automatically reduced the nutritional status of the food which cannot be compensated with the low coast food available from the market. But in the case of economically advanced group like Mullakuruman and Kurichiyan the situation is different. They have their own land for cultivation and with the better economy they managed every thing from the market. There is more number of literates in these groups with better economy and we cannot deny the fact that health and education are proportional both directly and inversely.

When analyze the comparatively better health status of Kerala women in general, it is found that rise in number of institutional deliveries is one of the factors. But the case is different for tribal women. Fifty percentages of them are not attending the hospitals for deliveries. This is most common among primitive tribal groups where most of the settlements

Table 3
Health and Education Indicators for Kerala and India

	Adult literacy rate(+15yrs)%		*Life expectancy at birth(yrs)*		*Crude death rate*	*Infant mortality rate*	*total fertility rate*
	Male	*female*	*Male*	*female*			
India	44	72	64	62	9	71	3.1
Kerala	83	93	76	70	6	14	1.8

Crude death rates and infant mortality rates are per 1000 and female to male ratio is the number of women per 100 men.
Data Source: Dreze and Sen (2002).

are located in reserve forest areas or interior villages which is not accessible to hospitals in the case of emergency. According to National Family Health Survey (NFHS-11) 93% of births were institutional deliveries in 1998-99. Rise in the number of institutional deliveries has reduced both infant mortality rate and maternal mortality. Tribal women of Wayanad are an exception to this data as the infant mortality rate in Wayanad is 22 when compared to the state rate of 14 (Human Development Report 2005).

Kerala women give a high priority to their health problems. This is mainly because of the impact of their high literacy status and employment. But the situation is totally different in the case of tribal women. Tribal women of Kerala had low literacy with lower sex ratio and low child sex ratio showing low status of females. The infant mortality and foetal wastage are also high among tribal women with a high proportion of reproductive morbidities.

The world economic forum has introduced a new methodology to measure the gender gap by incorporating five dimensions of female empowerment namely, economic participation, economic opportunity, political empowerment, educational attainment and health and well-being (World Economic Forum 2005). The tribes of Kerala have been exposed to formal education only recently. Their response to formal education and schooling are different from one another as they are from different social, cultural and economic backgrounds and exposed to a variety of socio-cultural situations. Wide disparity exists in the literacy rate as between the general population, Scheduled Castes and Scheduled Tribe population. While the national average literacy rate in 2001 was 52.21 per cent, it was lower for the Scheduled Castes (37.34 per cent) and the lowest for the Scheduled Tribes (29. 60 per cent).

Table 4
Literary Rates According to Gender and Community, Kerala: 2001

Category	*male*	*female*	*combined*	*Rank of Kerala among other states*
Total literacy rate	94.2	87.7	90.9	1
Literacy rate of SCs	88.1	77.6	82.7	1
Literacy rate of STs	70.8	58.1	64.4	5

Source: Census of India 2001 Primary Census Abstract.

It is a fact that literacy rate among the tribal has gone up yet the decadal rate of growth of literacy is very slow as compared to the literacy rate of the general population. The literacy rate has increased by 6.78% in the decade 1971-81 and 16.00% during 1981-91 for the general population but in the case of Scheduled Tribes, the literacy rate has risen by 5.05% and 13.25% only for the period 1971-81 and 1981-91 respectively. The gap between literacy rates of general population and STs

Table 5
Crude Literacy Rate Among the SCs & STs in India

year	*source*	*Scheduled Castes*		*Scheduled Tribes*		*others*	
		male	*female*	*male*	*female*	*male*	*female*
1981	census						
all areas		30.9	10.8	24.5	8	52.3	29.4
Rural		27.9	8.5	22.9	6.8	46.1	21.7
1983	NSS						
all areas		NA	NA	NA	NA	NA	NA
Rural		35.6	13	30.5	11.5	50.7	26.3
1987-88	NSS						
all areas		47.5	24.6	46.7	28.2		
Rural		37.5	15.5	32.5	13.4	50.7	30.5
1991	Census						
all areas		49.9	23.8	40.6	18.1	52.7	32.2
Rural						47.4	25.4

Source: Vimala Ramachandran 2002.

has increased from 20% in 1981 to 23% in 1991. It has a high female literacy rate of 86.2%, but literacy position is more unsatisfactory in case of ST females which are only 18.19% as against 39.23% for non ST women. i. e out of every 10 ST women are illiterate.

The crude literacy rate of the Scheduled Tribe females according to the above table shows an increase from 8 to 18 in 1981 to 1991. But this is low when compared to the Scheduled Castes and the general population. Education of the Scheduled tribe females is still an unsolved problem in Kerala because there are large percentage of dropouts and stagnation among female students. Parents are not interested in sending their children to schools as they have to look after the young ones when the parents are out for labour.

Table 6
Literacy Among Different Social Groups and Selected Districts of Kerala, 1991

District/state	*Literacy of Gen. population*		*Literacy of SC/ST population as %of literacy of general population*			
	male	*female*	*male SC*	*male ST*	*female SC*	*Female ST*
Kerala	93.62	86.16	78.98	57.40	75.47	50.52
Wayanad	87.59	77.69	80.07	55.13	75.81	47.03
Trivandrum	92.84	85.76	80.75	76.01	79.31	67.61
Malappuram	92.08	84.09	76.80	44.31	74.17	37.45

Source: Government of Kerala, 1993.

The national policy on empowerment of women in its introduction states, the principle of gender equality is enshrined in the Indian constitution in its preamble, fundamental rights, fundamental duties and directive principles. The constitution not only grants equality to women, but also empowers the state to adopt measures of positive discrimination in favor of women. Kerala is a state with an impressive array of achievements in the field of women development. Women in Kerala have made impressive gains in health and education, particularly when compared to other parts of the country. The gender gap in literacy rates is much smaller in Kerala, compared to other regions in India. Education of women has been linked to the low fertility rates, which together are key indicators of the emancipation of women (Dreze and Sen, 2002). But in spite of all these achievements, the conspicuous absence of tribal women in the public sector and economic marginalization remains as a controversy to Kerala model of development. The tribal had low literacy with lower sex ratio showing low status of females within the tribal system and very low child sex ratio. The infant mortality and foetal wastage were also high among tribes along with a high proportion of reproductive morbidities among the women.

III

Ecological equilibrium plays a vital role in the socio-cultural stability and health aspects of the tribal communities. In the case of technologically less developed groups, food habits and subsistence pattern are mainly centered on food gathering. They developed techniques of food gathering as an adaptation to the surrounding ecosystem. When the environment is rich and resourceful, the food procurement technologies become simple, easy and less time consuming. Where as when it is deficient in resources, the inhabitants will have to find different and complex ways of food procurement strategies for a minimum survival. In most cases it is the duty of the women to make two ends meet their requirements.

In Wayanad, agricultural labourers like Paniyan and Adiyan get 100 to 120 days of labour in a year. The females are able to get more labour opportunities than males. This is because non-tribal female labourers are not adapted to wetland paddy cultivation practices where as Adiyan and Paniyan females are highly skillful. It is reported that small cultivators pay the labourers a higher wage as they provide only few days work. But those who work on regular basis under cultivators having larger landholdings receive wages little lesser than the wage paid in general. Such labourers are paid advances also. It is found that tribal women are used to such kind of work as they get engaged on most of the days which affects their health both physical and mental.

In olden days whenever an animal is hunted, it was divided into many portions. The important portions like, liver, heart and thigh were kept for gods. The rest of the portion was divided among the members. One portion was set apart for the chief. The portion set aside for the god was also taken by the chief later. A small portion was set aside for the old and disabled men and women of the settlement. The portions of the god and the chief were cooked by the chief's wife separately and were kept on a plantain leaf together with rice in their sacred house. This was kept there for an hour propitiating their deity and the ancestral spirits. After that the food was served to the members of the family. The gathered surplus roots and tubers were also distributed. This type of distribution system is an adaptive strategy for managing a situation of food scarcity and also a social event which demonstrates relatedness, affection and concern. They not bothered about the quality or quantity of the collected items but consider this cosmic economy of sharing or distribution as an economic arrangement in an indefinite ecosystem.

In the past tribal communities of Kerala except a few, did not produce anything. They completely depended on the resources of nature for their livelihood. Today, hunting and trapping of birds and animals for food procurement was almost completely stopped owing to the restrictions imposed by the state forest department and also shortage of games in the forest. The collection of MFP has also reduced owing to the degradation of the forests. In this complicated situation they have to act as a medium of compromise between nature and culture and forced to become better managers of resources that are available. The shortage of traditional natural resources generated a condition to accept other economic activities especially agricultural labour under non-tribal and some of the tribal landlords. All these circumstances are leading to a kind of economic shock among the tribal people especially among women which the Govt should take into consideration before planning and implementing the development programmes.

The 2001 census showed that work participation rate of women in Kerala is lower than the all India average and the unemployment rates are the highest in the country. But in the case of tribal females, opportunities for labour are more when compared to their male counterparts. Females are more adapted to wet land cultivation and the recently introduced cash crop agriculture. After a period of harvest the husband joins with his wife for other works like thrashing, making bundles and packing the grains in bags. Usually the wife recommends her husband to the master for labour. In a household where husband has to endure long spells of unemployment while his wife keeps working. So by all means, women are an economic asset to the family as they also bring bride price and tribal people of kerala attach any special preference to boys when compared to other tribes of India. Traditionally in most of the tribal societies, the members were organized under the head of the household, who was usually the eldest male. But now a day the authority is seen shifted to a person who contributes larger share to the family income and most families it is women. She is the decision maker though her husband is alive. This is the result of increasing participation of women in the economy and the growth of personal economic independence.

The process of education and female literacy do not commensurate with the all round educational facilities available. Food gatherers and wage labourers have late enrolment in schools and their drop out rate is high. A scrutiny on the school going children and their academic performances reveal that their standard is staggeringly poor. The parents so far could not transpire the message of female education to their children as like the non-tribes of the area. Children from Koraga, Kattunaicken,Adiyan ,Paniyan, Cholanaicken and Kurumba tribes do not have a stimulating atmosphere for qualitative education especially for girls. If female education is considered possibly the best available indicator of women's status, the tribal women of Kerala at present will not come within the parameters of development.

Social justice for tribes is a term much discussed in the academic and administrative circles now a day. The denial of social justice to women is a major issue because it may lead to frustration of major aspirations of substantial segment of the society. In the society of Adiyan (agricultural labourers), the womenfolk enjoyed equal partnership in all walks of life. In the present day plural society of wayanad, the Adiyan women aspire to a higher level if living standards. The work group comprising of tribal and non-tribal of both the sexes engage in agricultural works provide ample opportunities for intermingling. A number of them are also employed as servant maids in non-tribal areas and households bringing about the atmosphere of sexual exploitation resulting in some of them becoming unwed mothers. Thirunelli village in Wayanad where Adiyan are numerically predominant is a pilgrim place and also a picnic spot. Large number of people from the plains is visiting this area as tourists. Exposure to tourists culture also lead to the birth of unwed mothers and the visitors leave the place forever after their 'pilgrimage'. When we analyze the social and legal status of the child born to an unwed mother, he/she will be a question in front of the society along with all sorts of discriminations resulting in personality disorders and unpredicted future.

Discussions are taking place at various levels about the nature and mode of empowerment for tribal women as a means of dealing with problems which are varied and multidimensional. First strategy is to take special measures to eliminate discrimination, eradicate illiteracy, and increase enrolment and retention rates of tribal girls. Education is the pivot of women's empowerment because it enables them to respond to opportunities, to challenge their traditional constraints, and there by a change in outlook.

BIBLIOGRAPHY

Bird, Nurit. Beyond the Original Affluent Society-A Culturalist Reformulation, *Current Anthropology.* Vol. 33, No. 1 Feb.

Bindu, B. (1998), Socio-Economic Change Among Three Wayand Tribes. A study of Kattunaicken, Adiyan and Mullukuruman in Eco-cultural Context. (Unpublished Ph.D thesis submitted to Calicut University).

Bindu, B. (1997), Ethnographic Notes on the Kattunaicken-A Food Gathering Tribe of Wayanad, Kerala, *Journal of Human Ecology,* Vol. 8 July.

Bindu, B. (2001), Kattunaicken Kinship-An Analysis. Calicut University Research *Journal,* Vol. 2 April.

Dreze, Jean and Sen, A. K. (1995), India: Economic Development and Social Opportunity, Oxford University Press, New Delhi.

Government of India, Census of India (2001), Primary Census Abstract.

Government of Kerala (2001), Directorate of Economics and Statistics, Thiruvananthapuram.

Government of Kerala (1994), Economic Review, State Planning Board, Trivandrum.

Government of Kerala (1994), Social Safety Net-Improvement of Primary Education in Wayanad District of Kerala State, DPEP.

Human Development Report (2005), State Planning Board, Govt. of Kerala.

Sarkar, Sourindranath (1965), Psycho-Dynamics of Tribal behaviour, Calcutta, J. N. Basu and Co.

Parvathamma, C. (1984), Scheduled Castes and Tribes-A Socio-Economic Survey, Ashish Publishing House, New Delhi.

Vyas, N.N. and R.S. Mann (1980), Indian Tribes in Transition, Rawat Publications, Jaipur.

Meera Bai, M. (2006), Women and Economic Reforms-Kerala Experience, Serial Publications, New Delhi.

Ramachandran, Vimala (2002), Gender and Social Equity. Hierarchies of Access. The European Commission.

Mathur, P.R.G. (1977), Tribal Situation in Kerala, Historical Society, Trivandrum.

Draft Project Report Vol. 1 (1994), Department of General Education, Government of Kerala, March, p. 38.

10

DEMOGRAPHY, SOCIO-ECONOMIC AND HEALTH CONDITIONS OF THE FOUR PRIMITIVE TRIBES IN NILGIRI HILLS OF TAMILANDU

T.S. Naidu & G. Palanisamy

INTRODUCTION

The tribals are, by and large, children of nature, their life style being conditioned by their eco-system. At present there are approximately 200 million tribal people, roughly 4 per cent of the global population. According to 1991 Census, the population of the Schedule Tribes in India was 67.76 millions, constituting about 8.08 per cent of the total population, approximately one tribesman for every thirteen Indians. In Tamil Nadu there are about 5.75 lakhs, of Scheduled Tribes widely dispersed in 21 districts of Tamil Nadu. They are the most vulnerable sections of the population and they are exploited by the most age old social and cultural handicaps coupled with environmental factors. They were socially as well as economically weaker than the rest of the population. Articles 14 (4), 46, 244 (1) and 339 of the Indian constitution speak of special provisions meant for the administration and control of Scheduled areas and tribals therein, for their welfare and protection.

Knowledge about the demography, living conditions and ecology profile of the study area and sample primitive tribal households facilitates proper understanding of the present living conditions of the primitive tribes in the study area. An attempt has been made to present the demographic characteristics of the tribes in section one. In section two it deals about the social conditions of the tribes and section three analyses the economic conditions of tribes and section four deals with the health condition of the primitive tribes.

SOURCES OF DATA AND METHODOLOGY

The tribals chosen for the study are the primitive tribes of the Nilgiri hills of Tamil Nadu. The tribes included are the Todas who are pastroliths by occupation, Kotas, horticulturists, Irulas food gatherers and Paniyas food gatherers and labourers. 51 tribal villages are covered in the study area. 4, 19, 15 and 13 villages are covered in Kota, Toda, Paniya and Irula tribes respectively. In selected villages, 710 household are selected to study the socio–cultural, ecology and health and nutritional status of the selected primitive tribes. Out of 710 households, 120, 110, 230 and 250 Kota, Toda, Paniya and Irula households are covered respectively. In the study are 3074 individuals were examined to know the general health conditions among the all tribes. 581, 493, 1065 and 935 individuals covered in Kota, Toda, Paniya and Irula tribes respectively.

The research team used three types of questionnaires for data collection. The household questionnaire, the pregnant women and lactating mother questionnaire, the Infant and children (1-6 years) questionnaire. The research team had stayed with the tribes and conducted the study, also 4 visits were made to study the growth and development of the health status of the tribes.

DEMOGRAPHIC CHARACTERISTICS

Type of Family

Table 1 shows the type of family by tribe-wise. Out of the total 710 total households 547 (77.04 per cent) families are nuclear families followed by joint family (20.99 per cent) broken family (1.83 per cent) and only (0.14 per cent) extended family. In Kota tribe 89 (74.17 per cent) and 31 (25.83 per cent) are nuclear and joint families respectively. In Toda tribe 74 (67.27 per cent) and

36 (32.73 per cent) are nuclear and joint families respectively. There are no extended and broken families among Kota and Toda tribes. In Paniyas and Irulas tribes (77.39 per cent and 82.40 per cent of families are nuclear families. There are no extend families among Irula tribe.

Table 1
Type of Family by Tribe

Tribes	*Open-Field*	*Open*	*Latrine*	*Public*	*Total*
Kota	31 (25.83)	89 (74.17)	–	–	120 (100.00)
Toda	36 (32.73)	74 (67.27)	–	–	110 (100.00)
Paniya	48 (20.87)	178 (77.39)	1 (0.43)	3 (1.30)	230 (100.00)
Irula	34 (13.60)	206 (82.40)	–	10 (4.00)	250 (100.00)
All Tribes	149 (20.99)	547 (77.04)	1 (0.14)	13 (1.83)	710 (100.00)

Age and Sex Composition

Age and sex composition of the various tribes are given in Table 2 Nearly one third (31.45 per cent) of the all tribal population are in the age group of 0-14 years, 31.35 per cent of them are in the age group of 15-29 years, 19.65 per cent of them are in the age group of 30-44 years, 12.11 per cent are in the age group of 45-59 years and 5.44 per cent are above sixty years.

One third of the male and female population of all tribes are in the age group of 0-14 years, 29.81 per cent of the male and 32.84 per cent of the female are in the age group of 15-29 years, 19.59 per cent of the male and 19.70 per cent of the female are in the age group of 30-44 years and 11.82 per cent of the male and 12.38 per cent of the female are in the age group of 45-59 years. Male and female population in the age group of sixty and above are 6.25 per cent and 4.66 per cent respectively.

Nearly one fourth 23.75 per cent and above one third 35.28 per cent of the Kota population are in the age group of 0-14 years and age groups 15-29 years respectively 18.07 per cent, 14.63 per cent and 8.27 per cent of Kotas population in the age group of 30-44, 45-59, and 60 and above years respectively. Only a very small proportion of the existing population is surviving in the age group of 0-14 years and 15-29 years. Among the males 16.37 per cent are in the age group of 30-44 years and 16.01 per cent are in the age group 44-59 years. One third of the Toda population in male and female population in the age group of 0-14 years and 15-29 years. In 30-44 age group equal distribution (19.65 and 19.69 per cent) in male and female population. Among the male 9.83 per cent in the age group 45-59 years, 5.13 per cent in the age group of 60 and above. Among the female 10.03 per cent and 6.18 per cent in the age groups of 45-49 years and 60 and above respectively.

The total population of the Paniya sample households are 1065 persons of which males account for 540 (50.70 per cent) and females for 525 (49.30 per cent). The age and sex composition pattern of the Paniya population reveals that 38.89 per cent males and 30.28 per cent females are in the age group of 0-14 years 24.07 per cent males and 32.96 per cent of females are in the age group of 15-29 years. In 30-44 years age group, 20.74 per cent and 20.76 per cent males and females population respectively 11.67 per cent and 13.15 per cent males and females population respectively in the 45-59 years age group. Only 4.63 and 2.85 per cent male and female population respectively in the 60 and above age group.

A total population of the Irula sample households 935 persons of which males account for 451 (48.24 per cent) and females for 484 (51.76 per cent). The age and sex composition pattern of Irula population reveals that one third of the malè and female in the age group of 0-14 years. 29.93 per cent males and 31.41 per cent females are in the age group of 15-29 years. Only 6.87 per cent males and 4.14 per cent females in the age group of 60 and above age group. Sex ratio of a population is usually expressed as the number of females per 1000 males. The over all sex ratio of the sample population is 1041. Irula has the highest sex ratio of 1073 and Paniya has the lowest sex ratio of 972. Kota and Toda has sex ratio of 1067 and 1106 respectively.

Table 2
Age and Sex Composition of the Sample Population by Tribe

Age Group	*Male* *No. of Persons*	*Male* *Percentage*	*Female* *No.of Persons*	*Female* *Percentage*	*Both* *No.of Persons*	*Both* *Percentage*	*Sex Ratio*
KOTA							
0-14	65	23.14	73	24.34	138	23.75	1123
15-29	99	35.23	106	35.34	205	35.28	1070
30-44	46	16.37	59	19.66	105	18.07	1282
45-59	45	16.01	40	13.33	85	14.63	888
60 +	26	9.25	22	7.33	48	8.27	846
Sub Total	281	100.00	300	100.00	581	100.00	1067
	(48.36)		(51.64)		(100.00)		
TODA							
0-14	68	29.06	82	31.66	150	30.43	1205
15-29	85	36.33	84	32.44	169	34.28	988
30-44	46	19.65	51	19.69	97	19.67	1108
45-59	23	9.83	26	10.03	49	9.94	1130
60 +	12	5.13	16	6.18	28	5.68	1333
Sub Total	234	100.00	259	100.00	493	100.00	1106
	(47.46)		(52.54)		(100.00)		
PANIYA							
0-14	210	38.89	159	30.28	369	34.64	757
15-29	130	24.07	173	32.96	303	28.45	1330
30-44	112	20.74	109	20.76	221	20.76	973
45-59	63	11.67	69	13.15	132	12.39	1095
60 +	25	4.63	15	2.85	40	3.76	600
Sub Total	540	100.00	525	100.00	1065	100.00	972
	(50.70)		(49.30)		(100.00)		
IRULA							
0-14	147	32.59	163	33.67	310	33.16	1108
15-29	135	29.93	152	31.41	287	30.69	1125
30-44	91	20.18	90	18.59	181	19.35	989
45-59	47	10.43	59	12.19	106	11.34	1255
60 +	31	6.87	20	4.14	51	5.46	645
Sub Total	451	100.00	484	100.00	935	100.00	1073
	(48.24)		(51.76)		(100.00)		
ALL TRIBES							
0-14	490	32.53	477	30.42	967	31.45	973
15-29	449	29.81	515	32.84	964	31.35	1146
30-44	295	19.59	309	19.7	604	19.65	1047
45-59	178	11.82	194	12.38	372	12.11	1089
60+	94	6.25	73	4.66	167	5.44	776
Grand Total	1506	100.00	1568	100.00	3074	100.00	1041
	(48.99)		(51.01)		(100.00)		

Marital Status

The Table 3 reveals that married persons account for 48.63 per cent while 45.71 per cent are unmarried. There are 737 married

Figure 1
Age and Sex Composition by Tribe

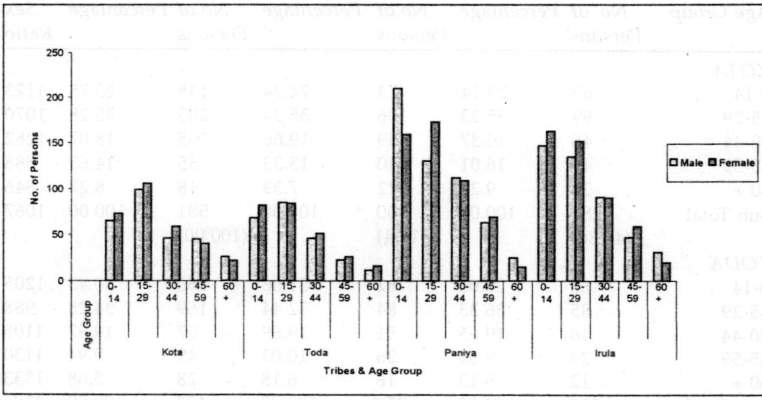

persons, 742 unmarried persons and 25 widowers among the males constituting 48.93 per cent, 49.27 per cent and 1.67 per cent of the total male population respectively. There are 758 married persons, 663 unmarried persons and 134 widows among the females constituting 48.34 per cent, 42.29 per cent and 8.54 per cent of the total female population respectively.

In Kota tribe 45.95 per cent are married male 48.75 per cent and female 43.34 per cent), 49.56 per cent are single (male 47.34 per cent and female 51.66 per cent) and only 4.31 per cent and 4.66 per cent). Among the Toda tribe the percentage of married, single and widow/widower are 51.32 per cent (male 54.71 per cent, female 48.27 per cent) 41.78 per cent (male 44.01 and female 39.76 per cent) and 6.47 per cent (male 0.85 per cent and female 11.58 per cent) respectively.

Among the Paniya the married, unmarried, widow/widower and divorced population consists 46.76 per cent, 47.42 per cent, 4.78 per cent and 1.04 per cent respectively 44.81 per cent of the male and 48.76 per cent of the female are married. The male and female are married. The male and female percentages of the unmarried are 54.26 per cent and 40.38 per cent respectively. In female 8.95 per cent and 1.91 per cent are widow and divorced respectively. Among the Irula the

Table 3
Marital Status by Tribe

Marital Status	*Male* No. of Persons	*Male* Percentage	*Female* No. of Persons	*Female* Percentage	*Both* No. of Persons	*Both* Percentage
KOTA						
Married	137	48.75	130	43.34	267	45.95
Unmarried	133	47.34	155	51.66	288	49.56
Widow/Widower	11	3.91	14	4.66	25	4.31
Divorced	–	–	1	0.34	1	0.18
Sub Total	281	100.00	300	100.00	581	100.00
TODA						
Married	128	54.71	125	48.27	253	51.32
UnMarried	103	44.01	103	39.76	206	41.78
Widow/Widower	2	0.85	30	11.58	32	6.49
Divorced	1	0.43	1	0.39	2	0.41
Sub Total	234	100.00	259	100.00	493	100.00
PANIYA						
Married	242	44.81	256	48.76	498	46.70
UnMarried	293	54.26	212	40.38	505	47.42
Widow/Widower	4	0.74	47	8.95	51	4.78
Divorced	1	0.19	10	1.91	11	1.04
Sub Total	540	100.00	525	100.00	1065	100.00
IRULA						
Married	230	50.99	247	51.04	477	51.01
UnMarried	213	47.23	193	39.87	406	43.43
Widow/Widower	8	1.78	43	8.89	51	5.46
Divorced	–	–	1	0.20	1	0.10
Sub Total	451	100.00	484	100.00	935	100.00
ALL TRIBES						
Married	737	48.93	758	48.34	1495	48.63
UnMarried	742	49.27	663	42.29	1405	45.71
Widow/Widower	25	1.67	134	8.54	159	5.17
Divorced	2	0.13	13	0.83	15	0.49
Grand Total	1506	100.00	1568	100.00	3074	100.00

percentage of married, unmarried and widow/widower are 51.01 per cent (male 50.99 per cent and female 51.04 per cent), 43.43 per cent (male 47.23 per cent, female 39.87 per cent) and 5.46 per cent (male 1.78 per cent and female 8.89 per cent) respectively.

Above data shows that married persons are more in Toda tribe, unmarried persons are more in Kota tribe and divorced persons are more in Paniya tribe.

Educational Status

Literacy Status of the various tribes of the study area is depicted in table 1.4. Out of 3074 total persons, 48.27 per cent are illiterates among males constitutes 42.69 per cent and female constitutes 53.63 per cent. 22.97 per cent are primary school educations 25.30 per cent of the male and 20.73 per cent of the female), 23.09 per cent are Secondary School educators (25.90 per cent of the male and 20.41 per cent of the female) and 5.67 per cent are higher educators (6.11 per cent of the male and 5.23 per cent of the female) are there in total persons.

In Kota tribe 20.99 per cent are not enter into school (20.28 per cent of the male and 21.67 per cent of the female) and 14.29 per cent are studied upto primary (16.37 per cent of the male and 12.34 per cent of the female). Secondary and higher educations accounts for 47.68 per cent and 17.04 per cent respectively. Male secondary and higher educators accounts for 44.84 per cent and 18.51 per cent respectively. In female secondary and higher educators accounts for 50.33 per cent and 15.66 per cent respectively.

One third (34.48 per cent) of the population in Toda tribe are illiterates 26.49 per cent and 41.69 per cent illiterates are male and female respectively. 29.62 per cent persons are studied upto primary (28.63 per cent of the male and 30.51 per cent of the female. Secondary and higher educators accounts for a 30.63 per cent and 5.27 per cent respectively.

Among the Paniya tribe, illiterate are the predominant (68.35 per cent, male are 62.96 per cent and female 73.90 per cent) followed by primary (21.78 per cent, 26.11 per cent of the male and 17.34 per cent of the female) and secondary school educators 6.68 per cent, 7.96 per cent of the male, 5.34 per cent of the female). Higher educators occupies only 3.19 per cent. In Irula tribe illiterates are 49.62 per cent followed by primary educators 26.21 per cent, secondary educators 22.56 per cent and only 1.61 per cent are higher educators.

Table 4
Education Status by Tribe

Educational Status	*Male* No. of Persons	*Male* Percentage	*Female* No.of Persons	*Female* Percentage	*Both* No.of Persons	*Both* Percentage
KOTA						
Illiterates	57	20.28	65	21.67	122	20.99
Primary	46	16.37	37	12.34	83	14.29
Secondary	126	44.84	151	50.33	277	47.68
Higher	52	18.51	47	15.66	99	17.04
Sub Total	281	100.00	300	100.00	581	100.00
TODA						
Illiterates	62	26.49	108	41.69	170	34.48
Primary	67	28.63	79	30.51	146	29.62
Secondary	90	38.47	61	23.55	151	30.63
Higher	15	6.41	11	4.25	26	5.27
Sub Total	234	100.00	259	100.00	493	100.00
PANIYA						
Illiterates	340	62.96	388	73.90	728	68.35
Primary	141	26.11	91	17.34	232	21.78
Secondary	43	7.96	28	5.34	71	6.68
Higher	16	2.97	18	3.42	34	3.19
Sub Total	540	100.00	525	100.00	1065	100.00
IRULA						
Illiterates	184	40.80	280	57.85	464	49.62
Primary	127	28.16	118	24.38	245	26.21
Secondary	131	29.05	80	16.53	211	22.56
Higher	9	1.99	6	1.24	15	1.61
Sub Total	451	100.00	484	100.00	935	100.00
ALL TRIBES						
Illiterates	643	42.69	841	53.63	1484	48.27
Primary	381	25.30	325	20.73	706	22.97
Secondary	390	25.90	320	20.41	710	23.09
Higher	92	6.11	82	5.23	174	5.67
Grand Total	1506	100.00	1568	100.00	3074	100.00

SOCIAL CONDITIONS

Type of Houses

Table 5 shows the type of houses among the four tribes in the study area. It is observed from the table that majority of the tribes are living in the tiled houses, 91.67 per cent of Kota, 84.55 per cent of Toda, 66.96 per cent of Paniya, and 82.40 per cent of

Figure 2
Educational Status by Tribe

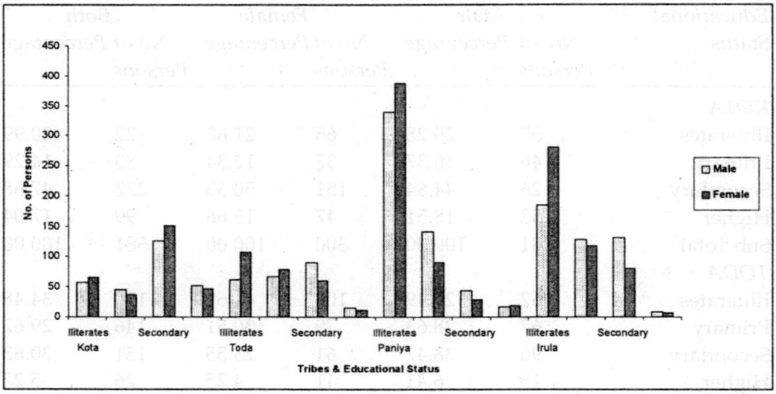

Irula. The numbers of tiled houses are more in the study area, because of the development schemes JRY and Hill Area Development Programmes the number of tiled home construction increased. Among the various tribes Paniya are having more number of thatched houses than the other tribes. Tribes who are inhabiting in pucca houses are 8.33 per cent in Kota, 3.64 per cent in Toda, 7.83 per cent in Paniya, and 10.40 per cent in Irula. 24.35 per cent of Paniya, 10.91 per cent of Toda and 3.60 per cent of Irula are living in thatched houses. The above data shows that thatched houses are not found in Kota.

Table 5
Types of House by Tribe

Tribes	*Types of House*				*Total*
	Pucca	*Tiled*	*Thatched*	*Stone*	
Kota	10	110	–	–	(100.00)
	(8.33)	(91.67)			
Toda	4	93	12	1	110
	(3.64)	(84.55)	(10.91)	(0.91)	(100.00)
Paniya	18	154	56	2	230
	(7.83)	(66.96)	(24.35)	(0.87)	(100.00)
Irula	26	206	9	9	250
	(10.40)	(82.40)	(3.60)	(3.60)	(100.00)
All Tribes	58	563	77	12	710
	(8.17)	(79.30)	(10.85)	(1.69)	(100.00)

Ownership of the Houses

Table 6 analyses the ownership of the houses by tribe-wise. Among all the tribes 52.11 per cent of the tribes are living in the Govt. houses, 42.54 per cent in own houses, 3.24 per cent in rented houses and only 2.11 per cent in constructed by N.G.O. The tribes who are living in their own houses are Kota 84.17 per cent, Toda 59.09 per cent, Paniya 31.30 per cent, and Irulas 25.60 per cent. Only tribes like Kota (8.33 per cent) Toda (1.82 per cent), Paniya (2.17 per cent) and Irula (2.40 per cent) are living in rented houses. The tribes who are living in Government houses are Irula 72.00 per cent, Paniya 60.43 per cent, Toda 39.09 per cent and Kota 6.67 per cent. Only Kota and Paniya tribe live in N.G.O constructed houses. The above data shows that more number of Irula and Paniya are living in Government houses than the other tribes.

Table 6
Ownership of the House by Tribe

	Ownership of the Houses				*Total*
Tribes	*Owned*	*Rented*	*Govt.*	*N G O*	
Kota	101	10	8	1	120
	(84.17)	(8.33)	(6.67)	(0.83)	(100.00)
Toda	65	2	43	–	110
	(59.09)	(1.82)	(39.09)		(100.00)
Paniya	72	5	139	14	230
	(31.30)	(2.17)	(60.43)	(6.09)	(100.00)
Irula	64	6	180	–	250
	(25.60)	(2.40)	(72.00)		(100.00)
All Tribes	302	23	370	15	710
	(42.54)	(3.24)	(52.11)	(2.11)	(100.00)

Electrification of Houses

Electrification of houses by Tribe-wise is shown in the Table 7. All the tribes who are living in electrified and non-electrified houses are 41.13 per cent and 58.87 per cent respectively. The tribes who are living in electrified houses are Kota 85 per cent, Toda 66.36 per cent, Paniya 4.78 per cent and Irula 42.40 per cent. The tribes who are living in non-electrified houses Paniya 95.22 per cent, Irula 57.60 per cent, Toda 33.64, per cent and Kota 15 per cent. Only 11 households are living in electrified houses because they are living in very remote area.

Table 7
Electrification of Houses by Tribe

Tribes	*Electrified*	*Non Electrified*	*Total*
Kota	102	18	120
	(85.00)	(15.00)	(100.00)
Toda	73	37	110
	(66.36)	(33.64)	(100.00)
Paniya	11	219	230
	(4.78)	(95.22)	(100.00)
Irula	106	144	250
	(42.40)	(57.60)	(100.00)
All Tribes	292	418	710
	(41.13)	(58.87)	(100.00)

Ventilation Facilities

It is observed from the Table 8 that majority of the tribes are living in having ventilation facilities to their houses. In all Kota tribes are having ventilation facilities. Irula, Toda and Paniya tribes having ventilation facilities 93.20 per cent, 88.18 per cent and 80.43 per cent respectively.

Table 8
Ventilation Facilities by Tribe

Tribes	*Yes*	*No*	*Total*
Kota	120	–	120
	(100.00)		(100.00)
Toda	97	13	110
	(88.18)	(11.82)	(100.00)
Paniya	185	45	230
	(80.43)	(19.57)	(100.00)
Irula	233	17	250
	(93.20)	(6.80)	(100.00)
All Tribes	635	75	710
	(89.44)	(10.56)	(100.00)

Water Facilities

Government agencies provide water facilities like tap, bore and well. Traditionally the tribals depended on their traditional water resources such as river, pond and spring. During summer seasons they face great difficulty to get protected water because many of the streams and ponds will dry. Table 9 explains the availability of water facilities by tribe-wise.

The table indicates that all the sample tribes are using tap water, well water and spring water 55.49 per cent, 27.04 per cent and 15.63 per cent respectively. In Kota tribe out of 120 households 97 households (80.83 per cent) 20 households (16.67 per cent) and only 3 households (2.50 per cent) are having water facilities by Tap, spring and well respectively. In Paniya tribe 65.22 per cent households are using well water and 30.87 per cent households are used spring water. In Irula tribes 87.60 per cent of households are using, tap water. Above table shows that Paniya tribes are not getting protected water for drinking, still they are depending on well, spring and tap water.

Table 9
Water Facilities by Tribe

Tribes	*Well*	*Tap*	*River*	*Pond*	*Spring*	*Borewell*	*Canal*	*Total*
Kota	3	97	–	–	20	–	–	120
	(2.50)	(80.83)			(16.67)			(100.00)
Toda	22	70	–	–	18	–	–	110
	(20.00)	(63.64)			(16.36)			(100.00)
Paniya	150	8	–	1	71	–	–	230
	(65.22)	(3.48)		(0.43)	(30.87)			(100.00)
Irula	17	219	6	–	2	4	2	250
	(6.80)	(87.60)	(2.40)		(0.80)	(1.60)	(0.80)	(100.00)
All Tribes	192	394	6	1	111	4	2	710
	(27.04)	(55.49)	(0.85)	(0.14)	(15.63)	(0.56)	(0.28)	(100.00)

Toilet Facilities

From the above table it can be examined that among all the four selected tribes majority of the tribes have open field toilet facilities. Out of the total 95.49 per cent of the households have open field toilet facilities. Only Toda tribe (2.73 per cent) have public toilet facilities.

ECONOMIC CONDITIONS

Labour Force Participation

According to Census, main workers are those who have worked or engaged in any economically productive activity for a major

Table 10
Toilet Facilities by Tribe

Tribes	*Open-Field*	*Open*	*Latrine*	*Public*	*Total*
Kota	110	7	3	–	120
	(91.67)	(5.83)	(2.50)		(100.00)
Toda	95	2	10	3	110
	(86.36)	(1.82)	(9.09)	(2.73)	(100.00)
Paniya	229	1	–	–	230
	(99.57)	(0.43)			(100.00)
Irula	244	4	2	–	250
	(97.60)	(1.60)	(0.80)		(100.00)
All Tribes	678	14	15	3	710
	(95.49)	(1.97)	(2.11)	(0.42)	(100.00)

part of the year or more than six months during the reference year. Marginal workers are those who have worked less than six months during the reference year. Non-workers are those who have not worked in any productive activity at any time during the reference year. According to the above definition, the population in the sample households has been classified into main workers, marginal workers and non-workers. Table 11 presents the labour force participation of the four tribes in the study area.

It is observed from the table that out of 3074 persons in the sample households, main workers constitute 45.86 per cent, and marginal workers 6.28 per cent. Non - workers account for 47.86 per cent of the population. Among the various tribes studied, Paniya tribe (55.50 per cent) have large number of workers, followed by the Irular (48.98 per cent), Kota tribe (34.94 per cent), and Toda tribe (32.04 per cent).

The table also explains the sex-wise labour force participation among the various selected tribes in the study area. In Kota tribe male and female main workers consists 32.75 per cent and 37.00 per cent respectively. In Kota tribe male and female non-workers consists 57.29 per cent and 54.33 per cent respectively. Toda tribe male main worker and non worker consists 44.88S per cent and 45.29 per cent respectively. Toda tribe female main worker, marginal worker and non worker consists 20.46 per cent, 15.06 per cent and 64.48 per cent respectively. Paniya and Irula male main workers 57.96 per cent and 51.21 per cent respectively and female main workers 52.95 per cent and 46.91 per cent respectively. Above data shows that among all the tribes Paniya tribe main workers (55.50 per cent) are more. Toda female workers and Kota male worker are less than the other tribes.

Table 11
Labour Force Participation by Tribe

Working Status	*Male*		*Female*		*Both*	
	No. of Persons	*Percentage*	*No.of Persons*	*Percentage*	*No.of Persons*	*Percentage*
KOTA						
Worker	92	32.75	111	37.00	203	34.94
Marginal Worker	28	9.96	26	8.67	54	9.29
Non–Worker	161	57.29	163	54.33	324	55.77
Sub Total	281	100.00	300	100.00	581	100.00
TODA						
Worker	105	44.88	53	20.46	158	32.04
Marginal Worker	23	9.83	39	15.06	62	12.58
Non–Worker	106	45.29	167	64.48	273	55.38
Sub Total	234	100.00	259	100.00	493	100.00
PANIYA						
Worker	313	57.96	278	52.95	591	55.50
Marginal Worker	9	1.67	39	7.43	48	4.50
Non–Worker	218	40.37	208	39.62	426	40.00
Sub Total	540	100.00	525	100.00	1065	100.00
IRULA						
Worker	231	51.21	227	46.91	458	48.98
Marginal Worker	6	1.34	23	4.75	29	3.11
Non–Worker	214	47.45	234	48.34	448	47.91
Sub Total	451	100.00	484	100.00	935	100.00
ALL TRIBES						
Worker	741	49.20	669	20.15	1410	45.86
Marginal Worker	66	4.38	127	11.28	193	6.28
Non–Worker	699	46.42	772	68.57	1471	47.86
Grand Total	1506	100.00	1568	100.00	3074	100.00

Occupational Status

Table 12 shows the occupational status by Tribe-wise. In all the tribes 93.08 per cent, 2.06 per cent and 4.86 per cent on primary, manufacturing and service sectors respectively. Paniyas both male and females depends only on primary sector, followed by Irula (both 96.10 per cent, male 94.94 per cent and 97.20 per cent), Toda (both 84.54 per cent, male 82.81 per cent and 86.96 per cent) and Kota (both 77.43 per cent, male 75.83 per cent and 78.83 per cent). In manufactory sector highest (both 6.62 per cent, male 7.50 per cent and female 5.84 per cent) in Kota followed by Toda and Irula tribe. In service sector Kotas (both 15.95 per cent, male 16.67 per cent, and females 15.33 per cent) are engaged.

Table 12
Occupational Status by Tribe

Occupational Status	*Male*		*Female*		*Both*	
	No. of Persons	*Percentage*	*No.of Persons*	*Percentage*	*No. of Persons*	*Percentage*
KOTA						
Primary	91	75.83	108	78.83	199	77.43
Manufacturing	9	7.50	8	5.84	17	6.62
Service	20	16.67	21	15.33	41	15.95
Sub–Total	120	100.00	137	100.00	257	100.00
	(46.69)		(53.31)		(100.00)	
TODA						
Primary	106	82.81	80	86.96	186	84.54
Manufacturing	8	6.25	5	5.43	13	5.91
Service	14	10.94	7	7.61	21	9.55
Sub–Total	128	100.00	92	100.00	220	100.00
	(58.18)		(41.82)		(100.00)	
PANIYA						
Primary	322	100.00	317	100.00	639	100.00
Manufacturing	–	–	–	–	–	–
Service	–	–	–	–	–	–
Sub–Total	322	100.00	317	100.00	639	100.00
	(50.39)		(49.61)		(100.00)	
IRULA						
Primary	225	94.94	243	97.20	468	96.10
Manufacturing	2	0.84	1	0.40	3	0.62
Service	10	4.22	6	2.40	16	3.28
Sub–Total	237	100.00	250	100.00	487	100.00
	(48.67)		(51.33)		(100.00)	
ALL TRIBES						
Primary	744	92.19	748	93.97	1492	93.08
Manufacturing	19	2.36	14	1.76	33	2.06
Service	44	5.45	34	4.27	78	4.86
Grand Total	807	100.00	796	100.00	1603	100.00
	(50.34)		(49.66)		(100.00)	

Land Holdings

Table 13 shows the land availability by tribe-wise. Out of 710 total sample tribes 481 households (67.75 per cent) are possessing land. 87.27 per cent, 84.17 per cent, 62 per cent and 56.09 per cent of Toda, Kota, Irula and Paniyas are possessing land respectively.

Table 13
Land Availability by Tribe

Tribes	*Yes*	*No*	*Total*
Kota	101	19	120
	(84.17)	(15.83)	(100.00)
Toda	96	14	110
	(87.27)	(12.73)	(100.00)
Paniya	129	101	230
	(56.09)	(43.91)	(100.00)
Irula	155	95	250
	(62.00)	(38.00)	(100.00)
All Tribes	481	229	710
	(67.75)	(32.25)	(100.00)

Land Value

Table 14 indicates that the average per household value is higher in Todas (Rs. 371052.08) followed by Kotas (Rs. 274356.44), Irulas (Rs. 195155.04) and Paniyas (Rs. 96592.36). All sample tribes per household land value is Rs. 214639.75. The highest average per capita land value is Rs. 79334.08, it is observed among the Todas, Rs. 54762.85 among the Kotas, Rs. 40934.96 among the Irulas and Rs. 25024.75 among the Paniyas. All sample tribes per capita land value is Rs. 47642.92. The table reveals that though some households are possessing land, they

Table 14
Estimated land Value by Tribe

Tribes	*Land Value*	*No. of Households*	*Per Households*	*Family Members*	*Per Capita*
Kotas	27,770,000	101	2,74,356.44	506	54,762.85
Todas	35,621,000	96	3,71,052.44	440	79,334.08
Irulas	25,175,000	129	1,95,155.04	615	40,934.96
Paniyas	15,165,000	157	96,592.36	606	25,024.75
All Tribes	1,03,671,000	483	214,639.75	2176	47,642.92

get marginal returns from those lands and hence they depend on wage employment in agriculture and other activities to eke out their livelihood.

Asset Values

The Table 15 gives the tribe-wise estimated asset values of houses and other assets of the sample households. Total asset value is high among the Kota (Rs. 100,24.100) followed by Irulas (Rs. 66,63500), Todas (Rs. 6523450) and Paniyas (Rs. 4969250). Asset value varies from household to household. Per household total asset estimated value of the tribes varies from Kotas (Rs. 83,534.17), Todas (Rs. 59 304.09), Irulas (Rs. 29,654) and Paniyas (Rs. 21,605.43). The per capita total asset values are same trend to per household. Per household and per capita house estimated value are higher among the Kota followed by Toda, Irula and Paniya. All tribes per household and per capita dwelling houses asset estimated values are Rs. 29,203.52 and Rs. 67,45.12 respectively. All tribes per household and per capita other assets estimated values are Rs. 10,487.00 and 2,422.19 respectively. Per household other assets values are higher among the Toda (Rs. 25,217.73) followed by Kota (Rs. 24,784.17) Irula (Rs. 4,748) and Paniya (Rs. 2,220.65). Toda, Kota, Irula and Paniya tribes per capita other assets values are Rs. 5,626.67, Rs. 5,118.93, Rs. 1,269.52 and Rs. 479.58 respectively. The above data shows that the Paniya other assets values are lower than the other tribes because the Paniya tribes are very backward P.T.G.

HEALTH

Table 16 shows the prevalence of diseases in the recent past three months of study among all the four tribes by age-wise. Out of total 3074 tribal individuals examined to check the health conditions 982 tribes are suffering from different ailments. Out of the 982 tribes there were 216 persons were suffering from cough, 166 were suffering from fever, 139 persons were suffering from body pain, 89 persons were suffering from stomach ache, 64 were suffering from headache, 50 persons were suffering from skin rashes and 37 persons were suffering from communicable diseases. In 0-1 year age group male infants

Table 15

Estimated Dwelling Houses and Other Asset Values by Tribes

Tribes	*Dwelling*			*Other Assets*			*Total Assets*		
	Total Value	*Per Household*	*Per Capita*	*Total Value*	*Per Household*	*Per Capita*	*Total Value*	*Per Household*	*Per Capita*
Kotas	70,50,000	58,700.00	12,134.25	29,74,100	24,784.17	5118.93	10,024,100	83,534.17	17,253.18
Todas	37,49,500	34,086.36	7,605.48	27,73,950	25,217.73	5,626.67	65,23,450	59,304.09	13,232.15
Irulas	54,76,500	21,916.00	5,857.22	11,87,000	4,748.00	1,269.52	66,63,500	26,654.00	7,126.74
Paniya	44,58,500	19,384.78	4,186.38	5,10,750	2,220.65	479.58	49,69,250	21,605.43	4,665.96
All Tribes	2,07,34,500	29,203.52	6,745.12	74,45,800	10,487.04	2,422.19	28,180,300	39,690.56	9,167.31

Table 16
Prevalence of Diseases in the Past 3 Months Among All Tribes

Ailments	*0-1*		*2-6*		*7-14*		*15-20*		*21-45*		*46 +*		*Total*
	Male	*Female*	*Male*	*Female*	*Male*	*Female*	*Male*	*Female*	*Male*	*Female*	*Male*	*Female*	
Headache	0	1	2	5	2	1	2	4	24	17	3	3	64
Stomach ache	2	1	6	3	9	9	4	7	24	17	5	2	89
Body pain	0	1	6	3	5	2	6	5	23	39	18	31	139
Cough	6	2	20	11	10	12	11	13	39	51	26	15	216
Fever	3	3	16	9	7	5	3	6	33	52	15	14	166
Gastgric	0	0	0	0	3	0	1	0	6	9	8	2	29
Dysentry	1	1	2	2	2	2	1	2	13	10	1	3	39
Asthma	0	0	0	0	3	0	0	1	3	1	4	2	14
Skin Rash	0	1	3	2	3	5	7	3	12	11	2	1	50
Dental Carries	1	0	1	1	0	0	0	0	4	1	0	0	8
Communicable Diseases	0	1	2	1	4	1	0	1	13	10	3	1	37
Others	1	1	6	4	7	21	5	9	28	24	9	15	130

suffering from cough (6), fever (3), stomach ache (2) and female infants suffering from fever (3) and cough (2). In 2-6 years age group males suffering from cough (20), fever (16), body pain (6), stomach ache (6) among females suffering from cough (11), fever (9), and headache (5). In 7-14 years of age group higher incidence of cough and fever was observed between the male and females. In 21-45 years of age group males were suffering from cough (39) followed by fever (33), headache (24), stomachache (24), body pain (23) and dysentery. In females suffering from fever (52), cough (51), body pain (39), headache (17), stomachache (17) and dysentery (10).

In 46 and above years of age group, 26,18, 15 and eight males were suffering from cough, body pain fever and gastric problems respectively, 31, 15, 14 and three females were suffering from body pain, cough, fever and headache respectively. The above data shows that majority of the tribes are suffering from body pain, cough and fever.

All the tribals, irrespective of the environmental conditions, culture was found to suffer from different ailments, which was common to all age groups and sex.

Measures undertaken by the tribes for the prevention of the diseases among the tribes for past three months were also recorded presented in the Table 17.

Table 17
Measures Undertaken for the Prevention of the Diseases in the Past 3 Months Among the Tribes

Tribes	*No Treatment Availed*	*Magico Religious*	*Home Remedy*	*Indigenous Medicine*	*Modern Medicine*	*Total*
Kota	1	2	1	3	66	73
	(1.37)	(2.74)	(1.36)	(4.11)	(90.42)	(100.00)
Toda	6	1	21	12	101	141
	(4.26)	(0.71)	(14.89)	(8.51)	(71.63)	(100.00)
Paniya	1	2	10	1	99	113
	(0.89)	(1.77)	(8.85)	(0.88)	(87.61)	(100.00)
Irula	2	–	5	–	264	271
	(0.74)		(1.85)		(97.41)	(100.00)
All Tribes	10	5	37	16	530	598
	(1.68)	(0.84)	(6.18)	(2.68)	(88.62)	(100.00)

Form the study samples it is observed that 598 tribals were taking different of medicines to cure the diseases an attempt has been made to analyse the pattern of medicines taken by the patients. Out of the 598 persons 88.62 per cent persons are taken modern medicine, 6.18 per cent person are taken home remedy, 2.68 per cent persons are taken indigenous medicine, 1.68 per cent persons are taken no treatment and only 0.84 per cent persons are taken magico religious. The data shows that majority of the tribes are preferring to have modern medicine.

DISCUSSION

All the four tribes under taken for study comes under the category of primitive tribes. All the four tribes are inhabiting in the Nilgiri hills in different altitudes. All the four tribes changed to a great extent because of the interaction with the plain people and the introducing of various developmental schemes by the Government for the development of health, education and economy. Inspite of introducing various developmental schemes, the tribes are still under poverty line.

Overall age and sex composition shows that 36.89 per cent of the sample population are economically dependent, among them 31.45 per cent are young dependent and 5.44 per cent are old age dependent. 63.11 per cent of the total sample population are independent group. In Kotas 32.02 per cent and 67.98 per cent are economically dependent and independent respectively. In Todas 36.11 per cent and 63.89 per cent are economically dependent and independent respectively. In Paniyas economically dependent are 38.40 per cent and 61.60 per cent are independent. In Irula tribe economically dependent are 38.62 per cent and 61.38 per cent are independent. More than half of the female population (52. 54 per cent) are in their reproductive age. Kota tribe female population 55 per cent are in their reproductive age, followed by Paniya tribe (53.72 per cent), Toda tribe (52.13 per cent) and Irula tribe (50 per cent). The data shows there is an imbalance in the sex ratio. The female population is less among all the tribes (except the Paniya) The literacy level among all the four tribes is very low. The female literacy level is very low (42.69) comparatively to male population (53.63).

The analysis made in the present article shows their conditions of living. Majority of the tribes are presently living in the tiled houses and thatched houses constructed by the Government under various developmental schemes. Only 41.13 per cent of the house holds are having electricity for their houses.

Drinking water is the major problem still 45 per cent of the tribes depend on well, river, pond and spring water. Only 1.55 per cent of the tribes are getting the protected water in their houses, the rest of them are getting water from outside.

Toilet facilities are very poor 95.49 per cent of the tribes go for toilet in the open fields\forest. The dependency on the forest by the tribes also reduced to a great extent only 13.52 per cent of the tribes are depending on the forest for their livelihood, but most of the tribes depend on forest for the fuel wood.

The data shows that majority of the tribes are aware of the modern medical treatment. Out of 3075 population examined 982 of them are suffering different type of diseases, which are related vitamin, protein, iron deficiencies and skin infections. There is urgent need to provide iron, calcium and vitamin tablets through the Primary Health Centres and Anganwadi Centres.

Changes in traditional occupations can be seen among the four tribes. The Toda a pastoral tribe changed their occupation to agriculture as major occupation and animal husbandry as secondary occupation. The Kotas an artisan community adopted horticulture as a main occupation. The Irula and Paniyas who are food gathering and hunting tribe changed to daily wage labourers. 67.75 per cent of the tribes are possessing agricultural land but only Todas and Kotas are cultivating the lands to some extent. The Irulas and Paniyas are not doing agriculture because the land they possess is barren land it will not suitable for agriculture.

REFERENCE

U.N. Report (1984), Health Status of Women, Improving Concepts and Methods for Statistics and Indicators on the Situation of Women, Studies in Methods Series, F. No. 33.

Government of India (1988), Tribal Development–A Statistical Profile, Backward Proper of Tribal Development No. 12, Ministry of Home Affairs, New Delhi.

P.V. Manoranjan Sahay (1993), "Health Status of Tribals in India, Social Change–Issues and Perspectives", *Journal of the Council for Social Development,* Vol. 23, No. 283, June-September, pp. 172-176.

T.S. Naidu (1999), Strategic Planning for the Future Development of the Tribes in India, Pondicherry University.

T.S. Naidu (2002), Women and Child Health Among the Primitive Tribes of Tamil Nadu, Pondicherry University.

11

ANTHROPOLOGY AND HIV/AIDS: CRITICAL ISSUES AND CHALLENGES IN A VULNERABLE REGION OF NORTH BENGAL

Samar Kumar Biswas

I
HEALTH–ANTHROPOLOGY–HIV / AIDS

Health is a common theme in every society and they have its own belief and practices regarding health, disease and treatment. From the time immemorial man has been interested in trying to control diseases. The medicine man, the priest, the herbalist and the magician all undertook in various ways to cure man's disease and to bring relief to the sick. In ancient times, health and illness were interpreted in a cosmological and anthropological perspective. Medicine was dominated by magical and religious belief and it was the integral part of ancient culture and civilization. Henry Siegerist, the medical historian has stated that every culture had developed a system of medicine and medical history is but one aspect of the history of culture. Dubos says that, ancient medicine was the mother of sciences and played a large role in the integration of every culture. During the past few decades the concept of health has emerged as a fundamental human right and a world wide social goal. In 1977 the 30th World Health Assembly decided that the main social target of the Government and World Health

Organisation in the coming decades should be "the attainment by all citizen of the world by the year 2000 of a level of health that will permit them to lead a socially and economically productive life", for brevity, called "Health For All". World Health Organisation has defined Health as a "state of complete physical, mental and social well being and not merely an absence of disease or infirmity (WHO, 1997). In recent years new philosophy of health has been acquired as stated below:

- Health is a fundamental human right.
- Health is essence of productive life and not the result of ever increasing expenditure on medical care.
- Health is intersectoral.
- Health is an integral part of development.
- Health is the central to the quality of life.
- Health involves individual, state and international responsibility.
- Health and its maintenance is a major social investment.
- Health is a world wide social goal.

But there are a number of factors which are a great hindrance for health and these factors are creating a number of health hazards to the people.

Normally the health, medicine, treatment is the subject of medical sciences and the doctors treat us. But health is very much a part of social sciences. Particularly medical anthropologists, who are actively engaged in studying health and illness, are increasingly realizing that biological and social factors need to be considered if we are to reduce human suffering. Socio-cultural dimension of health is it myth of reality. It depends on human behavior and attitude, and sometime people do not accept the modern treatment and it is not for financial condition. Health is definitely a part of social science. Some populations have an appalling incidence of infant deaths due to diarrhea. The origin of this situation is mostly biological, in the sense that the deaths are caused by bacterial infection. But they are so many infants exposed to those bacteria? Usually the main reason is social. The affected infants are likely to be poor. Because they are poor, they are likely to live with infected drinking water. Similarly malnutrition may be the biological result of a diet poor in protein, but such a diet is usually also a cultural phenomena, reflecting a society with class of people with very unequal access to the necessities of life. In many ways, therefore, medical anthropology, and anthropology in general are developing in the direction of a "bio-cultural synthesis". Epidemics of infectious disease have killed millions of people within short periods of time throughout recoded history. The Black Death- bubonic plague- killed between 25 and 50 per cent of the population of Europe, perhaps 75 million people, during the fourteenth century; an epidemic during the sixth century killed an estimated 100 million people in the Middle East, Asia and Europe. The current state of medical science and technology may lull us into thinking that epidemics are a thing of the past. But the recent and sudden emergence of the disease we call AIDS reminds us that new diseases, or new varieties of old diseases can appear at any time. Like all other organisms, disease- causing organisms also evolve. The human immunodeficiency virus (HIV) that causes AIDS emerged only recently. Virus and bacteria are always mutating, and new strains emerge that are initially a plague on our genetic resistance and on medical efforts to contain them.

The dimension of Anthropology has diversified into a number of problem oriented issues over a past few decades. In the era of post modernism far from being contented with the accurate presentation of cultures, anthropologists have taken on the responsibility of making interventions not only in the field situation but also in policy making at the national and international level. The practise of anthropology can be easily justified on the count that in depth anthropological knowledge about the culture of people for whom policies are designed can contribute towards effective plan formulation and execution of critical decisions. The role of anthropology in AIDS research and the impact of AIDS on the discipline of anthropology appear to be a complex more so because the AIDS epidemic cuts across cultural and geographical territories. Being global the crisis over AIDS is multicultural and multidimensional which appeals local attention and awareness on the one hand and world wide alarm and initiative on the other. Global inequalities of class, gender and ethnicity as related by poverty, powerlessness and stigma propel the spread of HIV. Anthropologists witness to suffering, their concern and engagement, are potent elements in the research process and in advocacy in national and international areas. The combined knowledge of theory and practise in the field of international research on AIDS is a significant contribution to anthropology in the 21st century.

The term HIV denotes HUMAN (isolated to the human species) IMMUNE-DEFICIENCY (lacking the ability to the fight off infectious agents) VIRUS (a disease causing agent); and AIDS denotes ACQUIRED (must do something to contract) IMMUNE (ability to fight off infectious agents) DEFICIENCY (lack of) SYNDROME (Cluster of symptoms that are characteristic for a disease). AIDS is a modern epidemic, which was first scientifically detected in the most developed and advanced country, the United States in 1981 and no country today has escaped the scourge of this disease. By the early 1990's HIV/AIDS has been officially reported by 164 countries. From a disease of affluence it has shifted to a disease of poverty, at least in term of location and most affected populations. The HIV/AIDS epidemic represents the most serious public health problem in India and here the first positive case was detected on April, 1986 in Madras among the commercial sex workers (CSWs). Then 10 prostitutes were detected as sero positive for AIDS by Center for Advanced Research in Virology, CMS. But the first developed AIDS patient was identified in 1987. It is estimated that as on mid 2001, 3.97 million Indians were infected with the virus. Unlike other epidemics in human history such as cholera, plague, small-pox, polis, etc. which generally affect the poor and marginalized sections of the society, AIDS infusion transcends the entire barrier those of rich or poor, class or caste, race or nationality. According to the report from India and Southern African Summit (WEF), 100 million HIV infections expected by 2004 and in 1995, 1,400 children were born with

HIV every day. In 2001 the total HIV / AIDS affected people in India was 5100000 in number.

The AIDS virus causes a weakness of the immune system. When it infects the body, it prefers to attack certain cells of our defence system. These cells are called helper T cells which are a fundamental part of our immune system. The AIDS virus almost fully specializes on these white blood cells since these helper T cells have CD4 molecules on the surface to which the AIDS virus binds. AIDS is the late stage of infection with the HIV. Generally the symptoms of the disease start after two or three years of infection. But it can take around 7-10 years to develop after infection with HIV. The minor signs such as persistent cough, chronic diarrhea, persistent fever, generalized itchy skin, swollen glands appear. It is very difficult to identify an infected person. HIV is transmitted through semen and vaginal fluids, infected blood or blood products, infected mother to her baby- before birth, during birth or through breast milk. HIV can be passed on because the virus is present in the sexual fluids and blood of infected people. If infected blood or sexual fluid gets into your blood, then you will become infected. Among identified risk behaviours the most important are: multipartner sexual activity (both male and female partner) without use of condoms or any other safety device; sharing the unsterilized needles or disposable syringes by IDUs; PBDs who sell blood in many non licensed blood donating clinics. These behaviours or practices are highly influenced by migration, socio-cultural practices, sexuality and sexual behavior i.e. premarital and extramarital sexual relation, prostitution or call girls, professional blood donors, truck drivers, injecting drug users, powerlessness and social instability, etc, and these are the most probable risk factors. It is revealed that the groups mostly affected by HIV / AIDS are- the migrants, sex workers, injecting drug users (IDUS), PBDs, and truck drivers. But now a-days it is not only confined among them it is rapidly spreading among the common mass and mostly it is getting transmitted from those above mentioned groups. Millions of people around the world already have the symptoms of AIDS, and millions more are infected with HIV but do not know they are infected. It is not only a great fear for human society but also human civilization. The HIV/AIDS patients or infected persons are not equally distributed in all the regions or the states or the countries, because HIV is only transmitted by some way and it mostly happen due to some practices or involvement which may be cultural or others. This article is an attempt to give a brief note on HIV/AIDS with its global and Indian scenario. In this context due to lack of sufficient data, the probability of HIV/AIDS infection in Siliguri areas which is considered as the largest urban centre of North Bengal and second in West Bengal has been discussed through highlighting on the basis of major risk factors.

II
SITUATION OF HIV/AIDS

GLOBAL SCENARIO OF HIV/AIDS

According to the estimates from the Joint United Nations Programme on HIV/AIDS (UNAIDS) and the World Health Organisation (WHO) 37 million adults and 2.5 million children were living with HIV at the end of 2003. This is more than 50 per cent higher than the figures projected by WHO in 1991 on the basis of the data then available. The total AIDS death in 2003 was 3 million among whom 2.5 million were adults and 500,000 below 15 year age group. According to the report of India and Southern African Economic Summit (World Economic Forum) it was expected that by 2004, 100 million people would be the sufferer of this disease throughout the world and estimated that 7.7 million people would alive with HIV; 2 per cent people belonging to 15-45 years age group of the world would be the HIV carriers; More than 90 per cent with HIV must be in the poorest nations and 20 million children under 15 would loss mothers to AIDS. By July 1996, 3 million children were infected from their mothers, among them 85 per cent were confined in Sub Saharan Africa. In 1995, 1400 children were born with HIV every day with HIV infection. Among the total victims of the world half of them belong to less than 25 years. In this regard the HIV/ AIDS scenario of some specific countries and regions of the world has been discussed in brief to evaluate the status of AIDS:

South–East Asia: Only in India there were five million HIV people. The epidemic was in far earlier stage than in Africa.

China: In 1993 there were 10,000 HIV people but in 1995 it was increased up to 100,000 and now it is rapidly increasing/ spreading among them.

United States: In every year 20,000 people were getting infected and there was near about 1 million HIV people.

Africa: Larger numbers of HIV/AIDS people were in Africa and it was their major problem. Here highest number of death was caused by this reason. There were 24 million HIV infected people where women were more infected than men. It is very important that average 5 per cent people were HIV infected in every age year of the 15-49 years age group.

Botswana: In urban areas 40 per cent pregnant women was HIV infected; and the average sufferer was 18 per cent.

Uganda: Here 15 per cent of the average population was suffered from HIV.

Kenya: Business survey found that AIDS costs were almost 4 per cent of the Annual profits.

South Africa: Here 6 per cent population had HIV. Its rates rose 35 per cent among present women. It had been noticed that the rates among the people of Kwa Zulu Natal was 20 per cent and the rates among the mine workers was almost 20 per cent.

Zimbabwe: Here 17 per cent populations were suffering from HIV. One antenatal clinic had reported that 60 per cent pregnant women in that area were suffering from HIV.

Zambia: Barclays Bank of Zambia reported that most of its senior managers were died by AIDS.

Malawi: The overall sufferer was 13 per cent of the total country's population and among them 30 per cent school teachers were infected.

The latest statistics regarding HIV/AIDS can give the more clear picture which are given below:

Table 1
Maximum HIV/AIDS Prevalence Rate

Rank Country	Prevalence Rate	Rank Country	Prevalence Rate
1. Botswana	38.80	9. Malawi	15.00
2. Zimbabwe	33.70	10. Mozambique	13.00
3. Swaziland	33.40	11. Central African rep.	12.90
4. Lesotho	31.00	12. Cameroon	11.80
5. Namibia	22.50	13. Djibouti	11.75
6. Zambia	21.50	14. Cote d' Ivoire	9.70
7. South Africa	20.10	15. Gabon	9.00
8. Kenya	15.00	16. India	0.80

Source: Chronicle India, 2006.

Table 2
Maximum HIV/AIDS People

Rank Country	HIV People	Rank Country	HIV People
1. South Africa	5,000,000	9. Zambia	1,200,000
2. India	3,970,000	10. Mozambique	1,100,000
3. Nigeria	3,500,000	11. Cameroon	920,000
4. Kenya	2,500,000	12. United States	900,000
5. Zimbabwe	2,300,000	13. China	850,000
6. Ethiopia	2,100,000	14. Malawi	850,000
7. Tanzania	1,500,000	15. Cote d' Ivoire	770,000
8. Congo Rep.	1,300,000		

Source: Chronicle India, 2006.

Table 3
Maximum HIV/AIDS Death

Rank Country	HIV Death	Rank Country	HIV Death
1. South Africa	360,000	9. Zambia	120,000
2. India	310,000	10. Uganda	84,000
3. Zimbabwe	200,000	11. Malawi	80,000
4. Kenya	190,000	12. Cote d' Iivoire	75,000
5. Nigeria	170,000	13. Burma	65,000
6. Ethiopia	160,000	14. Mozambique	60,000
7. Tanzania	140,000	15. Thailand	55,000
8. Congo Rep.	120,000		

Source: Chronicle India, 2006.

INDIAN SCENARIO OF HIV/AIDS

India has a population of one billion around half of them are adult and sexually active group. The first HIV positive case was detected in 1986 and since then the infection has been reported in all states and union territories. The spread is

Table 4
Feature in SAARC Countries-People Living with AIDS

	SAARC Country	*People*
1.	India	5100000
2.	Pakistan	74000
3.	Nepal	61000
4.	Bangladesh	13000
5.	Sri Lanka	3500
6.	Bhutan	Below 100
7.	Maldives	Below 100

Source: Chronicle India, 2007.

Table 5
Feature in ASEAN Countries-People Living with AIDS

	ASEAN Country	*People*
1.	Thailand	5,70,000
2.	Myanmar	3,30,000
3.	Vietnam	2,20,000
4.	Cambodia	1,70,000
5.	Indonesia	1,10,000
6.	Malaysia	52,000
7.	Philippines	9,000
8.	Singapore	4,100
9.	Laos	1,700
10.	Brunei	200

Source: Chronicle India, 2007.

diversified in nature. India has a sharp increase in the estimated number of HIV infections, from a few thousand in the early 1990s to an estimate between 3.8-4.6 million children and adult in 2002. In 2003 the total number of said infected was around 5.1 million and approximately 75 per cent of them were male population. The prevalence in six states viz. Maharastra, Tamil Nadu, Andhra Pradesh, Karnataka, Manipur and Nagaland was more than one per cent. The distribution is given below-

The highest numbers were in Maharastra and Gujarat in the west; Tamil Nadu and Andhra Pradesh in the south; Manipur in the north east. In the southern states the infections are mostly due to heterosexual contact, while infections are mainly found amongst injecting drug users in Manipur and Nagaland. Now some of the statistics regarding people infected by HIV/AIDS in India is given below:

Table 6
Breakup of States

Category	*State and Union Territory*
High prevalence state	Tamil Nadu, Maharastra, Karnataka, Andhra Pradesh, Manipur, Nagaland.
Moderate prevalence state	Goa, Gujarat, Pondichery
Highly vulnerable state	Assam, Bihar, Delhi, Himachal Pradesh, Kerala, Madhya Pradesh, Punjab, Rajasthan, Uttar Pradesh, West Bengal, Chhatisgarh, Jharkhand, Orissa, Uttaranchal
Vulnerable state	Arunachal Pradesh, Haryana, Jammu and Kashmir, Meghalaya, Mizoram, Sikkim, Tripura, Andaman and Nicobar island, Chandigarh, Dadra and Nagar Haveli, Daman and Diu, Lakshwadeep.

Source: *Chronicle India, 2006.*

Table 7
Estimated Numbers of Adults and Children Living with HIV/AIDS, (End of 2003)

Group	*Living with HIV/AIDS*
Adults	5,000,000
Women	1,900,000
Children	120,000
Total	5,100,000
Adult HIV prevalence estimate	0.9%

Source: UNAIDS/WHO, epidemiological fact sheets on HIV/AIDS and Sexually Transmitted Infections, 2004.

These calculations are based on the previously published estimates for 1999 and 2001 and recent trends in HIV/AIDS surveillance in various populations. Adults are defined as men and women aged 15 to 49. These estimates include all those with HIV infection, whether or not they have developed symptoms of AIDS.

Table 8
Cases of AIDS (End of December 2004) in India

Gender	*Cumulative AIDS cases*
Male	69559
Female	27419
Total	96978

The statistics for AIDS cases may be a poor guide to the severity of the epidemic, as in many situations a patient will die without HIV having been diagnosed, and the cause of death attributed to an opportunistic infection, such as tuberculosis or PCP.

Table 9
Breakup of Cases

Transmission Categories	*Number of cases*	*%*	*Age group*	*Male*	*Female*	*Total*
Sexual	83239	85.83	0-14	2440	1658	4098
Prenatal	3343	3.45	15-29	19654	12173	31827
Blood and blood products	2009	2.07	30-49	42049	12107	54156
Injecting drug users	2617	2.70	≥ 50	5416	1481	6897
Others (not specified)	5770	5.95	Total	69559	27419	96978
Total	96978	100%				

Table 10
HIV / AIDS in India

State/Union Territory	*AIDS Cases*
Andhra Pradesh	10293
Assam	225
Arunachal Pradesh	0
A & N Islands	33
Bihar	155
Chandigarh (UP)	1053
Delhi	945
Daman & Diu	1
Dadra & Nagar Haveli	0
Goa	490
Gujarat	4869
Hariyana	385
Himachal Pradesh	223
Jammu & Kashmir	2
Karnataka	2102
Kerala	1769
Lakshwadweep	0
Madhya Pradesh	1292
Maharastra	12783
Orissa	128
Nagaland	650
Manipur	2866
Mizoram	100
Meghalaya	8
Pondichery	302
Punjab	292
Rajasthan	1153
Sikkim	8
Tamil Nadu	44492
Tripura	5
Uttar Pradesh	1383
West Bengal	2397
Ahemdabad M C	462
Mumbai MC	6112
Total	96978

Source: NACO, 31 August 2004, Monthly update on AIDS.

HIV Estimates, 2003: The prevalence rates below are taken from data collected during screening of women attending antenatal clinics, meaning that these prevalence rates are only relevant to sexually active women.

Table 11
HIV Prevalence in India

State/Union Territory	*HIV Prevalence (%)*
Andhra Pradesh	1.25
Arunachal Pradesh	0.38
Assam	0.00
A & N Inlands	0.50
Bihar	0.00
Chandigarh	0.50
Chattisgarh (UN)	1.00
Daman & Diu	0.50
Delhi	0.13
D & N Haveli	0.13
Goa	0.50
Gujarat	0.40
Haryana	0.25
Himachal Pradesh	0.00
Jammu & Kashmir	0.00
Jharkhand	0.00
Karnataka	1.25
Kerala	0.33
Lakshwadweep	0.00
Madhya Pradesh	0.00
Maharastra	1.25
Manipur	1.25
Meghalaya	0.00
Mizoram	1.38
Mumbai	1.25
Nagaland	1.25
Orissa	0.00
Pondichery	0.13
Punjab	0.00
Rajasthan	0.13
Sikkim	0.13
Tamil Nadu	0.75
Tripura	0.00
Uttar Pradesh	0.00
Uttaranchal	0.00
West Bengal	0.50

Source: NACO, 2004, State Wise HIV Prevalence (1998-2003).

Some areas report an HIV prevalence rate of 0 in antenatal clinics. This does not necessary mean that there is no HIV in the area, as some of them report the presence of the virus at STD clinics and amongst injecting drug users.

CURRENT ESTIMATES AND FUTURE PROJECTIONS

Globally India is second only to South Africa in terms of the overall number of people living with the disease.

- NACO estimated that there the number of Indians living with HIV increased by 500,000 in 2003 to 5.1 million. Around 38 per cent of these people were women.
- In November 2004, NACO published the number of AIDS cases reported. The total of AIDS cases in India was 87,596 of whom 24,504 were women. This data also indicated that 37% of reported AIDS cases were diagnosed among people under 30.
- The UN Population Division project that India's adult HIV prevalence will peak at 1.9% in 2019. The UN estimates that there were 2.7 million AIDS deaths in India between 1980 and 2000. During 2000-15, the UN projects 12.3 million AIDS deaths and 49.5 million deaths during 2015-50.
- A 2002 report by the CIA's National Intelligence Council predicted 20 million to 25 million AIDS cases in India by 2010, more than any other country in the world.

HIV/AIDS IN SOME SPECIFIC STATES/AREAS IN INDIA

The spread of HIV within the country is as diverse as the societal patterns between its different regions, states and metropolitan areas. In fact, India's epidemic is made up of a number of epidemics. This epidemic gets transmitted from state to states mainly through heterosexual transmission and injecting drug use. In this regard the most important causes related to HIV/AIDS transmission would be quite clear through the discussion of mostly affected states as given below:

Andhra Pradesh: Andhra Pradesh has one of the fastest increasing HIV/AIDS prevalence in India. In 2002 the ANC prevalence rate was 1.25 per cent and NACO has estimated that more than 400,000 people are living with HIV in Andhra Pradesh, the second highest number after Maharastra state. This is 10 per cent of the total HIV cases in India and ninety per cent of the infections in the state occur through sexual transmission (Shafeeq, 2003). Andhra Pradesh is a Hindu state in the southeast of the country with a total population of 75.7 million.

Tamil Nadu: When surveillance systems in the southern Indian state of the Tamil Nadu, home to some 60 million people, showed that HIV infection rates among pregnant women were rising, tripling to 1.25 per cent between 1995 and 1997. The ANC prevalence in Tamil Nadu was 0.88% in 2002, although an infection rate of 33.8 per cent was recorded at the one surveillance site for injecting drug users. By September 2003 Tamil Nadu had reported 24,667 cases of AIDS, the highest number reported to NACO by any state.

Karnataka: Karnataka has a population of 52.7 million and is a diverse state in the southwest of India. Here the mean prevalence among ANCs was 1.13 per cent in 2001 and 1.75 per cent in 2002. In 2001 there were four districts with an ANC prevalence of 2 per cent or more, and these are located in the southern part of the state, in and around Bangalore, on the border with Tamil Nadu, or in northern Karnataka's "devadasi belt." Devadasi women are a group of women, who historically, have been dedicated to the service of gods. These days, this has evolved into sanctioned prostitution-as a result many women from this part of the country are supplied to the sex trade in big cities such as Mumbai.

Maharastra & Mumbai: Mumbai (Bombay) is the capital city of Maharastra state and is the second most populated city in India with a population of 16.4 million people. Maharastra is a very large state of three hundred thousand square kilometers and it has a total population of 96.8 million. The 2002 ANC prevalence rate for the state of Maharasthra was 1.25 per cent and the prevalence for the city of Mumbai 0.75 per cent.

Goa: Goa is in the southwest of India and is best known as a tourist destination and tourism is so prominent that the number of tourists almost equals the population of the state which is 1.34 million. HIV infections have increased noticeably in Goa in the past couple of years. The ANC prevalence rate increased from 0.5 per cent in 2001 to 1.38 per cent in 2002.

Manipur: Manipur, a small state of 2.4 million people in the north east of India, has the highest concentration of HIV/AIDS infection in India. The geographical nearness of Manipur to Burma and therefore to the Golden Triangle drug trail, has made it a major transit route for drug smuggling, with drugs easily available. However, the transmission route of HIV/AIDS in the state is no longer confined to injecting drug users. It has spread further to the female sexual partners of IDUs and their children (Info Change, 2003). The ANC prevalence in Manipur in 2002 was 1.12 per cent and among injecting drug users at three surveillance sites the HIV prevalence was an extremely high 39.06 per cent.

Mizoram: In 1998, in the small north eastern state of Mizoram which has a population of less than a million, the epidemic took off quickly among male injecting drug users; with some drug clinics registering HIV rates of more than 70 per cent among their patients. In 2002, ANC prevalence was 1.50 per cent.

Nagaland: Another small north-eastern state, with a population of 2 million, and where injecting drug use has again been the driving force behind the HIV epidemic. In 2002, the ANC prevalence was 1.25 per cent and the HIV prevalence among the injecting drug users was 10.28 per cent.

III
THE GROUPS MOST AFFECTED BY HIV/AIDS

The HIV/AIDS is still largely concentrated in at-risk populations, including commercial sex workers, injecting drug users, and truck drivers, the surveillance data suggests that the epidemic is moving beyond these groups in some regions and into the general population. It is also moving from urban to rural districts (USAID, 2003). Dr. R. Feachem says "in some parts of India, particularly the states that are reporting the higher prevalence, the tipping point is long past. I think there is absolutely no doubt that the virus is moving into the general population". In July 2003, Dr. Meenakshi Datta Ghosh, project director for NACO, stated that HIV/AIDS no longer affects only high-risk groups or urban populations, but is "gradually spreading into rural areas and the general population". Some of the most affected groups by HIV/AIDS are discussed below:

Migrants: Migration of economically productive sections of the population is a common phenomenon all over India. According to the 1993 National Sample Survey in India, 24.7 per cent of the population had migrated, either within India, to neighbouring countries or overseas. Applying this percentage to the mid-2003 population (PRB, 2003) about 264 million Indians are mobile. "Being mobile in an of itself is not a risk factor for HIV infection. It is the situations encountered and the behaviours possibly engaged in during mobility or migration that increases vulnerability and risk regarding HIV/AIDS". Most of the migrant workers are highly mobile and often live in unhygienic conditions in urban slums. Long working hours, relative isolation from the family and geographical mobility may foster casual sexual relationships and make them highly vulnerable to STDs and HIV/AIDS. Migrant workers tend to have little access to HIV/AIDS information, voluntary counseling and testing and health services. Cultural and language barriers worsen their lack of access to such services as do exist. Returning or visiting migrants, many of who do not know their status, may infect their wives or other sex partners in the home community.

Sex workers: Although sex work is legal in some states, associated activities including soliciting and brothel keeping are penalised. Often women get involved with sex work because of poverty or marital break-up or they are forced into it. Mumbai has the country's largest brothel based sex industry, with over 15,000 sex workers. It is estimated that in the region of 70 per cent of the sex workers in Mumbai are HIV- positive. Sex workers in Mumbai are controlled by madams, pimps and moneylenders and because of this, reaching sex workers with HIV prevention is a major challenge. A study in Surat found that HIV prevalence among sex workers had increased from 17 per cent in 1992 to 43 per cent in 2000.

Injecting Drug Users (IDUs): HIV infections among IDUs first appeared in Manipur. In Manipur city, the level of HIV infection increased from 61 per cent in 1994 to 85 per cent in 1997 and in 1998 it was 80.7 per cent. Injecting drug use is also a major problem in urban areas such as Mumbai, Kolkata, Delhi and Chennai. Generally, syringes and needles are purchased from pharmacies without any need for prescriptions, and although they are regarded as inexpensive many drug users tend to focus on buying the drug rather than purchasing new injecting equipment. The sharing of equipment among India's IDUs is widespread. Recent data indicate that most IDUs had at some stage shared their needle and syringe.

The majority of drug users in India are male. According to a study in the capital of Manipur, the prevalence of HIV infection in female IDUs was 57 per cent compared to 20 per cent among female non IDUs. In the northeast of India, there are increasing numbers of young widows of addicts, many who are HIV-positive as a result of having been infected by their husbands. With the reported increase of HIV infection among wives and children of IDUs, this is highlighting the crucial need to reach the sex partners of IDUs with prevention, education, care and support services.

Truck Drivers: India has one of the largest road networks in the world and an estimated 2 to 5 million long distance truck drivers and helpers. The extended periods of time that they spend away from their families place them in close proximity to "high-risk" sexual networks, and often results in them having an increased number of sexual contacts. During their journeys the drivers often stop at 'dhabas', roadside hotels that usually provide food, rest, sex workers, alcohol and drugs. They pick up the women, use them and leave them at some other 'dhaba', where they are used by other drivers and local youths. As a result, truck drivers are crucial in spreading STDs and HIV infection throughout the country. A study published in 1999 showed that 87 per cent of the drivers had frequent and indiscriminate change of sexual partners, and only 11 per cent of them used condoms although their AIDS knowledge was fairly good. HIV prevalence patterns in truckers have tended to mirror the local epidemics. "There is no entertainment. It is day-in-day-out driving. When they stop, they drink, dine and have sex with women. Then they transfer HIV from urban to rural settings" (Christensen, 2002). There has been a number of major HIV/STI prevention projects aimed at truckers. Some of these projects include not just truckers, but also other stakeholders such as gas station owners and employees. A specific example from Mumbai is the AIDS Workplace Awareness campaign which is mandatory and which targets the drivers at the regional transport authority, where the drivers get their licenses renewed annual.

IV
VULNERABLE AREA IN NORTH BENGAL- PROBABILITIES OF HIV/AIDS

It is quite clear that the above mentioned states are mostly affected mainly due to besides social and cultural practices; the other major risk factors like prostitution, pre marital and extra marital sexual relations, call girls, professional blood donors, huge migrants/migration, tourists, injecting drug users, truck drivers are very much common. The HIV/AIDS is not always equally distributed; because the variations are mainly depend on the basis of contact or practices or pressure with those types of risk factors. Again the virus is carried by man and it is also spread through some practices of man, that means it is very much depend on availability of risk groups/factors and if it is more, then it may be said that there is a great probability to spread and affect the people and ultimately it start to spread among the common people of neighbouring states or regions like epidemic in nature. In this context somebody opined that the epidemic is moving beyond these risk populations in some regions and into the general populations. It is also moving from urban to rural population. In West Bengal the HIV prevalence was 0.50 per cent and the HIV/AIDS cases were only 2397 (NACO, 2004), obviously it is quite low in respect of some other states. But this matter should not be ignored because there is not any assurance that the HIV/AIDS cases will not be increased in near future. The HIV/AIDS prevalence or cases may increase rapidly if there is the continuous pressure of these risk populations/groups/factors on the common masses of any area and it can be seen in Siliguri areas. Now Siliguri is the largest urban centre of North Bengal and 2nd largest in West Bengal is very much important regarding the concerned discussion. For rapid /spreading/increase of HIV/AIDS, all of the favourable conditions i.e. every risk groups or factors or possibilities i.e. geographical location, transport-communication, tourist, migrants, truck drivers, hotels-bars, sex workers, drug users and so on are very much available here. Siliguri is termed as the gateway to the hills. It links many districts of West Bengal, North East states and Bihar including neighbouring countries like- Nepal, Bhutan, Bangladesh and even China, Myanmar and Thailand also. Major drug addicted areas are very close to Siliguri. This gate way is very much used for drug and other smuggling. Though data is not sufficient but on the basis of risk factors/groups it may be said that the situation of Siliguri is more vulnerable to HIV/AIDS infection. In this context due to lacking of sufficient data mainly a hypothetical analysis has been done on Siliguri town considering the probable risk factors-these are discussed below one after another:

(i) Locational Importance and Urban Development: Siliguri is considered as the second largest urban center of West Bengal. It is located in the Darjeeling district at the foothills of Darjeeling–Himalayan region. It is well communicated with a number of Indian states and with neighbouring International countries. Among the states of India Assam, Bihar is adjacent to Siliguri and other North–Eastern states are well communicated with it. International countries like Nepal, Bhutan, and Bangladesh are located quite adjacent to Siliguri and it takes a travel of only few hours to reach in the said countries. China, Myanmar is also associated with Siliguri through Nepal and North Eastern states respectively. The hill stations of North Bengal and Sikkim like Darjeeling, Gangtok, Mirik, Kurseong, Kalimpong has its worldwide recognition and their communication only be availed from Siliguri town. The natural beauty of Terrai-Dooars region could be enjoyed through a little journey from Siliguri. The entire trade route of

north eastern India and the trade with international countries are communicated through urban Siliguri. For these factors it is recognised as the gateway of north eastern India. Siliguri is well communicated through transportation, railways and airlines. The economic characteristic of Siliguri is service cum trade and commercial cum industrial. A number of ethnic groups are living in this urban center with their own cultural heritage and diversification that is why it is often regarded as a cultural marginal area. In 1907 it was a swampy malarious village with a population of 784, and it was declared as a town for the first time in 1931 census. But in 2001, the scenario has been totally changed where the 40.90 sq. km. areas has been covered by 472,374 people; and the density of population was 11,171/ sq.km. Surrounded areas upto 10 mile radius has been considered under the greater urban agglomeration. According To Census 2001, the total slum population of Siliguri was 173121. There were total 159 slums among whom 151 were documented and 8 were undocumented. Basically the concerned populations were non skilled, marginal and manual labourers and most of the male and female had to depend on different temporary works. Besides locational importance and fast growing urbanization, there are a number of factors which are similar to the globally accepted prime causes of HIV/AIDS infection.

(*ii*) *Migration:* From the above, it is clear that the migration is very much common here. The population of Siliguri is overwhelmingly made up of migrants, who prefer to come to Siliguri for various reasons of which political turmoil at the time of partition of India in 1947 and at the time of the Bangladesh war in 1971, and the continuous political unrest within the north east states and neighbouring country of Nepal and till the Bangladesh face quite important. In search of new occupational pursuit people from adjacent hilly areas, districts, states and countries come to Siliguri frequently and mostly start to live permanently. Among them, mainly the uprooted people are forced to reside in the slum areas. Here sometime they often get involved in extra marital affairs and frequent adultery practices. Often unsafe biological practices are very much common in these areas and the people get involved with a number of partners. A remarkable number of peoples are undocumented and come here due to several political instability as well as economic uncertainty. Separation from their family, socio-cultural norms and loneliness there grows a sense of anonymity which offers more sexual freedom and inadequate financial resources, make the highly mobile migrants more vulnerable to adopting high-risk sexual behaviour.

(iii) Tourists and Tourism: The hill stations of Darjeeling-Himalayan region and Sikkim have world wide recognition. People from all over the world come here to visit those places and they often visit the adjacent Tibettan region also. The reserve forest areas of Dooars also attract a huge number of people from the entire world. To reach at those places Siliguri is the main and only transit station for onward journey from plains to hills as well as north east. Naturally the concerned tourists halt here before further journey. Data available from the Siliguri Municipal Corporation reveals that upto January 1997 near about 10 lakh tourists have visited in the said region and they had halted in different hotels and lodges in Siliguri. In those hotels the tourists enjoy by their own means.

(iv) Hotel-Bar-Lodge: The demand of tourism has made a rapid flourishment of hotels-bars and lodges in Siliguri town. Presently there are 4 three star hotels (with bars), 125 registered hotels and restaurants (some with bars) and other 70 unregistered hotels and lodges. Some unofficial sources it has been known that in most of these hotels the tourists are being entertained with prostitutes and call girls. Besides these, often the teenagers and adults from the high class society go through illegal sexual affairs in these hotels. The local newspapers often flash out several incidents of such happenings. Thus, there is a high probability of the spread of HIV/AIDS through these sources.

(v) Prostitutes-Call girls: In Siliguri, during 2004, officially 47 prostitutes as well as call girls were registered. But unofficially it has been reported that huge number of women from surrounding suburban and adjacent village areas a large come everyday in Siliguri and they stay whole night for the same i.e. sex trade. They have a direct contact with different

hotels and lodges. Mainly they are involved with the entertainment of the tourists. But one of the most alarming facts is that often both the married and unmarried women of posh business families are also working as call girls. Thus, premarital and post marital illegal sexual affair is rising here at an alarming situation.

(vi) Impact of Nepal: In Nepalese context, poverty, the open conflict, gender inequalities combined with low level of literacy are the key risk factors that are likely to accelerate the spread of HIV/AIDS. The prospective for the spread of this disease in Nepal is large because of the widespread existence of commercial sex workers, high rate of sexually transmitted diseases, low level of acceptance of the concerned protective devices and a large group of intravenous drug users. In May 2005, Nepal's Ministry of Health reported 4,999 HIV infections and 888 AIDS cases. It is estimated that 0.5 per cent of population in the age group of 15-49 years in Nepal are HIV positive and the male to female ratio of the infection is 3:1. The most vulnerable to the disease are street children, migrant children scavengers, hotel and restaurant workers, transport workers, refugees, industrial labours, construction workers, police, military, prisoners and the people living in urban slum areas due to their low level of earning and subsistence living. Every year about 800,000 people cross the southern border as seasonal migrant labour and come to India. A huge section of them come to Siliguri for the same. The migrant labours live without their spouses for a long time and it compels them to establish sexual relationship with female sex workers. The mobile transport workers during their long routes establish sexual relationship in different red light areas at their night halt stations. This communication is mainly taking place through Siliguri town and thus the Nepalese drivers are often in sexual relationship with the prostitutes of Siliguri and may spreading the germ of this virus here. Besides these, more than 200,000 Nepalese women are involved in prostitutions in India and a large section of them can be found in the red light areas of Siliguri and adjacent sub-urban areas. Thus, the overall situation of Nepal has a very serious impact on Siliguri, especially

considering the AIDS situation because it is quite adjacent to Siliguri and a huge number of Nepalese people have a daily communication with Siliguri.

(vii) Role of Truck Drivers: Siliguri is the prime and only transit trade route of entire north east India. That's why to reach north east and so on trucks from all over the country passes through Siliguri town. Besides this, according to the record of A.R.T.O. Siliguri, upto 2005 the license of 7561 goods vehicles had been issued. The report of Government check post highlights that near about 2000 National permit trucks pass over Siliguri every day. Often the concerned drivers go through break journey in different 'dhabas'. In this way they frequently go to the red light areas and get involved in sexual relations. They also have a relationship with the commercial sex workers available in the highways. These highway commutes mostly indulge in unsafe sex and are capable of proliferating HIV/AIDS in farthest places. Their lack of awareness makes them more susceptible. Especially in this context the mobile transport workers of Nepal are highly vulnerable because it is the shortest international communication route.

(viii) Flow of Drug-Drug Cultivation-Injecting Drug Users of North-East: The states of north eastern India like Manipur, Mizoram and Nagaland are well communicated with Siliguri town. The geographical nearness of Manipur to Burma and therefore to the golden triangle drug trial (i.e. Myanmar/Burma, Laos and Thailand), has made it a major transit route for drug smuggling. With the developing transport communication of Siliguri the drug smuggling is spreading its roots here and due to this easy availability some of the teenagers are getting involved with this addiction through needle sharing among intravenous drug users (IDUs). This was first recorded in Manipur and presently it is recognised as a big problem in metropolitan cities. It is very much used in north east regions. The concerned practitioners use this method as a less expensive way of addiction. It has been noticed that the major drug addicted areas are the hill stations of North Bengal specially-Darjeeling, Tindharia, Matigara, Kurseong, Naxalbari, Gangtok, Jalpaiguri, Coochbihar etc. *(http://www.wbvha.org/sebayan.htm).* It is one of the

major problems in Nepal. There are about 2, 00,000 drug addicts where 30,000 are injecting drug users and among them 40 per cent are HIV affected. Those people often come to Siliguri as migrant labour, casual worker and even for educational pursuit. Especially in some educational institutes of Darjeeling and Siliguri the teenage population is gradually getting enmeshed in this addiction, so, there may have a high probability to get infected with HIV/AIDS very soon.

(ix) Blood Donors: The professional blood donors (PBDs) as well as people undergoing blood transfusion, dialysis and blood product receives are considered to constitute the second highest group(14.35%) for HIV/AIDS in India. They are often internal drug users and having proximity with commercial sex workers. Around the medical institutions of Siliguri a large number of PBDs are found and they are highly susceptible in this concern.

CASES RECORDED SO FAR

The Department of Community Medicine of North Bengal Medical College in Siliguri had reported during May 2004 to April 2005, suspected 312 persons from different parts of North Bengal came to know that either they are infected by HIV or not. Through proper blood test it was confirmed that among them 52 persons were HIV positive. In 2002, out of 141 the same was identified among 15 persons. Again, during 2005 the CMO (H) of Jalpaiguri hospital had confirmed through Eliza test that among every 1000 blood donors 3 persons are HIV positive that means the probability of HIV sufferer in Jalpaiguri may be very alarming and remarkable. Another, June 2005, Dr. U. Biswas, super of Alipurduar hospital in Jalpaiguri district said that in this locality the geographical location, hotels-bars, antisocial activities/smugglings, drivers, illegal sexual relations are the main causes for the rapid increasing of HIV/AIDS. In this context an example is given here-a young boy of Alipurduar during 1997-98 went to Manipur for working in a hotel and that time he committed sexual affairs with a Manipuri girl and later he is infected by HIV. Then he came back in his native Alipurduar houses but he and his family members were boycotted by his locality.

V
SOCIO-ECONOMIC IMPACT OF AIDS AND REMARKS

In the context of Indian society the impact of AIDS is multidimensional. Among the nuclear families if the concerned male is infected then it creates a serious challenge on the bread earning of them. Besides, medical expenditure is another burden. On the other hand in the joint families the disease affected is merely looked with sympathy. Till date AIDS is a social stigma in Indian society and particularly in the rural areas the infected person and also some time his/her family members are almost forced to isolate from the rest of the neighbours. With the rapid proliferation of AIDS in India the development of adequate medical infrastructure is an urgent one, but the expenditure is very tough to manage for the Government. The demand of Indian labour is very high in abroad but if the spread of AIDS continues by leaps and bounds then the host countries will not pay the interest to involve the infected labours of India in their country. It is a loss from the economic perspective. Another major issue lies in the familial integrity. Indian middle class families are bounded by value orientations. If they found that their life partners are suffering from this disease it makes them psychologically separated from each other and it determines that AIDS has a very deep rooted socio-cultural impact in the Indian society.

In recent times AIDS is increasing at an alarming rate throughout the entire world. Though biological factors are the main causal issues related with HIV / AIDS but we cannot ignore the concerned cultural factors. Poverty, deprivation, social insecurity are the main issues which forces a man to get divert from his normal courses of life. Lack of economic stability forces a man to leave his family and search for occupation even farthest from his residence. But his mental needs cannot attain its proper requirements at all and that's why he is forced to come in contact with antisocial activities. Even in the most developed countries of the World the teenagers are in hunt to enjoy a little moment to forget their busy schedule and try to keep them away far from mental tension. It is provoking them to use drugs and come into the nexus of sex traders. Thus HIV/AIDS has become a more social problem rather than biological one. Even till date in India HIV/AIDS is recognised as a social stigma and the concerned sufferer are maltreated very much.

The prevention of AIDS does not demand only medical or biological awareness but social awareness is also foremost important in this regard. Proper education to child and youth may aware them to recognise the fundamental relationship of human society. Educational awareness may properly help an individual to recognise his basic requirements of life and the ways he must choose to achieve his goal. But he has to be alert that his way of approach must not be against the rule of nature or against the morality of humanity. Simultaneously we have to be co-operative with the sufferers and we have to show them a new way of life to overcome their mental depression. It is to be mentioned here that an HIV/AIDS sufferer is more mentally weak rather than he is biologically. Thus we have to make them mentally strong enough that he may find new ways of life in future. The main problem oriented issues of our country like poverty, unemployment, exploitation must be prevented and the youth and child must be given a better future so they can flourish themselves. This social problem must be sorted out with heartiest efforts from the members of the society and their ways of livelihood altogether.

REFERENCES

Amatya, S. (2005), (March-September), *Gender and HIV/AIDS in Nepal: Some Observations (139-152), Indian Anthropologists* (Vol. 35 No. 1&2), *Journal of Indian Anthropological Association.*

Basset, M. *et al.*, (1993), *Separation from Wife, High Risk Behaviour and HIV Among Male Urban Workers in Harare, Zimbabwe,* VIII International Conference on AIDS and STD in Africa, Marrakech, December 12-16.

Chaudhuri, B. (2003), *Health, Forest and Development: The Tribal Situation* , Inter India Publications, New Delhi.

Chronicle India (2006), Chronicle Books, New Delhi.

Chronicle India (2007), Chronicle Books, New Delhi.

Cravero, K. (2000), *Globalisation Trends and HIV/AIDS, UNAID Report.*

Dennis, A. (2001), *Global Sex,* University of Chicago Press, Chicago.

Ember, C., M. Ember, P.N. Peregrine (2002), *Anthropology* (10th ed.), Pearson Education Asia.

http://www.globalchange.com/aiddoc.htm, 31.3.2005. *AIDS Statistics.*

http://www.avert.org/indiaaids.htm, 31.3.2005. *Indian HIV & AIDS Statistics.*

http://www.avert.org/indiaaids.htm, 31.3.2005. *HIV & AIDS in India.*

http://www.wbvha.org/sebayan.htm, 30.3.2005. West Bengal Voluntary Health Association.

Misra, K.K. (2005), *Anthropology New Global Order and Other Essays,* Concept Publishing Company, New Delhi.

NACO (National AIDS Control Organisation) : *www. NACO.nic.in*

Park, K. (2000), *Park's Text Book of Preventive and Social Medicine* (17th ed.), Banarsidas Bhanot Publishers, Jabalpur.

Roy, C. (2005), (March-September). *Human Rights and HIV/AIDS with Special Reference to Women (97-110),* Indian Anthropologists (Vol. 35 No. 1&2), *Journal of Indian Anthropological Association.*

Siliguri Municipal Corporation (2005), *Official Data.*

Sinha, S.P. (1999), *India sits on AIDS Bomb,* B.R. Publishing Corporation, Delhi.

Sirohi, A. (2005), *Encyclopedia of Social Welfare: Modern Perspectives on Social Work* (Vol. 3), Dominant Publishers, New Delhi.

UNAIDS, December (2003), *Report on the Global HIV/AIDS Epidemic 2002.*

Verma, R.K., P.J. Pelto, S.L. Schensul, A. Joshi (Eds.) (2004), *Sexuality in the Time of AIDS: Contemporary Perspectives from Communities in India,* Sage Publications, New Delhi.

12

HOUSEHOLD LEVEL IMPACT OF HIV AND AIDS : A STUDY OF HIGH PREVALENCE STATES IN INDIA

Roli Misra

The human immunodeficiency virus (HIV) causes Acquired Immune Deficiency Syndrome (AIDS), which is a condition in humans wherein the immune system begins to fail, leading to opportunistic infections that can be life threatening Infection with HIV can occur by the transfer of blood, semen, vaginal fluid, Cowper's fluid or breast milk, the major routes of transmission being unprotected sexual intercourse, infected blood transfusion and transfer from an infected mother to her baby. HIV and AIDS are a serious challenge for the developing as well as the developed world and have emerged as one of the major public health challenges in India in recent years. India, with an estimated 5.206 million people living with HIV in 2005, accounts for nearly 69 per cent of the HIV infections in the South and South–Asian region. India has six high prevalence states viz. Andhra Pradesh, Karnataka, Maharashtra, Tamil Nadu, Manipur and Nagaland. When HIV prevalence in any state is five per cent or more among high risk groups (like commercial sex workers, and those attending Sexually Transmitted Diseases (STD) clinics and one per cent or more among the low risk population (like women attending antenatal clinics (ANC), then the state is considered to be in high prevalence (Table 1).

Table 1
HIV Prevalence Rates for Six States–2005 (in per cent)

States	*STD Clinics*	*ANC Clinics*
Andhra Pradesh	22.8	2.00
Karnataka	12.0	1.25
Maharastra	10.4	1.25
Tamil Nadu	8.4	0.25
Manipur	7.2	1.50
Nagaland	1.7	1.43

Source: NACO.

These six states together accounted for nearly 83 per cent of the AIDS cases in India as on 31 July 2005. Nearly 56 per cent of the cases were in the age group of 30–49 years. If the age group 15–29 years is also evaluated, then nearly 89 per cent of the cases will belong to the age group 15–49 years, which are the most productive years. Since most HIV infected individuals are in their prime productive years, HIV is considered to be a serious threat to economic growth. It is in place to mention that there have been region–wise differences in the dominance of a particular mode of transmission for instance, in Southern states main mode of transmission is unprotected sex while in the North–Eastern States of India it is mainly due to injecting drug use This is especially true in the States of Manipur and Nagaland, which lie adjacent to the drug trafficking 'Golden Triangle Zone (Solomen et.al. 2004). Further, in recent years the infection has spread from urban to rural population and from high risk behaviour groups to the general population Hence, the problem of HIV and AIDS has deep social and economic roots and therefore, its impact has severe socio–economic consequences also.

PURPOSE, SCOPE AND METHODOLOGY OF THE STUDY

The objective of this paper is to asses the impact of HIV and AIDS on health of the population and also to throw light on the weak public health system of the country. This paper also attempts to assess the financial burden on the HIV affected households. The findings of this study may help in urgent policy action in order to mitigate the negative impact generated by HIV and AIDS.

This study is based on the household survey conducted by NCAER in the six high prevalence states of Andhra Pradesh, Tamil Nadu, Karnataka, Maharashtra, Manipur and Nagaland covering urban and rural areas (Table 2). Voluntary Counseling and Testing Centres (VCTC). Counselors acted as field investigators for this survey which drew samples mainly from various government health facilities and the care and support homes run by the NGOs located in various areas (Table 3). The sample size taken for the purpose of study was 2,385 persons living with HIV and AIDS (PLWHA).

Table 2
Districts Selected for Conducting the Survey

State	*Districts*
Andhra Pradesh	Hyderabad, Warangal, East Godavari, Guntur, Krishna, Chittoor, Cuddapah
Karnataka	Bangalore, Belgaum, Dharwad, Bellary, Dakshina Kannada, Mysore
Maharashtra	Mumbai, Nagpur, Nashik, Aurangabad, Pune, Satara, Sangli
Manipur	Imphal East and West, Chandel, Thoubai, Bishnupur, Churachandpur
Nagaland	Dimapur, Kohima, Tuensang
Tamil Nadu	Chennai, Namakkal, Tiruchirappali, Theni. Erode, Tirunelveli

Source: UNDP, 2006.

Table 3
Distribution of Sample HIV Households by Place of Interview

Place of Interview	*Rural*	*Urban*	*Total*
VCTC	17.4	11.7	14.2
TB Hospital	6.2	3.3	4.6
Care and Support Home, Community Care Centre and Drop in Centre	13.8	11.9	12.7
General Hospital	11.2	9.8	10.4
Antenatal and Maternity Ward	3.2	3.3	3.3
ARV collection Centre	1.3	2.5	2.0
Network of positive people's Office	5.8	6.3	6.1
NGO Office	4.5	7.6	6.3
Residence	35.5	42.0	39.2
Others	0.90	1.53	1.26
Total	100	100	100

Source: UNDP, 2006.

DISCOVERING HIV STATUS

An HIV affected person does not know his/her HIV Status unless he/she goes for a blood test. This could be either after a prolonged illness, or at the time of donating blood or during pregnancy.

Table 4
Distribution of PLWHA by Ways of Discovering their HIV Status

Discovering HIV Status	*Rural* *Men*	*Women*	*Urban* *Men*	*Women*	*Total* *Men*	*Women*
Voluntary Testing	31.0	55.8	45.6	58.3	39.3	57.2
After Prolonged Illness	63.3	28.0	48.7	23.8	54.9	25.7
During Pregnancy–spouse/self	0.9	11.5	0.5	12.3	0.7	12.0
Blood Test at the time of joining a job	1.1	0.2	1.7	–	1.4	0.1
Others	3.8	4.5	3.5	5.6	3.6	5.1
No. of Years since HIV was detected						
Less than a year	59.3	57.7	43.7	45.5	50.4	51.0
1–3 years	29.1	26.7	39.0	38.7	34.8	33.3
3–5 years	7.6	11.1	12.1	11.5	10.2	11.3
5+	4.0	4.5	5.1	4.3	4.6	4.4
Place of Testing						
Government Hospital	52.9	67.5	58.5	64.6	56.1	65.9
Private Hospital/ Clinic	47.1	32.5	41.5	35.4	43.9	34.1
Mode of Infection						
Sexual Contact (Heterosexual)	76.1	89.3	67.1	87.3	71.0	88.2
Sexual Contact (Homosexual)	1.7	1.9	2.7	1.2	2.3	1.5
Blood Transfusion/ donation	3.3	2.1	2.4	2.6	2.8	2.4
Needle Sharing	13.9	2.6	24.0	2.8	19.7	2.7
Others	5.0	4.1	3.8	6.1	4.3	5.2
N (Number of Persons)	577	468	766	576	1343	1044

Source: UNDP, 2006.

From table 4, it can be observed that while nearly 55 per cent men who had tested positive had gone in for test after a prolonged illness. This percentage is less than half in the case of women (26%). Few people came to know about their status from the blood test conducted at the time of joining a job. Around 12 per cent women discovered their status during pregnancy.

There have been various reactions from PLWHA when they first came to know about their positive status. More than 65 per cent were shocked, while 20 per cent were embarrassed, 11 per cent did not want to face their families and 12 per cent decided not to disclose their HIV positive status as they feared discrimination and rejection.

COPING MECHANISM ADOPTED BY PLWHA

The survey highlighted an important feature of Indian society i.e. strong family ties. The families of HIV positive cases were supportive inspite of slight hesitation initially by few. Around 74 per cent men and 70 per cent women got support from their families. It may be noted that where 12.4 per cent of women were supportive of their HIV–positive husbands, only 8.5 per cent husbands were supportive of their HIV–positive wives reflecting gender discrimination in this deadly area also.

Table 5
Distribution of PLWHA by Coping Mechanism Adopted to Get Over Initial Shock/ Disbelief (in percentage)

Characteristics	*Men*	*Women*
Counselling	39.7	32.0
Confidently	6.8	6.9
Family Support	17.7	11.9
Friends Support	1.6	3.8
Became Alcoholic	–	0.4
Decided to keep HIV Status Secret	1.0	0.5
Help others	0.2	0.3
NGO Support	1.9	1.6
Wanted to know hot to live with HIV Status	31.2	42.7
Total	100	100

Source: UNDP, 2006.

From this Table 5 it can be inferred that around 40 per cent of the HIV positive man and 32 per cent of the HIV–positive women reported that counselling helped them to overcome their initial state of shock. An interesting fact which was revealed was that nearly 35 per cent of the respondents wanted to know more about the infection and ways to lead a quality life despite being tested HIV–positive.

NATURE OF ILLNESS

More that 1/4 m of the women and 55 per cent men reported that they went for a HIV test because they had been suffering from prolonged illness as evident from table–6 and already discussed while discovering HIV status.

Table 6
Per cent Reporting Prolonged Illness by PLWHA

% reporting prolonged illness	*Men (55.0)*	*Women (26.7)*
Nature of Illness		
Respiratory Infection	4.6	3.0
Malaria	1.4	2.2
Fever	31.8	29.5
Headache, bodyache	2.4	3.4
Weakness	3.8	3.4
Loose Motion/ diarrhea	17.1	18.7
Typhoid	0.7	1.1
Jaundice	1.4	1.1
TB	24.4	20.1
Skin Disease	6.5	6.0
Gynecological Problem	–	3.4
Sexually transmitted diseases/RTI	1.6	3.0
Others	4.4	5.2
All	100	100
Number of Persons	738	268

Source: UNDP, 2006.

Having observed this table is can be inferred that undiagnosed fever has emerged as the most important reason for the PLWHA going in for the HIV test, next important reason being Tuberculosis (TB). In many countries HIV sentinel surveillance is carried out among TB patients to ascertain the level of HIV prevalence (Ahmad Zuber *et. al.*, 2003).

NO TREATMENT OF ILLNESS

The survey results show that all illness episodes are not treated (men 4.4 per cent and women 9.7 per cent). It can be said from the data from Table 7 in this table that illness at first instance is not considered serious and therefore has been reported as a major reason for not seeking treatment there is also a gender difference in seeking treatment, women being deprived treatment on account of financial constraints and lack of family co–operation.

Table 7
Reasons for no Treatment of PLWHA

	Men	*Women*	*All*
Illness episodes for which no treatment was sought	4.4	9.7	6.5
Reasons for not seeking treatment			
Illness not considered serious	79.7	63.2	69.8
No medical facility nearby	3.1	4.2	3.8
Financial Constraints	10.9	25.3	19.5
Doctors not willing to treat	–	1.1	0.6
Lack of time	3.1	2.1	2.5
No cooperation from family	–	2.1	1.3
Others	3.1	2.1	2.5
Total	100	100	100

Source: UNDP, 2006.

HOUSEHOLD EXPENDITURE INCURRED ON TREATMENT

The out–of–pocket expenditure incurred by the households includes amount spent on fees and medicines, clinical test, transport costs, bribes and tips. Household incur substantial expenditure even if the treatment is sought from a government health facility. However, there is a big gender gap in the average expenditure incurred per illness episode, while for men, it is Rs. 796, for women it is much lower at Rs. 487/– (Table 8).

Table 8
Expenditure Incurred by PLWHA for Treatment of Non–Hospitalized Illness Episodes by Source of Treatment (Rs.)

Source of treatment	*Rural*		*Urban*		*Total*		
	Men	*Women*	*Men*	*Women*	*Men*	*Women*	*All*
Government	510	301	650	347	589	324	482
Private	1179	759	1225	803	1202	781	070
Charitable trust/ NGO	245	132	352	577	305	342	322
Faith healer/ religious person	600	–	150	–	300	–	300
Others	452	431	92	1061	229	759	559
All	770	410	817	566	796	487	676
No. of episodes	641	449	764	439	1405	888	2293

Source: UNDP, 2006.

One thing needs to be mentioned here is that PLWHA do not have access to any health insurance cover. Hence, when it comes to hospitalization, government hospitals are preferred over private nursing homes. The direct cost of hospitalization includes amount paid as room rent, cost of medicine, doctor's fees, surgery, test. The average expenditure per hospitalization is Rs. 2,687 and there is again substantial gender gap in the average cost of hospitalization (Table 9).

Table 9
Average Expenditure Incurred per Hospitalization Case by PLWHA by Source of Treatment (Rs.)

Source of Treatment	*Men*	*Women*	*All*
Government	1533	1270	1440
Private	6255	3875	5645
Charitable trust/NGO	1701	1836	1738
Faith healer/religious person	1600	600	1267
ALL	3001	1984	2687

Source: UNDP, 2006.

The data indicates that average household expenditure per hospitalization is Rs 3,001 for men, this average is lower for women at Rs. 1,984/–indicating that higher percentage of women have sought treatment from the government hospitals instead of going to private nursing home/hospital.

It can be understood that it is difficult for any household to incur expenditures on treatment, therefore, they adopt various means to support their finances for this cause (Table 10). It has been estimated that more than 40 per cent of individuals who are hospitalized in India borrow money or sell their assets to meet the cost of care and on an average hospitalized Indians spend 58 per cent of their annual expenditure on hospitalization (11PM2005).

In 36 per cent cases the households meet their expenses from past savings and this percentage increases with increased incomes. However, all households in different income groups have resorted to borrowing and liquidation of assets.

Table 10
Source of Financing Hospitalization

Source of Financing	*Annual Household Income (Rs.)*					
	Upto 20000	20001- 30000	30001- 41000	41001- 84000	> 84000	TOTAL
Past Savings	20.0	31.2	38.0	44.4	52.4	35.9
Liquidation of Assets	11.7	14.2	8.4	8.8	2.4	9.7
Borrow from money Lender/other financial institutions	23.3	9.2	14.1	11.1	2.4	13.6
Loan from employer	–	2.8	2.1	1.4	2.4	1.6
Borrow from friends/ Relatives	27.2	28.4	29.6	24.1	26.2	26.9
NGO support	17.2	12.1	6.3	9.3	8.3	11.0
Others	0.6	2.1	1.4	0.9	2.4	1.3
TOTAL	100	100	100	100	100	100

Source: UNDP, 2006.

CONCLUSIONS AND POLICY IMPLICATIONS

In this study conducted by NCAER data used is from a primary survey of HIV households spread over the rural and urban areas of six high prevalence states in India to investigate the household level impact of HIV and AIDS. After having discussed the reasons for discovering HIV status, nature of illness, coping mechanism adopted and expenditure incurred by PLWHA, the following conclusions can be drawn:

(i) Even though the aggregate impact of the epidemic may not appear to be larger now, the impact on households affected by this epidemic is very severe as this impact is felt on consumption expenditure and savings.

(ii) The poor households and particularly the females are more vulnerable than the male members of the households indicating gender differences.

(iii) Social stigma and discrimination has emerged as a serious issue which prevents PLWHA from disclosing their states not only to community but also at times to family and spouses.

(iv) For the economy, incase the HIV spreads, it implies reduced availability of savings, which can result in reduced investment and economic growth.

The important policy implications from this study that have emerged in order to mitigate the negative impact generated by HIV and AIDS are as follows:

(i) Special social protection programmes are required to support the people and households that are hit by epidemic.

(ii) The PLWHA households need much greater support from the government in terms of access and affordability of medical care.

(iii) Given the low level of literacy rates in India especially among women, the major source of information regarding HIV and AIDS namely television and radio need to be used more intensively to spread awareness.

(iv) Priority should be given to educating people about *how HIV is not transmitted*–Efforts need to be made to create awareness about modes of transmission of infection, so that attitude of people towards PLWHA can be changed.

(v) Improving women's legal position relating to inheritance and property ownership as well as maximizing their access to credit and their income–generating ability are needed so as to empower women.

(vi) India can go on adopting an alternative approach that reduces risk–exposure. It can draw on Swedish approach, which views women being driven into prostitution as a form of "male violence" and men who buy sex as criminal offenders. The Swedish government help women get out of prostitution. Such an approach can really be an integral part of the alternative suggested in our country also.

REFERENCES

Bharat S., Aggleton P. and Tyrer P. (2001), "India HIV and AIDS Related Discrimination, Stigmatization and Denial", Geneva, UNAIDS.

IIPM (2005), Health on the Pill in the *Indian Economic Review,* Volume III, Quarterly Issue, 30th June.

Independent Commission on Health in India (2001), A Call for Rethinking: National AID Prevention and Control Policy and Programme.

Lalit M. Nath, The Independent Commission on Development and Health in India HIV/AIDS in India Some Issues.

NACO (2003), Evaluating Report.

NACO: Combating HIV/AIDS in India 1999–2000.

NACO (2005), Monthly Updates of AIDS.

UNAIDS and WHO (2005), "AIDS Epidemic Update: Special Report on HIV Prevention", Dicemlies, Geneva.

UNDP India (2006), "Socio–Economic Impact of HIV and AIDS in India".

WHO, (1999), "AIDS: The Challenge", Regional Office for South–East Asia, New Delhi.

Zuber Ahmed *et. al.,* (2003), "HIV Infection Seroprevalence in Tuberculosis Patients," *Indian Journal of Tuberculosis.*

13

DEVELOPMENT OF PRIMITIVE TRIBAL GROUPS IN KARANATAKA: SOME PRELIMINARY OBSERVATIONS

Nanjunda D.C.

INTRODUCTION

Tribal development has been given one of the major attention by all the Governments in India during all five years plan on account of the socioeconomic backwardness of the tribles. Also lot of provisions have been brought in to the constitution to safeguard their basic interests. A study team remarked that tribal welfare should aim at the prospective within reasonable time. Advancement of the social and economic life of the tribes with a view to their gradual integration with the rest of country on a footing of equality. It is noted that Scheduled Tribe (ST) population of India constitutes about 8.08 per cent of the total as per the 1991 census. Out of this more than 62 per cent tribes are spread only in Five states of the country. However, the total number of such ST is 635. All ST groups are entitled to have many benefits directly from the Governament, with reservations for them in many sectors of the development.

WHO ARE THE PRIMITIVE TRIBAL GROUPS (PTG)

The first attempt was made in 1931 to identify the PTG in the country. That group of tribles who have following characteristic features can be classified in to primitive tribal groups (1) still practicing pre-agricultural level of technology (2) extremely low level of literacy (3) near stagnant or diminishing populations. Till today 75 groups have been identified so far in 16 states and UTs. The problems of Indian tribes can be classified in to two types. (1) problems of major tribes and (2) problems of primitive tribes. But in India both of them are mixed up together and that's why no significant achievement could be made in solving the problems of primitive tribles. Now a days they are facing some serious problems like lack of basic facilities viz; no good houses, acute shortage of food, drinking water, power, medical facilities, unreachable to NGO's, lack of essential agricultural technology etc. In the resent past planning commission had issued some guide lines to the states that tribal development plan should be emphasizing on the following points (1) elimination of expatiation of all form (2) rapid social and economic development (3) improving their organizational capabilities and narrowing down the gap between the levels of development of the tribles and other are. Also commission suggested with ITDP an integrated area development plan fousing on the specific problems of the tribal people must be implemented.

AREA OF THE STUDY

Jenu kuruba and Koraga tribes have been identified as PTGs in the Karnataka State. Jenu kuruba tribe is concentrated around Mysore, Chmarajanager and Kodagu districts that are more or less 200 Km away from the Bangalore. Total population of this tribe is 24654 and the literacy rate is 18.35 per cent Usually they are living in hamlet made out of bamboo and huts with their and judicial system. They believe in magic, sorcery and witchcraft. Neither polygamy nor polyandry is practiced. Besides Working with Raton and bamboo, collection of minor forest products like herb, honey, roots fruits etc as their major occupations.

Koraga is a very primitive tribe in the Karnataka State. Mostly they are concentrated in Dakshina Kannada and some part of the Udupi district, which is around 450 Km away from the Silicon City-Bangalore. They very much believe in magic and witchcraft and local medicine men. The total population is 19784(2001Cencus) with 19.23 per cent of literacy. They have their own rich culture and traditional heritage. Their traditional occupation is basket making. Few percentage of the population lives in semi urban areas.

The author has had an intensive fieldwork in selected tribal areas where large concentration of the above mentioned tribes could have been found. The methodology included participant observation, micro and macro study, and focus group interview with tribal leaders, NGO's, local politicians, resources persons, and state officials.

LITERACY STATUS OF PTGS OF KARNATAKA

Table 1

PTG	*Total Population*	*Total Literate*	*Male-Literates*	*Female-Literates*	*Male*	*Female*	*Total*
Jenu kuruba	27597	4033	3172	2161	15.10	19.29	17.09
Koraga	11566	3543	1678	1865	27.82	29.38	28.06

Source: Mohanty, 2002.

RESULT AND DISCUSSION

Of course, Government has implemented various tribal welfare programmes through ITDP, but failed to show any interest in the feed back process. Success and failure of any policies and programmes depend on the participation of local people. Our study has shown that the non-tribal officials(22%) who don't have any first hand field experience about tribals are framing all these policies and programmes. Our study also reveled that agriculture, animal husbandry, cottage industries and forest development programmes have limited success so for because concerned policy do not have any scope for the people participation. Most odd thing we found those, even Governament officials did not have complete awareness about various tribal developmental schemes. Few NGO's (12%) working for the welfare of these tribals have suffering with many problems like lack of organizational programmes have limited success so for because concerned policy do not have any scope for the people participation. Most odd thing we found that even Governament officials did not have complete awareness about various tribal developmental schemes. Few NGO's working for the welfare of these tribals have suffering with many problems like lack of organizational efficiency, no trained Anthropologists and fund/grants on time. Some NGO's said they have to pay bribe to the concerned officials for the release of the money in the form of commission. Only 9.32 per cent of tribal people aware about some of the Governament schemes for their self-development. It shows the acute rate of illiteracy among these tribles. More than 77.74 per cent tribal people said medical facilities is beyond reachable to them. Also they said allopathic doctors are rarely visits to the primary health centers may be once/twice in a weak. During summer these people should walk many miles to get drinking water. Infectious diseases are most common among these tribles.

Attendance is very low in ASHRAM schools. Teachers says that acute poverty, lack of interest in both parents and children and superstitious believes are the most common reasons for the high rate of-drops out among tribal children. But on the other hand it is also true that most of the teachers are not showing any interest to teach tribal children. Many of them are working in these schools just for special remuneration by the Governament. Our study has shown that the sectional allocation of the tribal sub plan do not reflect the felt needs of the people and as such have not created the desired impact. More than that this study has revealed that there is no scope for a set planning for implementation, monitoring and evaluation of programmes in the tribal sub plan. Not only the PTG, even other tribal groups in the state have yet to seen the different faces of Basic Infrastructure. Governament has implemented many developmental schemes but the main problem seems to be that it has no any set channels to make reach these programmes to each and every tribal family. Our study has reveled that only more than 12-18 per cent of these groups has got some of the facilities like housing, power and water. Governament has a plan to mapping new under ground water areas with the help of Geo Information System. Many houses constructed by the Governament agencies have become already ruined due to low quality of work. More than two third (71%) families don't have power facilities. Now Governament has a plan to provide new solar technologies to the some of the hamlets that are not so easily reachable. People have to walk 2-3 miles to get drinking water. Most of the families are using water from near by ponds and open wells. So these people are facing acute health problems. Good drainage and toilet facilities have become nightmare. Many tribal leaders (21%) told that they tried their level best to bring these problems to the notice of the concerned officials but the result is a big zero. Some of them told local political leaders visits only during election time. But politicians and other people's opinion are that these people don't like to receive any new technology/things in to their life. Many of the GRAM PANCHYATHS (31%) are absolutely inactive due to the lack of fund and political consciousness. Roads and other communication systems are more or less absent. During rainy season all links between these tribes and the rest of the world will be completely out of order. State Governament has a plan to shift some families of these tribes and rehabilitate in new places with assured basic infrastructure. Families are protesting against this decision saying that Governament provide every basic infra structure in the new habitat first. Then we will ready to move from here.

Shifting cultivation still prevalent in these two tribal groups. So policy makers should seriously think to providing new agricultural technologies emphasizing on integrated forming system. Since these people does not shows any interest in using chemical fertilizers, sustaining agricultural through green manure can be promoted through field demonstrations. Now these PTG are facing acute shortage of the food. Hence the best probable alleviative before the Govt. and local NGO's is introducing new eco-friendly technologies for rice and other crop cultivation's. Many tribal people are getting different types of help from co-operative societies like LAMPS but it is not working round the year. Due to this now a days they are not getting any good prices for their products. So, they are very eager to sell their products directly to the market but the main problem is involvement of middlemen, as they are exploiting uneducated tribes in different ways. More odd thing is that these middlemen have good relation ships with developmental officials at various levels. Also 33 to 40 per cent tribal households have been affected by land alienation problem. Our study has revealed that about 77 per cent of land were alienated by the non-tribles there, by cause indebtedness among the tribles. The effort made by the Governament to tackle this problem is not even partially succeed because, some invisible hands are effectively functioning between rich non-tirbles and concerned Governament officials. This is the main hurdle in reaching all the schemes to the grass root level.[3] In case of promote of cottage industry, Governament has established Tribal Cooperative Marketing Development Federation of India Limited. The main work of this limited is to provide commercial market to the tribal products. Also it helps to promote enterpriunrship among tribals by providing soft loans. Apart from this Governament has newly introduced a project called Tribal Women Empowerment Project. But the main draw back is no provision of imparting training to the local artesian to up grade their skills. Some time there will be no enough supply of raw materials to the cottage industries. Since Governament has brought a strict forest conservation rules backed by the recent Supreme Court verdict many tribal people says, they are not permitted to collect any minor forest products. Then how can we get raw materials for our traditional work? Many NGO's said Governament should revise its forest polices and connect to the tribal welfare programmes.

CRUCIAL AREAS FOR URGENT ACTION

Economic Deprivation

Now-a- days most of these tribal families are living on the edge because of weakening of the subsistence based economy.

Basically their basic economies are depended on land, water and minor forest products. But recent restriction on the collection of minor forest products by the Governament has made an adverse effect on their self-sufficiency and high threatening their very existence. Also few of these tribal families are still practicing the hunting and gathering mode of economy. Due to the recent ban on collecting minor forest product for the commercial purpose by administration has made them their life still worst. The problem of food shortage has been gradually increasing. Shortage of raw materials has made cottage industry dead and local artisan as bonded laborers to rich non-tribal people. New forms of exploitation were super imposed older once. This is the time of the administration to think seriously about family based alternative income generation programme wherever the present occupation is dwindling and application of science and technology for manpower development.

LAND–ALIENATION

More than 90 per cent these two tribal groups are dependent on agriculture and allied activities. More are less their economy is primarily agro based. The major per cent of Jenu kuruba and 31.21per cent of Koragas have become absolutely land less labourers. This study has revealed that in many cases these tribles are the official landlords and the non-tribals are its virtual owners. Also it is noted that in certain cases certain type of land is owned by recognized village community and here land alienation is less. So the administration think more seriously about this problem by ceiling loopholes in the legal provision and immediate action should be taken to identify alienated land and restoring it to the tribals with delivery of possession. Also we observe that the rigid implementation of the forest conservation act without any regard of the local situation has worsened the relationship between forest dwellers and the officials. More than that, linked up with the alienation of land is the problem of indebtedness among the tribals, who have placed their lands with the local moneylenders. Our study has revealed that 61.32 per cent of jenukuruba and 59.21 per cent of koraga tribal people are severely suffering from indebtedness. Also study has shown that apart from poverty, ignorance of equitable price system, spending lot of money for various rituals, and remitting fines as set by their own local panchyanths or judicial system are other major problems of these tribals. It is necessary to have first hand knowledge of the causes of poverty and indebtedness of these tribal people and Governament immediately must take proper action to remove indebtedness among tribal people.

Problem of Shifting Cultivation

Despite, banning on the shifting cultivation still most of the families of these group are practicing shifting cultivation. This kind of cultivation is most common among the families who are living in hilly areas like Kodagu and Mangalore district of Karnataka State. The practice of shifting cultivation is done for two or there years regularly and, thereafter, that piece of land is left. Absence of wells irrigation faculties, fertilizer, and loose of soil fertility and damage by the wild animals, further deteriorates the agricultural yield and they're by increasing nutritional problems in these tribals.

Migration and Unemployment

This problem is not so common in above-mentioned tribals but due to drought and other reasons few families who are living very next to the border of the urban areas migrates in searching of jobs. Usually jenu kuraba tribes migrates to other places during harvesting (Coffee plantations) season for the employment. Koraga tribes migrates to the near by urban areas to work as wage labourers. Our study has revealed that most of these tribes are migrating in search of employment and whose descendants are hardly return to their home land. Since these tribes are hard workers they are very much exploited by the middlemen.

A RECONSIDERATION OF ROLE OF PANCHYATHS

73rd amendment panchyaths have more legal provisions to implement well fare programmes at gross root level. They can ensure effective participation of tribal people in to the process of planning, implementing and monitoring the various schemes. They can play a vital role during the framing of polices at higher level. To strengthen good relation ship between forest ant forest dwellers joint forest management system can be more effective under the supervision of the panchyaths. There by panchyaths can help tribal people to improve socio economic conditions. The proper management of forest produces could alleviate poverty, generate employment opportunities and improve quality of life. Some time primitive tribes are victims of the regional imbalance too. So panchyaths should act as a central monitoring agencies to check this problem by advising both the Governments as and when required and they should have qualified technical manpower to implement programmes more effectively. Also, together with local NGO's they can initiate more meaning full role in sustainable development of tribes. Panchyaths should take action to provide essential services such as road, drinking water, primary health centers etc to all tribal hamlets. Only 13 per cent of jenukuruba and 17.34 per cent of koraga have some awareness about the existences of panchyaths in their respective areas. Panchyaths officials say these tribes are not ready to come out of rigid traditional thinking and they are not interested in politics. Now a days jenu kuraba tribes are showing some interest in political consigns also.

DISPLACEMENT OF TRIBAL GROUPS

The Karnataka Governament has a plan to shift jenu kurbas to some other new places but these tribes are not interested in shifting to new places as lack of proper basic infrastructures. These tribes are not satisfied with new packages. Because most of tribal leader says, we are not ready to believe the Government and compensate money is not enough to live in urban/semi urban areas. Previous examples show tribles, displaced by the various reasons are become unemployed, debt bondage and destitute. They are not ready to loose their traditional resources of lively hood.

CONCLUSION AND POLICY IMPLICATIONS

We should always keep in our mind that the problems of the tribals are basically different in different region of the country. Before implementing any polices and programmes the executive agencies should identify the area of minimum and maximum resistance to innovations in their culture Also it should be followed recognizing vital linkages in their cultural fabrics. Even though the Government is spending lot of money under various tribal sub plans the result is not encouraging because these schemes are not geographically/ culturally specific and not need based one. Since the problems of both major tribals and primitive tribals are entirely different micro level analysis of the problem is most essential. Understanding of tribal organization and value through sustained scientific studies is most essential now a days. The tribals can avail of the welfare and development programmes only if the anti-exploitative measures are effectively tackled. The fundamental lacuna in all tribal sub plan is framing of polices with out involving any tribal members in the panel and not even at implementation stage. Also many of these programmes don't have any scope for identifying the integrative forces in tribal life. They are treating as just receiver of Benefits. Before taking any decision on tribal development administration should consult local NGO's who are working at grass root level. The so called primitive tribes who are usually less vocal than other major tribals have little or no contact with the administration and planners as a result of which they remain out side the pale of the developmental benefits. As much as possible new tribal sub plan should involve lot scope for self-management, ecological disequilibrium conscious efforts should be made to prepare the people psychologically to accept the change in environment. Our study has shown that how they would fail in mobilizing their local resources if they are completely depend on either, Governament/NGO's. The present situation demands a revitalizing of existing development. Owing to their numerical inferiority, the so-called primitive tribals are not so competent too resist the atrocities, and are not capable of creating a mechanism of self-defense except that of retreat to further remote are, which are not easily accessible. But more vigorous step has to be taken to bring them into the main stream of the Nation Public participation in each and every policies and programmes is highly essential. While implementing the tribal development plans, care should be taken that the cultural traits of primitive tribes are not disturbed with in the process of their interaction with the mainstream of nation life. More over watch on the trends set in motion, which should not destroy the social solidarity of the tribles and kill their zest for life should be the part and parcel of every tribal developmental policy. Also there should be lot of scope for prioritizing their needs, solving their own problems and raising their own resources to meet their urgent needs in all schemes. On the basis of allocation of funds, area specific and people specific tribal plan should be formulated. The so-called primitive tribes, particularly those, who depend on forest resources for their livelihood, have often had their way of life disrupted by a drastic change in the ecology. Formulation of welfare plans with a view to accommodating tribal needs with regional and national interest is most impordent. Thus integration not assimilation, should be the leading principal behind and tribal development policy. Finally, it is difficult to conceive of a trained mind, other than an Anthropologist, who can effectively tackle this problem with greater insight. Also it very essential to orienting the administrator to tribal life and culture in all aspects considered above and giving them special training for the tasks they have to undertake among the tribes.

As J., Nehru said we should not over administer these areas or overwhelm them with a multiplicity of schemes. We should rather work through, and not in rivalry to, their own social and cultural institutions.

REFERENCES

Mohanty, P.K (2002), *"Development of Primitive Tribal Groups in India,"* Kalpaz Publication, New Delhi.

Makhan Jha, (1995), *"An Introduction to Indian Anthropology,"* Vikas Publishng House, New Delhi.

Patel, M.L. (1994), *"Development and Dualism of Primitive Tribes"*, M.D Publications, New Delhi.

Sharma, (2002), *"Tribal Welfare and Development"* Sarup and Sons Publications, New Delhi.

Singh.B, (1977), "Tribal Development at Cross Road" *Man In India*. 57(3), pp. 229-247.

Verma, RC (1995), *"Indian Tribes Through the Ages,"* Publication Division, Ministry of I and B, Governament of India.

Planning Commission (1990), Draft Report on Eight Five Year Plan, Governament of India.

14

RELEVANCE OF TRADITIONAL HEALING CENTERS AND TREATMENT OF THE POSSESSED

Shobha Devi R. Patil & G.R. Krishnamurthy

INTRODUCTION

The cause and treatment of diseases have been of great concern to human beings since the existence of human world. The Atharvaveda one of the ancient Indian epics says that diseases are caused due to the influence of supernatural beings (evil spirits) upon the individuals. Even Hughes (1968) states that "In the non-western societies, when a wound does not heal, a sick man does not respond to treatment and when a normally expected and predictable does not happen, the people start explaining such conditions (illness) as an event occurring due to 'Spirit possession' of the individual. Further, he states that in these Societies, disease is frequently seen as a warning sign a visitation from punishing agents for a broken taboo, a hostile impulse or an aberrant urge to depart from the approved way. Often the therapy involves confession of the client and under such conditions the confession may relieve the client of one's diffused as well as focused anxieties and guilt. Accordingly various magi co-religious measures were under taken to cure the individual from his/her ill health".

In the olden days the treatment services were available in the religious places like temples and shrines and from the magicians. Besides Ayurvedic medicines were prescribed by the vaidyas and pandits in which case, the medical practice was normally inherited through their elders as a family occupation, without having undergone any formal in a school.

With the advancement of civilization and due to the influence of western culture on India , there has been gradual change in the peoples perception of the diseases and the treatments opted for the same. It could be stated here that in India we find Primary Health Centers are being established for every 30,000 population to cater to their health needs. Thus in the present day it can be observed that an effective infrastructure of modern health services, being developed through out India to cater to the needs of needy persons.

But it is not strange to see people going to modern doctor, as well as traditional healer, for relief even in the modern world. Ishwaran (1968) reports "today people when fall ill takes help of all agencies or means to get cured. First home medicine, propitiation to God and Goddess, temple priest, local exorcist, vaids or hakims to modern medical practitioners both within and outside the village". Further Randhava ct. al (1961) reported that a "majority of the possessed cases hail from rural areas and they are predisposed to religious ideas and practices" Chandrasshekar (1990) also states that the "Phenomenon of possession is very common in India, especially in rural areas. In every village one or two persons are said to experience possession by either spirits or God. He further reports that this syndrome is closely associated with mental health in India. Individuals who are oppressed by men and who are afraid to communicate directly, instead of developing neurotic symptoms, use possession phenomena for their benefit". Bidarakoppa and Marulasiddaiah (1979) have stated that" mental health needs of the vast rural population are almost untouched by psychiatric services, further not even proper estimation of mental health needs of them is being carried out. But the traditional healers and religious shrines, which are commonly found in rural setup, are providing mental health services to lead a happy life.

Keeping in mind the observations made by various researchers, the Authors developed an interest to take up a study, which may throw light on the causes for persistence of age –old practices in the modern scientific society. Hence, here an attempt is being made to study systematically, the nature of services and the outcome of traditional healing practices, in meeting the health needs of our people. Further, the present study may throw light upon understanding the useful techniques of the traditional healers, as well as it may help to bridge the gap between the two medical systems–traditional and modern.

Therefore through personal observation of the techniques and rituals practiced in the healing centers, the behaviours manifested by the cases were recorded and further used for analysis.

Besides, the traditional healers and the priests of the concerned shrines were interviewed. The main areas covered during investigation through unstructured interview were regarding; age, gender, educational status, occupation, secondary occupation, the number of years of being in traditional healing services, the techniques used, their beliefs and opinion about their services and their opinion about the client's coming to them etc. Through repeated visits, and by winning the confidence of the healers/priests in these centers, rapport was established with them, before collecting the data.

DESCRIPTION ABOUT THE TRADITIONAL HEALERS AND THEIR TECHNIQUES

Findings of the Study

Traditional Healer of Malapur, Dharawad

This healer is an old woman of about 80 years, in charge of a dargah (mohamoddan shrine) in Malapur area of dharawad city. She is a widow, having 3 children. She lives with her sons and grand children in her own house within the premises of the dargah. This dargah is reported to be a branch of Saint Doodpheer dargah of Lakshmeshwar (a village from the same district about 50 km. from Dharwad). This dargah was built about 6 decades back. Initially the healer's father was providing healing services to the needy.

After his death the present healer started her practice. This healer has been providing services for the past 3 to 4 decades.

HEALING TECHNIQUES USED BY THE HEALER

The healer gets individuals suffering from various health and interpersonal problems. She treats them only on Thursdays or on new moon days. The clients are expected to bring with them a few lemons and a particular (Marata) type of incense sticks, which emit a kind of pungent fume.

During one of her visits, the researcher observed that women came to the healer because of inter personal problems with their husbands, in-laws or because of their own ill health. If it is an inter personal problem, the healer takes the lemon and blesses it (muttering something) and gives back to the clients only to be tied in one of the corners of their house or to be worshiped by the client for 40 days, which is believed to help the client to overcome her problem.

In case of ill health healer collects the details as to the nature of the problem, attempts made prior to clients visit to the healer for treatment, etc. After that she returns the lemons blessed and gives ash of the burnt incense sticks, to the client to be consumed once or twice a day for 3 to 4 days.

In a few cases, taking clue from her client and relatives, she treats the clients as possessed individuals. In this context the healer follows the exercising techniques. The healer makes the client to cover her hand and also face with her sari-pallu (border of the sari). Then she puts her left hand on the client's head, lights the incense sticks and makes the client to inhale the strong pungent smell while coaxing her to reveal its (spirit's) identity. Ultimately (when it is too intolerable to inhale the smell) the client would take the name of some deceased persons who are known to the client and also to the members of her family to be the object possessing her (the client). The cause given for the same may be either the hostile feelings or the desire of spirits to have a dwelling place.

After the confession is made by the individual spirit as to the 'object and purpose of possession' the healer would ask the Spirit as to its desire to be pacified so that the Spirit would stop troubling the individual in future. At this juncture the Spirit may demand for egg, fruits, sweet, beedi, etc., to be supplied with or to be kept at the tri-angular corner near the grave yard which is about 2 km. away from the dargah, so that the trouble caused by the 'Spirit' would be removed. Accordingly, the client's family follows the instruction of the spirit to pacify it. And when the client kneels down completely with exhaustion, Healer pats the client on her back with the special broom made out of peacock's feathers as a mark of cleaning the client's body from the evil spirit and also to confer blessings of the holy spirit of the dargah. Further the healer asks the client pluck a few hairs from her head as an indication to have been freed from the possessing spirit. After that the healer puts the hair packed with a piece of paper in to a bottle and closes it tightly. The healer reports that she is arresting the spirit inside the bottle and throwing it away in an abandoned well, so that it would not trouble the client in future. She also ties a talisman on the forearm of the client, which is believed to provide additional protection to the client in times to come. In turn the client's family offers her kanike (gifts) liberally, for having got relief from their sufferings.

During her second visit, the researcher met with a lady who had come second time for treatment of her possession episodes. She was said to have been treated for possession episodes by the same healer a few months back, but had a relapse and had come again for relief. According to healer the relapse was because of pollution to talisman by the occurrence of death in the home or attending to funeral etc., but it was realized after verification that none of such events had happened in the case of this client. For that the healer gave the reason that, perhaps a person who had attended a funeral might have entered the client's house. Thus, the healer and the clients appear to have preconceived ideas about the possession phenomena, and the occurrence and relapse of possession in their own ways.

Traditional Healer of Yelavatti

Village Yelavatti is situated in shirahatti taluk of Dharawad District, Karnataka. The healer is aged about 50 years, studied upto S.S.L.C. (10th standard). He belongs to forward (Lingayath) caste, married, living with his wife, children and mother. He hails from rural agriculture family. He is said to be practicing magical rituals for the past 20 to 25 years. People with various health, economic, social and personal problems contact him for relief. People from Dharwad district, neighbouring Districts and States flock here seeking his services.

The traditional healer of Yelavatti claims to have undergone training from a Saint in Northern India. He has built a temple in the name of goddess Renuka in front of his house, with a big 'Hall' (measuring 25' x 18') with a 'Adishakthi' (Goddess of power) painting covering entire wall of one side of the hall. There is a concrete platform in the 'Hall' where he keeps sacred items like ash, talisman, herbs etc., for the purpose of treating his clients. He gives healing services to the people on every Thursdays and on new moon days.

Healing Techniques Used by the Healer

Based on nature of the problem presented by individuals and the details revealed about the treatment measures adopted by the family before the individual was brought to him, the healer tries to diagnose as to what could be the cause for the problem of the client. It could be either black magic or spirit possession or bad time. When 'spirit possession' is speculated the healer keeps his right arm on head of the client (spirit) to reveal its identity. When the client gives her original identification, he rejects it and further forces the client to answer and admit as to what Spirit it is? When did it enter the client? What is the purpose? And so on. Some times he puts the leading questions such as 'Are you from blood relatives, family, distant relatives, a neighbour, a villager or a friend?

If there is no admission from the client to any of these questions as to what sort of spirit one is, then he holds tightly pulling the client's hair, ties both sort of Spirit one is, then he holds tightly pulling the client's hair, ties both hands of the client to her back and forcibly makes her to kneel down to his feet and threatens the client (Spirit) to admit as to its source. Then he presses in front of the ear, which causes unbearable pain and goes on abusing and further threatening to apply very harsh and severe treatment to punish it, if the source is not revealed. By this time, the client is very tired and exhausted. Later she (client) submits to the commands of the healer and to the family members. She (spirit) declares as to who the spirit was? How and why it was troubling the client? After this revelation, the healer asks as to what is the desire of the Spirit? The Spirit may demand for fruits, sweets, egg, beedi etc., which would be supplied to pacify it or the spirit may demand for good behavior to be maintained by the dependents of the Spirit's deceased person. Once the desire of the spirit is fulfilled under the compelling environment, the Spirit agrees to leave the client unharmed in future.

After this the healer whispering a few incomprehensible words blows air on the face of the client. This is followed by tieing a talisman either on the forearm or on the ankle so that it would protect the client from the influence of evil spirits. At this state the client is totally exhausted and rests completely on the floor for 10 to 15 minutes. When the client wakes up, she looks dull and complains of pain in the hands and head, because of the twisting and tight holding of her and pulling of hair, etc. The client is given few blessed lemon and sacred ash (Vibhuthi), to be applied by the client after going home.

Outcome of the Treatment

At this healing center, two cases were studied by the author. Both of them were females and coming from rural background. They had received treatment for 'possession phenomena'–by this healer, and had left the center with the assurance that the 'Spirit' would not cause any trouble to the client in future. But both cases had come back with their problems (illness) within a short time of 30 days after their recovery from previous episodes and illness.

Therefore, it could be concluded here that the individuals try to draw the attention of others through manifesting some physical as well as emotional disturbances, which are usually attributed to 'evil spirit' influences upon the individual after some time, by their surroundings (family and neighbourhood). Thus when treatment is sought in this direction of driving away the evil spirit from the individual, the client would manifest the 'possession states' as per the stimulation, expectation and sometime even threat the client receives in such healing centers by the traditional healers would cause in 'possession episodes'. Similarly after the process is over the client would be declared to have been relieved of the 'Spirit' by the people around. The client may also show improvement in one's condition either for temporary or prolonged period, which perpetuates the superstitious belief among all the concerned.

But in reality it could be observed that the problem or possession attacks of the client is found to be disappearing either completely or partially depending upon the fulfillment of their needs or removal of the unpleasant life situation which was the underlying cause for their psycho-physiological disturbances and the manifestation of 'possession states'. Shobhadevi and Bidarakoppa (1994) have made similar observations in their study. As the treatment techniques used by traditional healers do not concentrate on tackling the underlying causes clients seem to return to the healers seeking further treatment after a short period of recovery from their distress.

TRADITIONAL HEALER OF BADAMI, DISTRICT BIJAPUR

Here, due to short of space without going into the details of the healing process, author is interested to mention some bold confessions made by the healer.

Interestingly, soon after the healer completed the healing procedure of one of the female cases, who was brought by her mother for her unrecovered ill-health, he reported that by using the same technique he would make same client not to confess of being 'possessed' by the Spirit. Accordingly he induced the trance (possession) state in the client and he insisted upon telling client that she is not possessed by any evil spirit but she is her-own-self. Ultimately, the client accepted that she is so-and-so and not an evil spirit.

Special Confession by Healer

The healer expressed that whatever he is practicing is only the blind faith. The techniques used by the traditional healers are all superstitious and farce. He further opined that 'Mata and Maddu' (Magic and Black Magic) are also farce. Every healer plays some trick and makes people believe whatever he says as truth. Although he is not personally interested in practicing this type of treatment techniques, he is forced to continue this practice because people ask for this type of service, based on their religious beliefs and practices. As in the present case, many people come to him seeking his service to drive away the 'evil spirit' from sick persons, which is assumed by the people as the cause for all their sufferings. Thus, the circumstances in which he lives have made him to oblige his clientele and follow some of the healing techniques against his personal interests/ beliefs.

Common features found in the healing techniques used by the traditional healers:

Background of the Clientele Coming to the Traditional Healers

1. The individuals come with a history of uncured symptoms of physical ill health and or emotional problems over a period of time.
2. The clients consult the traditional healers, as they believe that evil spirit is the cause for their sufferings. Carstairs (1995), Hughes (1968) have made similar observations in their study.

The Environment and the Techniques Used by the Healers

Once clients arrive at the traditional healing centers they are totally under the influence and control of the atmosphere prevailing in these centers and they obey commands of the traditional healers.

New clients get exposed to the behaviour of other 'possessed cases' during their visit. Besides they believe that traditional healer has the power to cure (relieve) them from their sufferings. Carstairs (1995) has made the observation that "the villagers believe that the traditional healer knows about the causes for their suffering. They Surrender totally to the healer". Thus the clients are mentally prepared for the manifestation of expected 'possessed' behaviour among themselves.

Further such clients visit the traditional healer along with their significant family member/s, which gives an opportunity to be with the family during the healing process. Acherkncht (1959) writes that "the therapeutic achievement of psychogenetic movement do not necessarily depend upon real etiological knowledge of casual treatment. It is quite possible that the therapeutic successes are essentially due to the same two mechanism of confession and suggestion, which are so little understood and which had been used with such success by the folk medicine man".

Hollingshead et. Al. (1958) state that "the cultural and socio-economic factors influence the kind of therapy doctors prescribe and patients accept. The need for treatment is often affected by such non-medical factors as Local customs, ability to pay, availability of psychiatrist and local definition of mental illness".

The following lines highlight traditional healers' approach to tackle the problem/s of the clients, observed by the researcher during the study. The clientele forms people coming from different socio-economic strata-Rural and Urban, Rich and Poor, Educated as well as illiterate.

1. The healer makes the client to come closer to him (face to face).
2. The healer keeps with him certain of the tools (lemon, sacred ash, sacred thread, talisman, etc.), which are considered as the powerful tools to drive away the evil spirit from the client.
3. He would ask the client and also his/her accomplice regarding problem, the measures undertaken by them, which help the healer to have detailed history of the individual.
4. He uses various psychological techniques like clarification, interpretation, persuasion, compulsion, cajoling, commands, threats of punishment, etc. which lead to confession of being 'possessed' by concerned individual/client.

5. The confession thus made gives relief to people assembled there. The family is in a position of getting relief that they have been able to provide appropriate services to the client. The client is in a position to get relief from one's pent up emotions and on the other hand be satisfied that his/her behaviour is in confirmation with the expectation of the social environment. The healer is in a position to be satisfied that he has been able to fulfill the expectations of his clientele and maintain his status as a person having special powers to relieve the individuals from clutches of supernatural (evil spirits) powers.

Thus manifestation of possession and relief from possession takes place according to the social expectations, and acceptance of particular behaviour in a conducive social environment.

Description about the Shrines/holy centers and the Services available to 'Possessed' persons.

In this part details of the shrines visited to study nature of cases coming to the shrines, the treatment services and facilities available to the clients there in general and to the 'possessed' cases in particular are being highlighted.

Karibasajja Shrine, Ukkadagathri, District Chitradurga

This shrine is situated on the bank of river Tungabhadra in Ukkadagathri village in Chitradurga District. The village is about 35 kilometers from Ranebennur, a Taluka headquarter in erstwhile Dharwad District. It is almost bordering Dharwad and Chitradurga Districts. The shrine is said to be 3 to 4 centuries old. It is popular all over Karnataka and neighbouring states as a healing center for the possessed persons.

COMMON BELIEFS SHARED BY THE DEVOTEES AND THE PRIESTS OF THE SHRINE

The priest and devotees reported that the Holy Spirit of late 'Saint Karibasajja' is residing at this shrine. This shrine is said to be having the power of causing miracles and cure diseases of the individuals who are devotees of this Saint. By way of treatment method sick persons are given talisman to be tied around their arm, waist or neck. Sometimes they are also given few blessed lemons, which are to be consumed by sick persons. In case of possessed cases Sacred ash (Vibhuti) and lemons are given which maybe either applied on the body or consumed by the possessed as a means of getting relief from their pain.

INITIATION AND BEHAVIOUR OF THE CLIENTS DURING POSSESSION ATTACK

The possessed behaviour is invoked at the time of evening pooja, which takes places around 7 p.m. every night. During pooja, two huge musical drums are played on by the drummers, devotional songs are sung by the devotees and shrine-bells are rung continually for nearly half an hour. While Mahamangalarati (waving of lamps) is offered to the holy Saint (considered as God), the 'possessed' brought over there slowly start swinging their body to and fro, letting loose their hair, rolling on the ground, somersaulting, abusing the relatives or the 'God' himself, with intermittent laughs and weeping. Occasionally, and excitement would continue for about half an hour to one hour, by then the clients get exhausted, lie down on the floor becoming totally calm and quiet. After some time (5 to 10 minutes) they start talking as if nothing had happened to them.

Clients do not recall as to what had happened to them during the attack. But they do complain of body ache, pain in the limbs. The clients remain normal at all other times and do their routine work normally.

It was learnt that possession attack/s normally does not manifest in their homes but only one or two days after coming over to the shrine. Otherwise while at home, the client keeps on complaining periodically certain psycho-physiological symptoms–like, pulling sensation in legs, stomach ache, loss of appetite, weakness, food refusal, being dull, fainting spells, etc. Client's family tries to help the sick person to recover through the use of locally available resources, like home medicine, visiting doctors, magicians, etc. but when the person does not improve they are brought to holy shrines, to relieve the sick person's affliction by evil spirit/s, which is believed to be causing distress. Therefore, when the respondents were asked as to why the possession takes place only at the shrine and not at home, the reply given by them was that, 'Ajja' (Holy Saint) does not allow the adamant devil/evil spirit to reside in the client's body in his premises. Therefore, the possession manifests at the shrine.

INDICATORS OF RECOVERY FROM THE 'POSSESSION STATES'

Normally such clients spend minimum 5 to 7 New moon days at the shrine, before they are relieved of their 'possession sates'. They may either stay over there throughout or visit the Shrine for two or three days during every new moon days and go back to their respective places. The shrine has one Sacred Iron Box called 'Arapettige' with a big thick Iron Handle. The Handle was observed to be woven with human hair around it. The 'possessed' when 'pass (squeeze) through' this Iron Handle on the new moon days it is believed by the people that possessed spirit would surrender to Holy Spirit Karibasajja and would not disturb the 'possessed individual' in future. As a mark of having left the body of client, possessed spirit is required to remove a few hairs from her head and tie it around the Iron Handle of the Sacred Box. After this he/ she (client) comes out from the handle slowly. Once this process is over, client is considered to be cured from the possession state. After this, client and his/her family members together offer prayers and offer some gift in kind or cash to the God, whose grace is believed to have helped them to recover from 'possession episodes'. While returning to their native place they take an vow that they would be visiting the shrine on every new moon day or on the day of annual festival, as per their convenience, to offer prayers. If they do not keep up their vow, respondents are afraid: the same spirit would attack the client again.

Some of the clients were found to have taken refuge in the shrine from quite few months. They were either widowed or deserted and without having any sustainable means of livelihood. Unlike in their home, they found this Shrine to be providing them security, calm and free atmosphere. They go out for coolie in the morning hours to earn for their livelihood and in the night they manifest possession attacks, lest they would be dislodged from the shrine.

Jod Gomat Dargah

Jod Gomat Darga is in Bijapur–a District head quarters in Karnataka. It is situated in the heart of the city amply provided with vast lush green lawn around. It is said to be about four centuries old named after Abdul Razak–a Dharmaguru (religious priest) of Adil Shah II, the Sultan (King) of Bijapur during the 16th century.

THE RITUALS TO BE OBSERVED BY THE DEVOTEES

As soon as the sick persons come to this dargah she/he is required to offer Ziyarat (prayer) and then buy a sacred thread from the priest and tie 40 knots and then tie it to the tomb of the holy saint. Tieng knots signifies 'tieing up the God' until forty days by which time they are supposed to be free from the possession symptoms or any other problem for which the individual has been brought here for relief. If the individual's problem is not solved within forty days, it is believed that, the thread tied to the tomb is said to strangle the holy spirit (God) itself. Thus whatever may be the client's problem; it should be solved within 40 days. Therefore, the clients suspected to be possessed by the evil spirits are expected to get possessed on the forthcoming new moon day.

THE BEHAVIOUR OF THE POSSESSED

When an individual is brought to this dargah with an assumption that the evil spirit is the cause for individual's sufferings (ill-health), the individual is expected to manifest 'possessed' behaviour one day or the other. Although this is a Muslim religious place, both Hindus and the Muslims come to this place seeking healing services. The 'Spirit' possessing the individual is said to manifest itself on the new moon day. The individuals during possession start dancing, carrying big stone on their head. At this instance, the 'object' of possession and the reason for possessing the individual are being revealed by the client (Spirit). After that the client would remain normal and maintain her usual self, until the next attack, which may happen in the evening when many people are around for the evening Ziyarat.

INDICATORS OF RELIEF FROM 'POSSESSION STATES' AMONG THE INDIVIDUALS

As the client's 'object' of possession is revealed during one of the 'possession states', the client also starts attending to the Ziyarat along with devotees, which is observed every evening within the courtyard of the dargah. During one of such Ziyarat, the clients who have come for treatment of possession by evil spirit would develop possession by the 'Holy Spirit', which is considered as an indication of being warded off evil spirit's influence among these individuals. From that day onwards, such clients are expected to visit this dargah every Thursdays or on the new moon days and give 'Hazari' (attendance), during which the cases manifest 'possession by the holy spirit' and offer solution to the problems raised by the people around her. It was also reported by the respondents that unless they observe this practice the cases would have relapse of possession by the evil spirit and would start having manifestation of the previous problems (ill-health) in their life. Therefore, lot of ex-clients assemble on Thursdays and on new moon days to offer their 'Hazari' services at the dargah.

BEHAVIOUR OF THE CLIENTS DURING 'HAZARI'

Normally the clients come to the dargah along with their family and friends. When the client sits for giving her 'Hazari' to the holy spirit, she offers her ziyarat first, later she starts making big yawning and belching sound for two to three times. After this she covers her face with pallu of her sari (border of the sari) and starts swinging her head around. At this stage, the people around her (normally her accomplice) start asking her suggestions to their problems; the clients would answer in a monotonous tone as to what should be done by them to overcome their problems. Once the questioning is over, the client would remain silent for some time, and return to her normal condition without having any strange feeling about her experiences. Further, the client's claim no memory for their experiences during 'Hazari' state. With this experience every one is happy and go back home with lot of satisfaction and happiness to themselves.

Therefore, it could be said here that the 'Hazari' behaviour of clients seem to benefit both clients as well as their relatives in long run.

Srikshetra Shrine, Ganagapura, District Gulbarga

This shrine is situated on the bank of the river Bhima in Ganagapura village about 27 kilometers from Gulbarga city in North Karnataka. This shrine is named after a holy Saint by name Sriman Narasimha Saraswati who is said to have lived here about six centuries ago. Many people from Maharastra and Karnataka visit this place for their health and other problems. The sick and their family reside in the open premises of the shrine. All devotees are offered with Madukari (free meal) only once during afternoon. Madukari is the food served by ex-clients of the shrine, who by offering free meal to the devotees try to fulfill their owe to the holy spirit, for having overcome their problem by the blessings of holy spirit of his shrine.

MANIFESTATION AND TREATMENT OF THE 'POSSESSED' INDIVIDUALS

The priests of this shrine say that they are not involved in the treatment of possessed person. Such persons are brought by their relatives voluntarily, they stay here, develop possession episodes and later get relieved on their own and go back home. Every thing depends upon the faith and devotion and the miracle of Holy Spirit that cures the devotees of their crisis (the crises could physical illness, mental illness, or some socio-economic problems). People believe in the Saint's existence even today in that shrine in disguise. He is reported to be residing in the Paduke (wooden sandals) of the Saint, which are being worshipped everyday in the shrine. He showers his blessings in the form of miraculous cure to all those who worship him with full devotion and reverence.

THE RITUALS OBSERVED BY THE DEVOTEES

Once the clients are brought here they are expected to bathe 2 to 3 times (have holy dips) every day in the confluence of river, which is about 3 kilometers from the shrine and offer prayers at the shrine. The sick persons have to strictly walk down the distance from the confluence of river to the shrine every time. The other pilgrims may go to and come back from the confluence, hiring a Tanga (a horse drawn cart). Further the devotees have to take 'Madukari' served every afternoon in the premises of the shrine. The devotees are not supposed to cook their private food here. Otherwise they have to depend upon fruits and food available in the shops/inns. Clients and devotees who have accompanied them should attend all the three prayers (early morning, noon and night pooja) performed in this shrine.

MANIFESTATION OF THE 'POSSESSED' BEHAVIOUR

Possessed behaviour among the clients is being induced during the pooja time when simultaneously the beatings of the drums, ringing of bells and singing of devotional songs by the priests and devotees take place. Totally a different picture appears to be created at the shrine then. The palanquin is taken around the sanctum of the temple 3 times. At this stage the clients start behaving in peculiar ways–swinging of the body around, rolling on the ground, somersaulting and sometimes abusing the relatives too. Some of them even start climbing up on the steel rails (pillars) dance and hang upon them for a few minutes. The clients would remain in this state of excitement for about half an hour to one hour. After this they calm down, some of the clients go to sleep for few minutes, before the normal self sets in, whereas, many of them immediately return to their normal selves. Possessed persons do not claim any memory into their experiences.

It has been reported that the clients frequent the shrine at least on 4 to 5 new moon days or on every Thursday for getting relief from the evil spirits.

INDICATION FOR GETTING RELIEVED FROM THE 'POSSESSION EPISODES'

Once the cases have been brought to the shrine with an assumption that the possession by evil spirit is the cause for the individual's sufferings, it is very much expected that the individual would manifest 'possessed' behavior at any time. Further family believes that the individual is going to be cured 'exorcised' from the evil spirit because they believe that the 'holy spirit' would help individual to be relieved through his miracle. Thus after manifesting such 'possession' behaviour for about 4 to 5 times, the case/client is considered to be fit to be relieved by the possessing spirit in the near future. Thus the whole process comes to an end when the client nails a lime, to an old neem tree situated in the premises of shrine. Later the client and family return home with contentment and happiness.

COMMON FEATURE OBSERVED IN ALL THE HOLY CENTRES

It was found that people belonging to varied socio-economic background visit these holy centres in search of solution to their problems (Possession or otherwise) in life.

1. All the three holy centres are built after the name of deceased Saint.
2. These centres are atleast 3 to 4 centuries old. During those days there was no scientific medical service available to the people for their various health problems. Further there were no appropriate social welfare services available to meet their various socio-economic and emotional problems. Thus holy centers formed as the supporting institutions for people who were in distress.
3. Holy centers provide an informal, peaceful atmosphere, where the clients (who are mentally and socially disturbed) can stay over for some days, free of cost, which probably provide peace and tranquility to them and which may help them to go back, start their life again with new enthusiasm and vigour.

4. It was found that priests of these centres were not involved in the healing process of "possessed" individuals.
5. Although the manifestation of the recovery from the possession states' were attributed to the miracle of the holy Saint of the centres, it was clear to the author that the free and very informal atmosphere found in these centers were responsible for providing catharsis to the individuals as they could ventilate many of their suppressed emotions and conflicts during their 'possession states'. Kakar (1980) and Sekar (1984) also agree with the present finding, Kakar (1980) has made similar observations from his study made on 'possession' at the temple of Balaji in Mehandipur, Rajasthan. He has concluded "the patient and his family members visit these healing centers as a last resort, when all the local resources are exhausted. When they decide to visit the centre, there is active participation in the treatment process. Further, the atmosphere existing in these Centres strengthens their hopes of recovery". Therefore, it could be stated here that unless they were brought to these holy centers for healing their emotions would not have had any let out, which might have in turn led to development of various psychological or neurotic behaviour problems and maladjustment and unhappiness.
6. It could be clearly stated that the age old beliefs and practices still prevail and are commonly observed among the modern civilized societies even today, because of the ineffective and inadequate services provided to the sick and distressed individuals through the modern health and social welfare agencies. Shobha Devi & Bidarkoppa (1994) have made similar observations in their study, as they found that although over 75% of the respondents studied by them had expressed that modern services were available in their place of living, but a very high majority of them i.e., over 87% of these respondents had expressed that they were not satisfied with the services available to them in the hospitals. Further, an insignificant number of them, i.e. only 4.6% of the respondents had received some help from government agencies for their socio-economic problems.

CONCLUSION

It could be observed from the present study that people irrespective of their socio-economic background visit the traditional healers and holy centers for getting relief for their health and related problems in life.

Further it could be said here that although many people visit the traditional healing centers for help, yet they are not being helped by these centers, in getting complete relief from their distress, as it could be observed that the clients who have been treated by the traditional healers and/or holy centers are required to visit them even in their future life, otherwise, it was reported by the respondents that they would have manifestation of same symptoms again.

Finally it could be said that the common man is not getting proper services either from modern or from traditional health services in overcoming their problems in life. Hence it is right time for the professionals, policy makers and the administrators to think in the direction of providing more holistic health and developmental services to meet the needs of common people in distress in society. For instance, providing health education and counseling services at PHC levels, as well as at Gram Panchayat level, may help these needy people in getting relief from their distressing life situation. Integration of traditional healers in the health service sector may also help in providing better services to persons seeking help for various health problems in their life.

REFERENCES

Ackerknecht (1959), "A Short story of Psychiatry", Hagners Publishing Co., Inc., New York, p. 84.

Bidarakoppa G.S. & Marulasiddaiah (1979), "Role of Religious Institutions in the Promotion of Social Welfare", *The Journal of Karnataka University. Social Sciences*, 15, pp. 27-37.

Arstairs G.M. (1955), "Medicine and Faith in Rural Religion in Indian Society", in Paul B.D. (ed.) Health Culture and Community: Russel Sage Publications, N.Y., pp. 107-134.

Hoolingshed *et al.*, (1958), "Social Class and Mental Illness" John Wiley and Sons, Inc., New York.

Hughes C.C. (1968), "Medical Care; Ethno Medicine", *International Encyclopedia of the Social Sciences*, Vol. 10, pp. 87-93.

Ishwaran K.C. (1968), "Shivapur, A South Indian Village Routlege and Kegan Paul", London, pp. 91-100.

Jaggi O.P. (1973), "History of Science and Technology in India", Vol. III, Folk Medicine–Atmaram and Sons, Delhi-6.

Kakar. S. (1980), "The Myth of Faith Healing", In Print March, pp. 74-91.

Randhawa M.S. *et. al.*, (1961), "Farmers in India", Indian Council of Agriculture Research, New Delhi.

Sekar K. (1984), "Social Work Ingredients in Traditional Healing", Ph.D. Thesis, National Institute of Mental Health and Neuro Sciences, Bangalore, Karnataka.

Shobha Devi Y.J. and Bidarkoppa G.S., "Possession Phenomena: As a Coping Behaviour", in Graham Davidson (Ed.) Applying Psychology Lessons from Asia-Oceania, Australian Psychological Society Ltd., pp. 83-95.

PART–III

APPROACHES

15

ROLE OF SHIRISHA–*ALBIZIA LEBBECK* (LINN.) WILLD.) IN THE MANAGEMENT OF TAMAK SWASA (BRONCHIAL ASTHMA)

Ramji Singh, S.K. Singh, O.P. Singh, Shriprakash, K.K. Rai, R.K. Tiwari & Aruna Devi

INTRODUCTION

Albizzia lebbeck (Linn.) Willd. is an indigenous drug of the family of Mimosaeae commonly known as 'Shirisha'. This plant is distributed allover India upto 900 m in the Himalaya. This plant has been used in Indian Medicine from pre-historic time for treating the conditions caused by poisons or toxins and it is a drug of choice particularly indicated for snake's bite, scorpion sting and insects bite, (Chopra, 1956) Charaka, the eminent authority of Ayurveda described this drug as 'Shriste-Vishghananam' i.e. the drug to be antidotes for toxins or poisons and recommended its use for the treatment of Bronchial Asthma.

This is a large, deciduous tree; leaves bipinnate, leaflets 8-18, subsessile, obliquely elliptic–oblong or obovate–oblong; flowers greenish yellow in globose heads; pods strap-shaped, 10-30 cm long, yellowish brown and seeds 6-10, pale-brown in colour.

The bark is astringent, bitter, acrid, sweet, mild thermogenic, expectorant, aphrodisiac, anti-inflammatory, anodyne, cephalic, ophthalmic, depurative, restorative and tonic. Pharmacological studies show this is antiprotozoal, hypoglycaemic, abortifacient, antiasthamatic, antiallergic, analgesic, antifertility, antifungal, antiovulatory, antibacterial, hypotensive, CNS depressent and bronchodialator. Toxicological study shows the clinical as well as experimental studies indicated the absence of any serious toxicity.

One can simply draw an inference from the above indication that it is likely to have good anti-allergic and antihistaminic property. The allergy is one of the important etiological factor for the causation of bronchial asthma and the histamine or histamine like substance, elaborated in the body as a result of allergic manifestation are found likely to be pre-dominant in all above conditions i.e. snake-bite, insects bite, bronchial asthma, eczema, urticaria, chronic rhinitis etc.

Keeping above facts in view,a pilot clinical study has been carried out to assess the effect of *A. lebbeck* (Linn.) Willd. in the patients of Tamaka Swasa (Bronchial Asthma).

MATERIAL AND METHOD

Criteria for Selection or Exclusion of the Patients for the Study

A series of 300 cases of different age and sex group with the complaints of paraxysmal dyspncea, having prolonged expiration, bronchi, clinically diagnosed, a case of Tamak Swasa (Bronchial asthma) were selected for clinical trial. Majority of the cases except few acute cases, were kept on O.P.D. level trial. All the registered cases were kept on detailed clinical information on the proforma specially prepared for this purpose.

Patients of tropical eosinophilia, having absolute eosinophilic count above 2000/cumm, were not included in this series. Patients of cardiac asthama, spontaneous pneumothorax, massive collapse of lungs, renal asthma, acute and chronic bronchitis were also excluded from trial series.

Criteria for Establishment of Diagnosis

(a) *Clinical:* A characteristic clinical picture of paraxysmal attack of dyspnoea, with short inspiration followed by prolonged expiration and presence of ronchi in the chest (whistling sound) was sufficient enough to diagnose the case.

(b) Haematological examination includes total and differential count and E.S.R. Increased Polymorph and Lymphocytes may be suggestive for severity of the disease. There was increased polymorph in acute condition while in chronic inflammation condition of the disease there would be tendency of lymphocytosis. Increased eosinophilia count may be suggestive of allergic nature of the disease.

(c) X-ray chest though would not be an important diagnostic parameter but to exclude Bronchial asthma from other lungs diseases to find out the shape and size of the heart, it could not be overlooked. In Bronchial asthma cases dilated bronchial tubes were found in majority of the cases.

(d) Pulmonary function tests-Includes, forced vital capacity and forced expiratory volume in/second. This pulmonary function tests, the most important diagnostic criteria were carried out in majority of the cases.

(e) Biochemical criteria-Blood histamine, histaminase, catecholamines and serum cortisol, as important parameter were adopted only in few cases.

Criteria of Assessment of Response of Therapy

Alongwith the record of subjective improvement, regarding cough, parxysmal dyspnoea, general feeling of well being and improvement in spasm and rhonchi in the chest, a few objective parameters were also adopted to objectify the improvement e.g. expiratory rate, breath holding time, ventillatory functions (FVE and FEV). The objective tests were repeated at interval of 2-3 weeks.

Biochemical Parameters as Stated Above Were Repeated Before and After Treatment Overall Assessment of the Results

1. *Relieved:* Patients declared to be relieved who showed partially disappearance of all the clinical features of the diseases and the rending of the in nesting actions done for the assessment, came within normal range.
2. *Improved:* In those cases where clinical features did not disappear completely and the investigations done for assessment though improved to some extent but did not reach within the normal range, were taken as improved.
3. *Unchanged:* Those in whom, there was no improvement in signs and symptoms as well as in investigations done after treatment, or in other has condition become worse, were grouped as unchanged.

Dose, Schedule, Vehicle and Duration of Treatment

The bark decoction of *Albizia lebbeck* (Linn.) Willd., prepared on the line of method described and the dose prescribed 25 ml. in divided doses. Patients were subjected for clinical trial for the period of 2-5 weeks or even more.

OBSERVATIONS AND RESULTS

Before discussing the response of the treatment of the trial drug *Albezia lebbeck* (Linn.) Willd. in cases of Tamaka Swasa (Bronchial asthma) it was necessary to put the case for observation on different incidences or causation as well as for the provention of the disease.

Going through the seasonal incidences of our trial cases, the incidence of bronchial asthma was found to be high in Winter and Rainy seasons in an average of 88.30% i.e. more than two third of the cases were proved to suffer from this disease in this period.

Sex incidences in our reported cases showed that male and female both sexes would be more or less equally involved with this disease.

Table 1
Age Incidence of Bronchial Asthma Cases

Age group in years	*No. of cases*	*Percentage (%)*
Up to 10 yrs	01	00.33
11–20 yrs	60	20.00
21–40 yrs	140	46.67
41–60 yrs	80	26.67
61–above	19	6.33
Total	300	100

Table 2
Sex Incidence in Cases of Bronchial Asthma

Sex	*No. of cases*	*Percentage (%)*
Male	205	68.33
Female	95	31.67
Total		

Table 3
Occupation Incidence in Cases of Bronchial Asthma

Occupation	*No. of cases*	*Percentage (%)*
Students	40	13.33
Farmers	60	20.00
Servicemen	65	21.67
Businessmen	45	15.00
Housewives	90	30.00
Total	300	100

Occupational trends of our trial series showed that all the classes of people as farmers, servicemen, businessmen and housewives were found to be affective in this disease. Here the incidences were found to be more in housewives in 30% of cases.

Table 4
Area Wise Distribution of Bronchial Asthma Cases

Area	*No. of cases*	*Percentage (%)*
Rural	135	45.00
Urban	165	55.00
Total	300	100

In our study cases, people of urban area were found more affected than the rural area. It was just possible for the urban people due to nearer hospitality facility.

Table 5
Duration of Diseases in Cases of Bronchial Asthma

Duration of diseases in years	*No. of cases*	*Percentage (%)*
0–2 yrs	150	50.00
> 2–4 yrs	80	26.67
> 4–6 yrs	60	20.00
> 6–above	10	3.33
Total	300	100

Going through the duration of illness of our registered cases it was observed that near about 56% of the cases were having history of disease > 0 – 2 yrs the remaining 50% were of longer duration and 26.67% of cases up to 2 years duration.

Table 6
Sign and Symptoms of Bronchial Asthma Cases Before & After Treatment

Sign and symptoms	*Before treatment*		*After treatment*	
	No. of cases	*Percentage (%)*	*No. of cases*	*Percentage (%)*
Paraxysmal attack of Dyspnoea	300	100	76	25.33
Cough	300	100	85	28.33
Prolonged expiration	300	100	60	20.00
Rhonchi in the chest	260	86.67	60	20.00
Congestion in chest	276	92.00	70	23.33
External dyspnoea	160	53.33	50	16.67
Insomnia	125	41.67	40	13.33
Fever	45	15.00	10	3.33
Crepts	85	28.33	30	10.00
Weakness	60	20.00	25	8.33
Barrel chest	42	14.00	42	14.00
Pigeon chest	10	3.33	10	3.33
Frequent coryza	125	41.67	–	–
Headache	40	13.33	–	–

Table 7
Blood Investigation Before and After Treatment in Cases of Bronchial Asthma

Values	*Before treatment*	*After treatment*	*Difference between before & after treatment*
Mean	9500/Cu mm	7750/Cu mm	1750/Cu mm
S.D.	± 2362.20	± 864.11	± 12.41
S.E.	–	–	11.65
t	–	–	24.42
P	–	–	< 0.001

Table 8
Eosinophil Count Before and After Treatment in Cases of Bronchial Asthma

Values	*Before treatment*	*After treatment*	*Difference between before & after treatment*
Mean	5.71	2.5	3.21
S.D.	± 4.37	± 1.22	± 3.78
S.E.	–	–	0.218
t	–	–	14.72
P	–	–	< 0.001

Table 9
Erythrocyte Sedimentation Rate Before and After Treatment in Cases of Bronchial Asthma

Values	*Before treatment*	*After treatment*	*Difference between before & after treatment*
Mean	23.5	1.6	7.5
S.D.	± 20.83	± 15.75	± 7.09
S.E.	–	–	.
t	–	–	18.34
P	–	–	< 0.001

Table 10
Report of Radiological Examination of Chest in Cases of Bronchial Asthma (200 cases)

Level of blood sugar (Fasting)	*Results*	
	Negative	*Positive for emphysema*
200	110	90

Table 11
Biochemical Investigation: Whole blood Histamine, Plasma Histaminase, Total Catecholaminase and Cortisol Before and After Treatment in Cases of Bronchial Asthma (100 cases)

Name of investigation	*Before treatment*	*After treatment*	*Reduction*
Histamine	15.56	7.34	8.22
Plasma Histaminase	358	179	179
Plasma Catecholaminase	27.56	28.65	–1.09
Plasma Cortisol	29.85	34.35	–4.50

Table 12
Effect of the Treatment on Vital Capacity Before and After Treatment in Cases of Bronchial Asthma

Duration	*Mean ± S. D.*	*t*	*P*
Before treatment	1900 ± 394	–	–
After 2 weeks treatment	2250 ± 453	2.85	< 0.01
After 4 weeks treatment	2900 ± 229	4.85	< 0.001

Table 13
Effect of the Treatment on Respiratory Rate in Cases of Bronchial Asthma

Values	*Before treatment 1*	*After2 weeks treatment 2*	*Difference between 1-2*	*After 2 weeks treatment 3*	*Difference between 1-3*
Mean	28	25	3	20	8
S.D.	± 3.05	± 2.42	± 1.79	± 1.89	± 2.36
t	–	–	29.13	–	58.00
P	–	–	< 0.001	–	< 0.001

Table 14
Effect of the Treatment on Breath Holding Time in Cases of Bronchial Asthma

Values	*Before treatment 1*	*After 2 weeks treatment 2*	*Difference between 1-2*	*After 2 weeks treatment 3*	*Difference between 1-3*
Mean	18	24	6	28	10
S.D.	± 4.35	± 3.27	± 3.11	± 3.55	± 3.88
t	–	–	33.52	–	44.64
P	–	–	< 0.001	–	< 0.001

There is a significant change in breath holding time, after treatment of cases breath holding time increased.

The study of age incidence showed that no age bar was for bronchial asthma, though maximum number of cases recorded in this series were between 20-40 years of age where the percentage of cases were 46.66%. Family history of asthma was found in 25 per cent of cases. Sex incidences in our reported cases showed that male were more proved to suffer from this disease where the percentage of incidences was 68-33. Here in our trial series lower female class incidences would be due to inability of female class to come to the hospital either due to Parda system or due to the poverty otherwise, as textual report reveals both sexes would be more or less equally involved with this diseases.

In our studied cases, people of urban and rural areas were found to be more or less equally affected. 10% of the cases were more from the rural area. It was just possible for the urban people due to nearer hospitality facility. Going through the duration of illness of our registered cases it was observed that 50 per cent of the cases were having history of the disease for less than 2 years and the remaining were of longer duration.

Occupational trends of our trial series showed that all the classes of people as students, farmers, serviceman, businessman and housewives were found to affected with this disease. Here the incidences were found to be more in housewives in 30 per cent of cases. It would be probably due to their constant exposure to smoke in kitchen.

More predominant and pronouncing signs and symptoms observed here in our cases were paraxysmal dyspnoea, cough, and prolonged expiration in 100 per cent of cases and Bronchial in 85 per cent of cases.

The haematological observation in this series revealed that the total leucocyte count was within normal range in 80 per cent of cases and remaining in 20 per cent it was on higher side probably due to secondary infection. Polymorph count was raised in 35 per cent of cases, Lymphocytes was raised in 28 per cent of cases and eosinophil count was found to be higher in 52 per cent of cases. Rise of Polymorph and Lymphocytes respectively indicate acute and chromic inflammation and rise of eosinophilic count was the indication of Allergic origin of the disease. E.S.R. was found upper level in 50 per cent of cases only.

The most importanat observation was the estimation of blood histamine, histaminese, catecholamine and plasma cortisol. Though, these imvestigations were donein limited 20 cases only but observation given important information. The histamine was found to be enormously raised. In our series it was noted to be 15.36 ± 9.23 ug/100 ml of blood which was almost double as per normal level. Histaminase, the enzyme responsible for destruction of histamine was found to be raised in diseased condition i.e. 356 ± 143.53, whereas normally reported was 112.35 ± 39.95 PU/ml. This was because of nature's attempt to counteract the histamine.

Similarly catecholamine and plasma cortisol were also found to be raised in cases of bronchial asthma. Here as per our observation they were relatively 26.68 ± 8.20 and 29.79 ± 10.2 ug/100 ml of blood. It appeared that they were raised as defence body machanism to counteract the etiopathological process in asthmatics, and with the failure of this mechanism the disease process persipitate.

General Effect of Treatment

After two-four week of treatment quick response was found in dyspnoea and cough in total 300 treated cases. 50 per cent of cases were found to be completely relieved from dyspnoea after 4 weeks of treatment out of which 45 per cent showed complete recovery even after 2 weeks of treatment. A little less about 40 per cent cases showed complete recovery from cough after 4 weeks of treatment and 30 per cent after 2 weeks of treatment. Bronchi was present in third of the total treated cases.

For the assessment of the result patients were classified as severe, moderate and mild, depending upon the severity of the symptoms. It was obvious with the perusal of the result that patients who were initially in severe group returns to normal and mild group after 4 weeks of treatment.

The respiratory rate and breath holding time, the important objective parameters were done before and after different duration of treatment and significant decrease in respiratory rate and increase in breath holding time both, after 2 and 4 weeks of treatment were found. In our treated series, the maximum respiratory rate was 28 per minute before treatment, which returned to 25 and 2 per minute respectively after 2 and 4 weeks of treatment. Similarly the mean value of breath holding time, which was 18 per second, went on increasing to 24 and 28 per second after 2 and 4 weeks of treatment. Improvement in breath holding time denotes improvement in functional capacity of lungs and the reduction in respiratory rate was the indication of symptematological improvement of the patients.

Effect of Treatment on Pulmonary Function Tests

The vital capacity and forced expiratory volume were have their vital importance to evaluate the changes in pulmonary function were adopted before and after different duration of treatment in 200 cases only.

The mean vital capacity of our cases before treatment was 1900 c.c. which came upto 2200 c.c. and 2900 c.c. in 1 second after 2 and 4 weeks of treatment. Similarly the mean of forced expiratory volume was measured to be 1255 c.c. initially which came upto 1425 and 1550 c.c. in one second. This trend response of therapy in vital capacity and forced expiratory volume is indicative of no spasm and clear air passage of the lungs.

Effect on Treatment on Histamine, Histaminase, Catecholamine and Plasma Cortisol

As per our observation there was raised tendency of histamine and histaminase and plasma cortisol in diseased cases. After treatment there were notable reduction in the mean average value of histamine, histaminase ± 07.26 and 178. The plasma cortisol showed resing tendency in mean average value upto 33.70. Catecholamine remain unchanged. Raised plasma cortisol after treatment was indication of adrenergic effect of *Albizia lebbeck* (Linn.) Willd. to stimulate the adrenal cortex to secrets plasma cortisol to provides a defence mechanism against the diseased process by exerting antiallergic, antihistaminic and anti-inflammation property.

Group	*No. of Patients*	*Result in %*
Relieved	140	46.66
Improved	115	38.33
Unchanged	45	15.00
	300	

OVERALL ASSESSMENT OF THE RESULT

Overall assessment of the results observed in treated cases with *Albizia lebbeck* (Linn.) Willd. showed response within four weeks of treatment. Complete relief was observed in 46.66 per cent, marked improvement in 38.33 and no improvement in 15 per cent of cases.

REFERENCES

Alberg H., Johanson H. and Werner I. (1972), Hyperthyroidism in Ashma. Lancet, 2, p. 381.

Augustin (1973), Immunology of Respiratory Tract, in Recent Advances in Medicine by Margaret, Turner Warwick.

Branszky L. (1959), Endocrinological Influences in the Modern Treatment of Asthma. 2nd Ed. Bristol, John Wright & Sons, Ltd.

Bernstein R.A., Liairelli L., Facktor M.A. (1972), Decreased Urinary Adenosine 3′ 5′ Monophosphate (Cyclic AMP) in Asthamatics. *Jour. Lab. Clinical Med.* 80, p. 772.

Blumenthol M.N., Mclean J., Mathews K., Sheldon J., Minneapolis Minn & Ann. Arbar (1965), *American Academy of Allergy,* Vol. 36, No. 2, *Jour. Allergy,* March-April.

Boyd W. (1970), A Text book of Pathology, 8th Ed., Lea and

Fabiger, Philadelphia.

Broket Hurst W.E. (1962), Slow Reacting Substance and Related Compounds. Progr. Allergy 6, p. 539.

Cabezas G.A., Graf P.D. & Nadel J.A. (1976), Sympathetic Versus Para Sympathetic Regulation of Airways in Dogs, *Jour. Appl. Physiol.* 31, p. 651.

Cecil and Loeb (1971), Text Book of Medicine, W.B. Saunders Co. and Igaku Shoin Ltd. London & Tokyo.

Citron K.M. & Pepys J. (1964), An investigation of Asthma Among the Tristan Da Cunha Icelanders. Brit. *Jour. Dis. Chest.* LVIII: 3.

Cookson D.V. & Reed C.E. (1963), Acomparision of the Effects on Isoproterenol in the Normal and Asthmatic Subject.

Criep L.H. (1931), The Effect of Bronchial Asthma on Heart. *Jour. Allergy* 2, p. 386.

Davidson (1974), Davidson's Principles and Practice of Medicine. 6th Ed., B.S. Edu.

Dunbar H.F. (1938), Psychosomatic Notes Relating to Syndromes of Asthma and Hayfever. Psychosomat. Quart., 7, p. 25.

Fein B.T. & Kamin P.B. (1965), The Climatic Factors in the Aetiology of Allergic Diseases. *Jour. Asthma Res.*, 3, p. 17.

Fergusson G.C. (1973), Alpha-1-Antitrypsin Deficiency and Intrinsic Asthma. Brit., *Jour. Dis. Chest.* 67, p. 71.

Fischel E.E. (1965), The Antigen-Antibody Reaction. *The Med. Clin. of North America.* Vol. 49, No. 6, Nov.

Grieco M.C. (1970), Current Concepts of the Pathogenesis and Management of Asthma. Bull. N.Y. Acad. Med., 46, p. 597.

Grieco M.C. & Pierson R. (1971), Mechnism of Broncho-Constriction Due to Beta Adrenergic Blochade. *Jour. Allergy Clin. Immunol.* 48: p. 143.

Hoene R., Coutu L., Horava A., Procopio P. Robert A. & Salgado E. (1952), Influence of ACTH on Anaphylactic Shock in Guinea Pigs. *Jour. Allergy.* 23, p. 343.

Holler (1959), Endocrinological Influenced in the Modern

Treatment of Asthma. 2nd Ed. Bristol, John Wright & Sons Ltd. (Cited by Banszky, 1955).

Howel J.B.L. (1971), Asthma–A Clinical Review. "Identification of Asthma". Ciba Foundation Study Group No. 38, Chuchill Livingstone, Edinburgh and London.

Humphrey J.H. (1951), The Effect of Cortisone Upon Some Experimental Hypersensitivity Reactions. Brit. *Jour. Exp. Path.,* 32, p. 274.

Ingmar M. & Helge C. (1965), The Intestinal Flora in Patients of Asthma and Rheumatic Arthritis. Acta. Allergologica. XX F.A.S.C. 2.

Ishizaka K. & Ishizaka T. (1967a), Catheterization of Human Reaginic Antibodies. Proceedings of the Sixth Congress of International Association of Allergy. Montreal. Nov., pp. 5-11.

Ishizaka K. & Ishizaka T. (1967b), Identification of the Antibodies as a Carrier of Reaginic Activity. *Jour. Immun.* 99, p. 1187.

Jones R.S., Wharton M.S. & Buston M.H. (1963), The Place of Physical Exercise and Bronchodialator Drugs in the Assessment of Asthmatic Child. Archs. Dis. Childh. 38, pp. 539.

Kagan S.G. & Weiss J.H. (1976), Allergic Potential and Emotional Precipitants of Asthma in Children. *Jour. Psychosom. Research.* Vol. 20, pp. 135-139.

Kirk Patrick C.H. & Keller C. (1967), Impaired Responsiveness to Epinephrine in Asthma. Amer. Rev. Resp. Dis. 96, p. 692.

Leigh D. & Manley (1963), Sellors in Chest Diseases. (In1956 cited by Perry and Holmes) 2, p. 476.

Lichenstein L.M.& Osler A.G. (1973), Cited by Jordan N. *et al.*: Thetrapy of bronchial Asthma. Med. Clin. North America. 57, 3, March.

Lockey S.D., Glennon J.A. & (1967), Comparison of Some Metabolic Responses in Normal and Asthmatic Subjects to Epinephrine and Glucagon. *Jour. Allergy.* 40, p. 349.

Makino S., Quellette J. & Reed C. (1970), Correlation Between Increased Bronchial Response to Acetylcholine and Admonished.

Metabolic and Eosinopenbic Response to Epinephrine in Asthma. *Jour. Allergy.* 46, p. 178.

Middleton E. Jr. & Finke S.R. (1959), Histmine and 5 Hydroxytryptamine in the Blood of Infants and Children. *Jour. Clin. Invest.* 38, pp. 595-604.

Parker C.D., Bilbo R.E. & Reed C.E. (1965), Methacholine Aerosol as a Test for Bronchial Asthma.

Price (1973), Price's Text Book of Practice of Medicine. E.L.B.S., 11th Ed.

Prigar S.J. (1960), Fundamentals of Modern Allergy. Mc. Graw Hill, p. 81.

Rackemann (1963), Classification of Asthma in Chest Diseases by Perry & Holmes Sellors, 2.

Reed C.E., Cohen M. & Enta T. (1970), Reduced Effect of Epinephrine on Circulating Eosinophils in Asthma and After Beta-Adrenergic Blockade or Bordetella Partussis Vaccine in Rats. *Jour. Allergy.* 46, p.90.

Robins S.L. (1974), Pathologic Basis of Disease. W.B. Saunders Co., London.

Schild H.G., Hawkins D.F. & Monger J.L. (1951), Reaction of Isolated Human Asthmatic Lung and Bronchial Tissue to Specific Antigen. Lancet 2, p. 376.

Serafini U. (1967), Studies on Histamine and Histamine Antagonists. Jorn. Allergy. 19, pp. 221-227.

Sharma P.C., Yelne M.B. Dennis (2000), Database of Medicinal Plant Used in Ayurveda. CCRAS, Deptt. of Ayush, Ministry of Health & F.W., Govt. of India, New Delhi, Vol. 1, pp. 445-453.

Szentivanyi A. & Szeckely J. (1974), Anaphylaxis and Nervous System. Part IV, Ann. Allergy. 16, pp. 389.

Thomas F., Dolan J.R. & Alan Meyers (1974), Bronchial Asthma and Allergic Rhinitis Associated With Inhalation of Pancreatic Extract. Amer. Rev. Resp. Dis., Vol. 112, Dec.

Tinkelman D.G., Michael J.C. & Cooper D.M. (1976), Inhibition of Exercise Induced Bronchospasm by Atropine. Amer. Rev. Resp. Dis., Vol. 114, No. 1.

Tiwari S.K. (1975), Bronchial Asthma. Ph.D. Trhesis, B.H.U., Varanasi.

Weiss J.H., Lyness J., Molk, & Riby (1976), Induced Respiratory Change in Asthmatic Leizer Children. *Jour. Psychosom. Research*. Vol. 2 (2), pp. 115-123.

Willis R.A. (1961), The Principles of Pathology. 2nd Ed., Butterworth & Co. Ltd.

Wittkower E. (1935), Studies on the Influence of Emotions on the Functions of Organs. *Jour. Ment. Sci.* 81, p. 533.

16

"CLINICAL TRIAL ON GUDUCHI CHITRAKA YOGA IN THE MANAGEMENT OF MADHUMEHA (*DIABETES MELLITUS*)"

Ramji Singh, S.K. Singh, Shriprakash, R.K. Tiwari & Aruna Devi

INTRODUCTION

Madhumeha (*Diabetes mellitus*) has been the medical problem since the ancient period. Many formulation are described in our Ayurvedic texts, which have been proved effective on even modern scientific parameters. In present era due to sedentary lifestyle and use of fast foods in the society, the problem has been increasing day by day. In Ayurvedic literature the reasoning factor of Madhumeha is given i.e.

"Asya sukhama Swapna sukhama Dadhini,
Gramyodakam uparasa prayasi |
Nawanna Panama Guna vaikritama Cha,
Prameha Hetu Kapha Kritta Sarvama | |

As shown above causative factors of Madhumeha the impact of modern civilization has absolutely changed our lifestyle. Most of people are forced to live mechanical life. As result physical activities of human being are considerably decreased. Ayurvedic text have described clearly mentioned that this disease is caused by genetic predisposition, eating high caloric diet, high carbohydrate diet and having sedentary habits.

The importance Ayurvedic drugs used in the management of *Diabetes* is also being recognized world over. This is more so because Ayurvedic drugs have no serious side effect. The drugs which have anti–hyperglycaemic action useful in the Madhumeha. In this context on ghanasatva of an Ayurvedic preparation comprising of Guduchi (*Tinospora cordifolia* Miers) and Chitraka (*Plumbago zeylanica* Linn) were put under trial on 36 cases at a dose of 500 mg thrice daily for 3 months. The result was encouraging both in reducing elevated blood sugar level as well as improvement in clinical signs and symptoms.

Guduchi-*Tinospora Cordifolia* Miers

Glabrous twinners, stem terete and sparcely lenticellate is distributed throughout, extending from the Himalayas down to southern part of Peninsular India.

Tinospora cordifolia Miers (Guduchi) stem is abundantly used in Ayurvedic system of medicine for its excellent efficacy in various urinary complications according to various authors of Ayurvedic Materia Medica. It is used as anti-diabetic, diuretic, antipyretic, antispasmodic, and stomachic. It is also used in chronic diarrhoea, dysentery, dyspepsia, fever, gonorrhoea, and in general debility. Rama Rao reported that boiled aqueous extract is used for leprosy.

Scientifically the alcoholic extract of the stem of *T. cordifolia* Miers. Shows some remarkable activity against *E. coli.* Gupta and Vishwanath have been reported that it contains some anti-tubercular substance which inhibits the growth of antibacterium tuberculosis (invitro). Gupta *et al.*, have been found reduction in the fasting blood sugar after the oral administration of the plant extract. They have been suggested the action of the drug due to its favourable effect of the endogenous insulin secretion. Broker and Bhatta reported that aqueous extract of the stem has a high phagocytic index.

Chitraka (*Plumbago Zeylanica* Linn)

Plant is distributed throughout the tropics and subtropics in India in wild and cultivated conditions.

This plant is branched under shrub; roots long, tuberous; stem striate; leaves simple, alternate, short–petioled, acute with entire or wavy margin, glabrous; flowers white in terminal spikes.

The therapeutic efficacy of root of Chitraka-(*Plumbago zeylanica* Linn) was also described by various Ayurvedic Physisians and which is stimulant, appetizer and antiphlegestic. It was also reported that the drug used in diarrhoea, dyspepsia, rheumatism, leprosy, paralysis and also useful in apses to promote suppuration. Brookil stated that the root shows abortificiant, activity due to its vesicant property. According to scientific report that the alcoholic and aqueous extract of the root showed anti-bacterial activity againt *Micrococcus pyogens* var. *aureus* common *Solminella typhi* and *Myobacterial phlei*.

In the present study the clinical trials on the aqueous extract of *Tinospora cordifolia* Miers and *Plumbago zeylanica* Linn. (in 1:1 ratio) in capsule form undertaken in acute and chronic Prameha (*Diabetes*) patients.

MATERIALS AND METHODS

Criteria for Selection or Exclusion of the Patients for the Study

A series of 36 cases of different age and sex group with complaints of Prabhut Mutral (polyurea), Atipipasa (polydispsea), Adhiksudha (polyphagia) were selected for clinical trial. Majority of the cases were kept on O.P.D. level trial. All the registered cases were kept on detailed clinical information on the proforma specially prepared for this purpose.

Especially Insulin dependent patients were not included in this trial series.

Criteria for Establishment of Diagnosis

Clinical

A characteristic clinical picture of Prabhut Mutrala, Atipipasa and presence Adhik-kshudha was sufficient enough to diagnose the case.

Urine Routrine & Microscopy Examination

Increased sugar level in urine may be suggestive of Madhumeha disease.

Biochemical Criteria

This includes fasting blood sugar and P.P. Increased blood sugar level was sufficient conformity diagnosis of the case.

Criteria of Assessment of Response of Therapy

Along with the record of subjective improvement, regarding cardinal symptoms of Madhumeha (*Diabetes mellitus*) observed maximum reducing the symptoms and general feeling of well being improved.

In urine examination Routine and microscopic observed the reduction of sugar percentage in urine. Average satisfactory reduction observed in urine sugar.

Biochemical parameters as stated above were repeated before and after treatment overall assessment of the results:

Good Response

Patients declared to be who showed disappearance cardinal symptoms of Madhumeha along with blood sugar level became normal or nearer to normal range.

Fair Response

In those cases where clinical features did not disappear completely and the investigation done for assessment through improved to some extent but did not reach within the normal range, were taken as fair response.

Poor Response

Those in whom, there was some improvement in cardinal symptoms of Madhumeha along with slight changes in urine sugar percentage and blood sugar level included in poor response group.

OBSERVATION AND RESULTS

Before discussing the response of treatment of trial drug "Guduchi Chitraka Yoga" capsule in cases of Madhumeha. It was necessary to put the case for observation on different incidences.

The study of age incidence showed that no age bar was for Madhumeha though maximum number of cases recorded in this series were between 41-60 years of age where the percentage of cases were69.44%. In trial series of Madhumeha family history of Madhumeha was found in 5.56% of cases, means out of 36 cases 2 were hereditary cases between the age group of 41-50.

General observations of the administration of Guduchi-Chitraka Yoga capsule in different cases are given below:

Primary stages of *Diabetes mellitus* (Acute cases) cases showed encouraging effects in reducing all the diabetic symptoms gradually. Regular administration of drug was found to be effective in reducing Atipipasa (polydipsia), Prabhut Mutrala (polyurea) and Adhik kshudha (polyphagia).

In this study we have observed satisfactory response in the following types of cases also i.e.

1. In chronic diabetic patients
2. Diabetes with other complications (Carbuncle and Prameha Pidika)
3. Old and debilitated cases

Regular administration of Guduchi-Chitraka Yoga capsule was also effective in reducing the urine sugar percentage and blood sugar percentage (fasting blood sugar). But in hereditary cases primary failure was noted in the patients who were addicted to Insuline therapy or modern oral anti–diabetic drugs from a longer period. But in later stages (1½ month after) satisfactory response observed in these types of cases also. In this trial also observed that patients who did not rigidly follow the diet and physical exercise (Hit Ahar Vihar) had not shown any remarkable response to drug or delayed response noticed in same cases.

Table 1
Age Incidence of Madhumeha (*Diabetes Mellitus*)

Age group in years	*No. of cases*	*Percentage (%)*
20-30	01	2.78
31-40	02	5.56
41-50	13	36.11
51-60	12	33.33
61-70	06	16.66
71-above	02	5.56
Total	36	100

Table 2
Sex Incidence in Cases of Madhumeha (*Diabetes Mellitus*)

Sex	*No. of cases*	*Percentage (%)*
Male	18	50
Female	18	50
Total	36	100

Sex incidences in our reported cases showed that male and female both sexes would be more or less equally involved with this diseases.

Table 3
Occupation Incidence in Cases of Madhumeha (*Diabetes Mellitus*)

Occupation	*No. of cases*	*Percentage (%)*
Students	–	–
Farmers	03	8.33
Servicemen	08	22.23
Businessmen	07	19.44
Housewives	18	50.00
Total	36	100

Occupational trends of our trial series showed that all the classes of people as farmers, servicemen, businessmen and house wives were found to be affected with this disease. Here the incidences were found to be more in housewives in 50% of cases.

In our studied cases, people of urban area were found more affected than the rural area. It was just possible for the urban people due to nearer hospitality facility.

Table 4
Area Wise Distribution of Madhumeha (*Diabetes Mellitus*)

Area	*No. of cases*	*Percentage (%)*
Rural	05	13.89
Urban	31	86.11
Total	36	100

Going through the duration of illness of our registered cases it was observed that near about 56% of the cases were having history of disease > 1–3 yrs the remaining 25% were of longer duration and 19.44% of cases upto 1 year duration.

Table 5
Duration of Diseases in Cases of Madhumeha (*Diabetes Mellitus*)

Duration of Diseases in years	*No. of cases*	*Percentage (%)*
0-1	07	19.44
> 1-2	08	22.23
> 2-3	12	33.33
> 3-above	09	25.00
Total	36	100

Table 6
Sign and Symptoms of Madhumeha (*Diabetes Mellitus*) Cases

Sign and symptoms	*No. of cases*	*Percentage (%)*
Prabhuta mutrala (Poly urea)	36	100.00
Atipipasa (Polydipsia)	34	94.44
Adhik kshudha (Polyphagia)	35	97.22

More predominant and pronouncing signs and symptoms observed here in our cases were Prabhut mutral (polyuria) in 100 % cases, Atipipasa (polydipsia) in 94.44% of cases and Adhikshudha (polyphagia) in 97.22% of cases.

In the present series of trial after administration of Guduchi Chitraka Yoga capsule in 36 patients from a perusal of the table, we may find that the clinical trial of the yoga has considerable effect in reducing the three cardinal symptoms of Madhumeha (*Diabetes mellitus*) as shown in Table 7.

Table 7
Effect of the Capsule Guduchi Chitraka Yoga in Reducing the Three Cardinal Symptoms of Madhumeha (*Diabetes Mellitus*) Cases

Cardinal symptoms	*Before treatment*		*After treatment*	
	No. of cases	*(%)*	*No. of cases*	*(%)*
Prabhuta mutrala (Poly urea)	36	100.00	10	27.78
Atipipasa (Polydipsia)	34	94.44	08	22.22
Adhik kshudha (Polyphagia)	35	97.22	06	16.67

Table 8
Effect of the Capsule Guduchi Chitraka Yoga on Urine Sugar Level in Madhumeha (*Diabetes Mellitus*) Cases

Level of urine sugar (Fasting)	*Before treatment*		*After treatment*	
	No. of cases	*(%)*	*No. of cases*	*(%)*
0-Nil	–	–	21	58.33
0.5-1.0 gm % (+)	08	22.23	11	30.56
>1.0-1.5 gm % (++)	12	33.33	04	11.11
>1.5-2.0 gm % (+++)	12	33.33	–	–
>2.0-Above % (++++)	04	11.11	–	–
Total	36	100	36	100

$\gamma^2 = 35.39$ $p < 0.001$ HS.
Chi – square test.

Table 9
Effect of the Capsule Guduchi Chitraka Yoga on Blood Sugar Level in Madhumeha (*Diabetes Mellitus*) Cases

Level of blood sugar (Fasting)	*Before treatment*		*After treatment*	
	No. of cases	*(%)*	*No. of cases*	*(%)*
80-Normal level	–	–	18	50.00
121-200 gm %	16	44.44	17	47.22
201-300 gm %	10	27.78	01	2.78
301-Above	10	27.78	–	–
Total	36	100	36	100

$\gamma^2 = 35.39$ $p < 0.001$

DISCUSSION

From the clinical trial carried, it was found that Guduchi-Chitraka Yoga capsule is effective in reducing the blood and urine sugar. This may be due to the exhaustion of the β–cells of Langerhans undergoing continued stimulation during prolong treatment with drug. However, the effectiveness of the drug is related to the various factors like Kala, Vayasatmya and Asatmya. Hereditary cases also studies with Guduch–Chitraka Yoga capsule and found temporary relief. Primary failure was noted in the patients who were addicted to Insulin therapy or modern oral anti–diabetic drugs from a longer period. This drug also proved in effective on those who inherited diabetes character and also on chronic and debilited patients.

CONCLUSION

It is concluded that the Guduch–Chitraka Yoga capsule shows very encouraging results in diabetic patients. It also caused in reduction of the urine out put (Mutra). The regular administration of the drug with Hit Ahar Vihar and physical exercises help in gradually reducing the percentage of urine sugar and fasting blood sugar in patients.

REFERENCES

Atkinson (1956), *Aust. J. Exp. Biol. Med. Sci.*, 34 (1), p. 17.

Bhatia B.B. & Lal, S. (1933), *Ind. Jour. Med. Res.*, (3), p. 777.

Broker Rajul & Bhatt J.V. (1953), *Ind. Jour. Pharmaco.*, 15, p. 309.

Burkill I.H. (1935), A Dictionary of the Economic Products of the Malay Peninsula, Vol. II, p. 1775.

Chopra R.N., Chopra I.C., Handa K.L. & Kapur L.D. (1958), Indigenous Drugs of India (2nd Ed.) U.N. Dhar & Co. Pvt. Ltd., Calcutta, p. 427.

Gupta K.C. & Vishwanathan, R. (1956), Anti–Biotics & Chemotherapy, 6, p. 194.

Chunekar K.C. (1960), Bhavaprakasha Nighantu. (Ist Ed.) Choukhambha Vidya Bhawan, Varanasi, pp. 188-228.

George *et. al.*, (1947), *Jour. Sci. Industr. Res.*, 68, p. 42.

Gupta S.S., Verma S.C. L., Garg V. P. & Mahesh R. (1967), Ind. *Jour. Med. Res.*, 35 (7), p. 733.

Gupta S.S., Verma S. C. L., Garg V. P. & Khandelwal P. (1965), Ind. *Jour. Physiol. & Pharmaco.*, 9, p. 9.

Gupta S.S., Verma S.C.L., Garg V. P. & Mahesh R. (1967B), *Ind. Jour. Physiol. & Pharmaco.* 1, p. 10.

Jaidev, V. (1966), Charaka–Samhita. Motilal Banarasi Das, Varanasi, Vol. I, p. 36.

Kirtikar K.R. & Basu B.D. (1975), Indian Medicinal Plants (2nd Ed.) Bishen Singh Mahendra Pal Singh, Dehra Dun, Vol. I, p. 79.

Koman M.C. (1918), Report on the Investigation of Indigenous Drugd, Govt. Press, Madras, pp. 16-28.

Kurup P.A. (1956), *Jour. Sci. Industr. Res.*, 15C, p. 153.

Rao Rama (1014), Flowering Plants of Travancore, Govt. Press, Trivendrum, p. 11.

Sharma P.V. (1975), Dravya Guna Vigyana, (3rd Ed.), Choukhambha Sanskrit Santhan, Varanasi, Vol. II, pp. 343-681.

Singh R.S. (1969), Vanoushadhi–Nidarshika (1st Ed.) Hindi Samiti Suchana Vibhag, Lucknow, Vol. I, pp. 126-141.

Watt J.M. & Breyer Brandwijk M.G. (1962), The Medicinal and Poisonous Plants of Southern and Eastern Africa, 2nd Ed., (E & S Livingstone Ltd., Edinburgh).

17

COPING STRESS: THE MANTRA OF SUCCESS

Anjali Ganesh & G.R. Krishanamoorthy

INTRODUCTION

Stress has become an important buzzword in the present day context because of its genuine and justifiable persistence in various walks of life. Work pressures, tight schedules, unacceptable peers, critical bosses, inefficient subordinates coupled with host of other irritants have a cumulative effect in making the life of an executive miserable and stressful. However, perception of events creates different reactions physically and psychologically activates stress. It is therefore highly individualistic in nature. So what is stressful situation to one may be a pleasant situation for another. In the words of John et. al., (1987), it is certainly wrong to conclude that stress is always bad. There is also a positive, pleasant side of stress caused by good things, which is called as 'Eustress[1]'. Another form of stress namely 'distress' is unhealthy for the individual and the organization as it leads to performance and other behavioural problems.

In fact, there is growing evidence that undue stress is related to disease that are major causes of heart diseases, hypertension, diabetes, cancer, stroke, suicidal tendencies and death. Therefore, it has become a topic of interest to medical professionals, social scientists, psychologists, business executives and even academicians. It is a known fact that the call centre industry is the one which has a maximum attrition rate compared to other service industries. Certainly the call centre industry promises to become a big white-collar labour intensive business. Though the pay and perks are lucrative, they definitely come at a stiff price. Peculiar working hours with shifts, showing artificial politeness to demanding and abusive customers, constant alertness, continuous use of voice, computers and telephones do not suit for the physique of the ordinary individuals. Those, whose body clock does not adjust to this routine, complain of insomnia, anorexia, nausea, stomach upset, and body ache. While peers and friends from other professions work during the day, call centre employees are obliged to do the reverse; social life of these professionals also takes a heavy toll. The pressure and demands of the job are so high that more than 70 per cent of the people over there feel stressed.

So, keeping this viewpoint, a micro study was undertaken in one of the call centres to understand the aspects of stress on those employees. This paper tries to highlight the causes of stress and coping strategies for stress.

OBJECTIVES

- To understand the dynamics of stress and factors responsible for generating high stress.
- To identify the impact of high stress on people's behaviour.
- To understand stress at workplace.
- To understand stress coping and stress management effectively.

SCOPE AND METHODOLOGY

For the purpose of this study, 'Manipal Informatics', a separate division of Manipal Press Ltd., which started its service on 1st April 2002 in Manipal, Udupi district, registered under Software Technology Parks of India, was selected. And 300 agents who have worked here for more than 6 months were selected and data was collected through predesigned questionnaire and interviews and later was tabulated and interpreted.

CAUSES OF STRESS (CONCEPTUAL STUDY)

Understanding the causes of stress, namely stressors enable us to tune our life to stress coping strategies.

Emotional Disturbances

Emotions are responsible for all the pleasures and the sufferings of life. Chopra and Sharma (2001), in their study mention that, emotional stress factors include fears and anxieties with which we struggle. Worrying unnecessarily about undone task or future uncertainties also trigger emotional stress factors.

Extra-Organizational Stressors, Organizational Stressors, Group Stressors and Individual Stressors

Extra-organizational stressors include things such as societal/ technological change, economic and financial conditions, family relocations and the like (John and Michael, 1980). As per John and Ganster (1993), organizational stressors like change in administrative policies, strategies, organizational structures, organizational processes and working conditions and such chronic occupational demands can lead to stress. Luthans (1998) expressed that, group stressors like lack of cohesiveness, lack of support interpersonal and inter-group conflict as well as organizational politics (Ferris *et. al.*, 1996) are the potential source of stress in the work environment. Individual dispositions such as Type A personality patterns, personal efficacy and psychological hardiness may all affect the level of stress in individuals.

Survivor Syndrome

When the organization undergoes downsizing, according to Caudron (1996), the survivors might have feeling of insecurity and role ambiguity that might lead to tension and conflict.

CHEMICAL REACTIONS

Chemical stressors are less under our control since we tend to consume it through food, water, smoke and other beverages.

Decision Stress

People normally experience ambiguity and conflicting job demands and too much responsibility with too little authority.

Apart from the above reasons the other problems in life such as commuting problems, phobia, onset of disease, experiencing pain and environmental situations are also stimulators of stress.

A study by Singh (1987) revealed that three motivational climates namely, 'Achievement', 'Expert influence' and 'Extension' increased satisfaction and decreased role stresses. On the other hand, climates of control, affiliation and dependency have opposite effect. Studies have also shown that if employees are given a sense of control over their work environment, such as, being given a chance to be involved in the decision making processes that affects them, this will reduce their work stress (Jackson 1988).

Thus, manager's functioning within an organization is to a large extent influenced by the stress experienced by him. The manner in which he is able to handle the stress to some extent depends on his/her internal and external orientation.

MAJOR FINDINGS

Stress At Workplace

An attempt was made to analyze stressors in the work place and the relevant data have been furnished in Table 1 by applying percentages.

Table 1 is self-explanatory. Majority of respondents have shown a tendency of negativism which itself is an indication that they are terribly facing work stress.

Impact of High Stress on People's Behaviour

About 48 per cent of the respondents felt that their behaviour is changed ever since they started working in call centres. Some of them experience sleeplessness, under eating or overeating, forgetfulness, confusion and the like. 20 per cent of the respondents who never had drinking habit resorted to alcoholism either on weekends or at the end of the day, which clearly indicates behavioural deviations, which are harmful. Behaviour is the major influencing factor for employee productivity and achievement of organizational goals. Behavioural change might trigger aggressive behaviour on the

Table 1
Stressors at Work Place

Determinants of Stress (Hassles or Stumbling blocks)	*Strongly Agree*	*Agree*	*Neutral*	*Disagree*	*Strongly Disagree*
	(In Percentages)				
Situations in Call Centres making the respondents workaholic	26	43	20	11	-
Perception of the importance of their services to the organization	6	38	4	52	-
Deadlines and time pressure	40	37	10	10	3
Trouble with work colleagues and boss	23	30	20	13	14
Trouble with client/customer	20	20	35	20	5
Technical breakdowns and associated with tasks not stimulating	16	28	12	24	20
Too many jobs to do at once and do not know where career is heading	22	38	22	12	6
Spouse is not supportive about work & family life adversely affects the work	18	33	28	11	10
Symptoms of stress (irritability, loss of appetite, physical stress of any kind)	56	31	-	13	-
Non-availability of time to pursue hobbies/interests and personal likings	22	50	19	9	-
Call centres have quick grievance redressal arrangements	12	18	30	22	18
Annual health check-ups and stress reduction programmes like yoga, meditation conducted in call centres	-	-	20	30	50
Feeling of tiredness, boredom and depression at the end of the day	12	33	28	17	10
Empowerment to participate in decision making process	8	34	26	14	18
Get sufficient breaks for relaxation and refreshing	10	15	15	35	25

part of the employees leading to interpersonal conflicts and lack of organizational citizenship behaviour. There is research evidence indicating a relationship between 'stress, absenteeism and turnover' (Lyman and Steers, 1973). The call centre employees are very much in news presently for all the wrong reasons such as offences like rape, customer cheating, data stealing, forgery and the like.

COPING STRATEGIES FOR STRESS

Many studies have suggested various coping strategies for stress. Goal setting, organizational behaviour modification, group dynamics, management of conflict, communication skills, political strategies, leadership styles, organization processes and design, decision making skills, control techniques, management of change and organization development techniques suggest ways to manage and cope more effectively with stress. Several theories are also being developed on the ways to cope with stress (Jeffrey, 1992). It is also proved that at the individual level certain activities like exercise, relaxation, behavioural self-control, cognitive therapy (Meichenbaum, 1992) and networking (Luthans *et.al.*, 1985) work the best.

The following models enable to understand how to cope with stress at the individual, group and organizational levels.

The manager with his internal strengths can make positive influence on the working environment. The Figure 1 clearly depicts how an individual with his personality attributes like

Figure 1
Managing Executive Stress: An Approach to Self Development–A Model

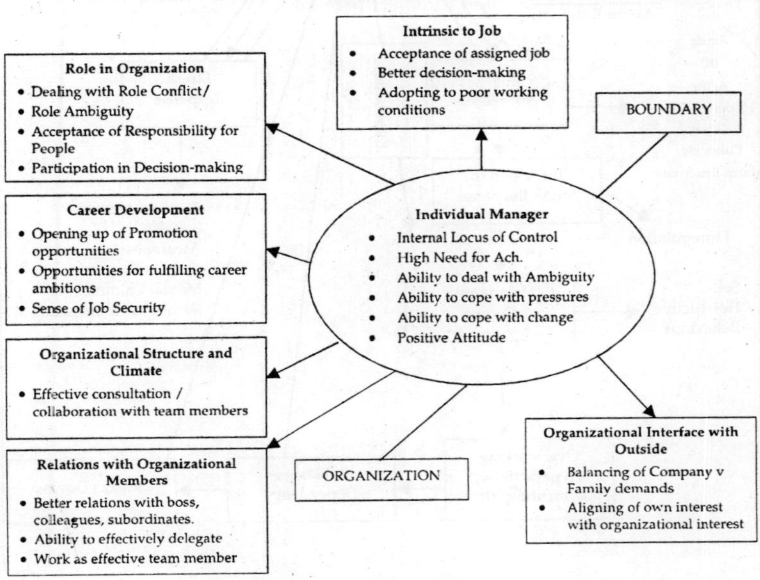

Source: Daisy (2002).

internal locus of control, high need for achievement and positive attitude counteract the negative impact of stress.

Figure 2 which delineates the negative repercussions of 'Reacting', while it is always easier to choose The right path, i.e., 'Responding' even though difficult to choose leads to improved health, problem solution and the overcoming of stress through mindfulness or awareness.

Figure 2
Coping with Stress: Reacting vs. Responding–A Model

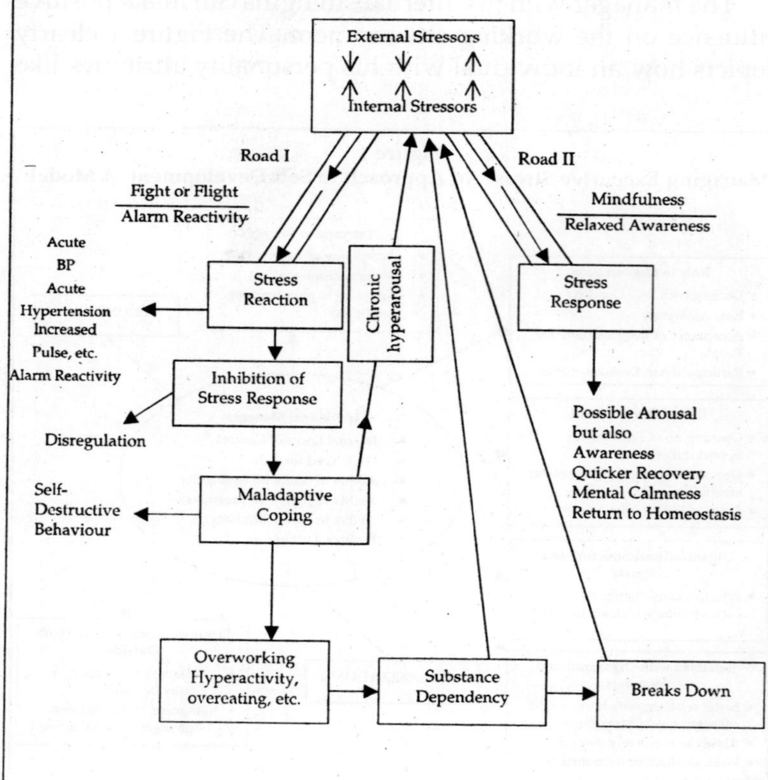

Source: Kabat Zinn 1990, from Rita Agarwal (2001).

FEW SUGGESTIONS

- Since call centre job is tiring, it requires longer breaks for the employees to feel refreshed.
- Work pressure should be equitably distributed to the employees.
- Separate formal grievance redressal committee and suggestion scheme to the HR managers to sort out the problems and demands of the workers should be set up.
- Annual health checkups and life style modification programmes must be conducted at call centres.
- Stress reduction programmes like yoga, meditation, relaxation and deep-breathing techniques must be imparted at call centres at formal level.
- Arrangement of monthly get together, recreation, games and talent shows will rejuvenate the employees from monotony and tardiness.
- Recognition of employees' performance by instituting awards and incentives act as morale booster, which can divert depression and disappointment in them.
- A department can be created which can deliver the service of employee bill payment, investment advice and portfolio management.
- Employee must resort to hobbies and other extra curricular activities during their free time to feel relaxed and happy.
- Effective time management and setting priorities to deal with the problems and having stable relationships help to fight out stress.

CONCLUSION

An individual must be well versed with the information about the job to understand whether he/she makes a proper fit into it. No matter whatever job the person opts, the stress factor is bound to be there at different intensities, based on individuals take towards it. It is necessary to aggressively seek copying strategies, which fit to particular situation or to person so as to achieve success throughout.

REFERENCES

Daisy Chauhan, (2002), Managing Executive Stress: *An Approach to Self Development*, Excel Books, New Delhi, p. 98.

D.H. Meichenbaum, (1972), "Cognitive Modification of Test Anxious College Students", *Journal of Consulting and Clinical Psychology*, 39, p. 370-378.

Dr. Rakesh Chopra, Santosh Sharma, (2001), *The Stress Cyclone*, Excel Books, New Delhi, p. 59, 64, 66.

Fred Luthans, (1998), *Organizational Behaviour*, McGraw-Hill International Edition, p. 334.

Fred Luthans, Staurt A. Rosenkrantz, and Harry We. Hennessey, (1985), "What Do Successful Managers Really do? An Observation Study of Managerial Activities", *Journal of Applied Behavioural Science*, 21(3), p. 255-270.

Gerald R. Ferris, Dwight D. Frink, Maria Carmen Galang, Jing Jhone, K. Michaele Kacmar, and Jack L. Howard, (1966), "Perceptions of Organizational Politics: Prediction, Stress-Related Implications and Outcomes", *Human Relations*, 49(2), p. 233-266.

Jackson, S.E., (1988), "Participation in Decision Making as a Strategy for Reducing Job Related Strain", *Journal of Applied Psychology*, Vol. 68, p. 3-19.

Jeffrey R. Edwards (1992), "A Cybernetic Theory of Stress, Coping and Well Being in Organizations", *Academy of Management Review*, p. 238-274.

John M. Ivancevich and Michael T., Matteson, (1987), *Organizational Behaviour and Management*, Business Publications, Plano, Tex., p. 211.

John M. Ivancevich and Michael T. Matteson, (1980), *Stress and Work*, Scott, Foresman, Glenview, III, p. 145.

John Schaubroeck and Daniel C. Ganster, (February 1993), "Chronic Demands and Responsivity to Challenge", *Journal of Applied Psychology*, p. 73-85.

Lyman W. Porter and Richard M. Stress, (1973), Organizational Work, and Personal Factors in Employees Turnover and Absenteeism, *Psychological Bulletin*, p. 151-176.

(Kabat Zinn, 1990), From Rita Agarwal, (2001), *Stress In Life and At Work*. Sage Publications, New Delhi, p. 191.

Shari Caudron, (1966), "Teach Downsizing Survivors How to Thrive", *Personnel Journal*, p. 48.

Singh, G.P. (1987), *Organizational Climate as Moderator of Role Stress–Job Satisfaction Relationship in case of Different Job Categories of Computer Professionals*, Ph.D. Thesis, University of Gujarat, Ahmedabad.

18

REVIEWING ORGANIZATIONAL STRESS AND CLIMATE: A CASE STUDY OF GOVERNMENT DOCTORS

Taruna & Archana Singh

An attempt was undertaken to Review Organizational Stress and Climate on a group of doctors. They were all subjected to an HRD workshop, which was conducted in a standardized form. Emphasis was to have a real interactive workshop where the group can reveal the reality. Pareek's O.R.S and MAO-C scale were used to identify the Stress and climate indices. Self Role Distance, Resource Inadequacy and Role Expectation Conflict were found to be the dominant stressors for the group. Among climate motives Dependency-Control motives were dominant.

INTRODUCTION

Organisations by their very nature tend to be complex entities.Howeever organisations are social systems, which combine science, people and technology and are formed on the basis of mutual interests. Consequently activities therein are governed by social and psychological law as well. Organisations are human entities therefore it is imperative to say that organisations are in a sense living organism with culture, climate, brains, complex systems. It is essential that we understand the dynamics of organisation and should refer it as organisms or living creature which means it behaves in similar ways as our biological mechanism as they are formed basically by the human beings.

Human behaviour in an organisation is influenced or directed by several physical and psychological factors, One of the key concepts to understand the integration is the role, It is through the role that the individual interacts with and gets integrated with the system,an individual at a time has to perform many roles, which is itself challenging and gives room for stress.

Stress has become the most pervasive fact of human life organizationally, all the job holders be it executives, middle level, supervisors or unskilled workers are exposed to stress in varying degree.Organisational stress these days has gained momentum and is most widely experienced due to the rapid changing environment manifesting into high competition and heavy demands on part of the employees.

Modern researches have proved that not only fine materials, sophisticated technology good working conditions make for progress and effectiveness of an organisations but employees, behaviour and the organisational climate plays a crucial role in determining effectiveness of an organisation.

Organisational Climate can be defined as the perceived attributes of an organisation and its subsystems reflected in the way it deals with members, group & issues. The perceived attributes related to organisational process to produce motivation or concerns, and climate can be characterized by these concerns.

Hence it stands rational to undertake the present study where there is an attempt to review the organisational stress and climate, which is highly significant in the present scenario where employees are constantly facing great difficulty in performing their roles and are sure to be engulfed into the clutches of stress. Climate also playing a critical role as it determines the general environment of the organisation which is again an inducing factor in experiencing stress.

Rationale of the Study

In the liberalized era of today that is highly competitive and demanding it attempts highly imperative to Undertake a study that "Reviews Organizational Stress and Climate", which are the significant factors, which affect the existence, growth and performance of the organization. And especially the group into study that is of the doctors is very important element of the society, hence, it stands imperative to review their stress level and climate motives. Although a plethora of researches have been conducted, very little effort has been made to peep into the dynamics of stress and climate for the present group into consideration to my best of knowledge. Hence this instigates more to conduct the study on the concerned group.

Objectives of the Study

1. To find out three highest stressors in respect of each participant through microanalysis and to calculate percentages of individuals afflicted by each of the stressors.
2. To find out the three highest stressor in respect of the total participants through macro analysis.
3. To find out the dominant, backup and dormant climate of the group.
4. To take a survey feedback to test the authenticity of the responses.
5. To suggest the ways to align the climate and to reduce stress.

Methodology

Two interactive HRD workshops were conducted on the thirty participants. For both the day's number of participants were fifteen. The workshop were conducted under standard conditions from 10 a.m. to 5 p.m. with a break of one hour (1 p.m.-2 p.m.) for lunch on both the days.

Profile of the Participants

All the participants were working as medical officers for the state govt. They were all having M.B.B.S. degree few of them even had their P.G degrees. All the participants were males.

Design of the Workshop

In the first stage, participants were acquainted with the concept of stress and organizational climate. They were given opportunities to speak on the challenges facing the organizations. Most of the participants had a negative meaning of stress. They were introduced to the new concept of stress i.e. the positive aspect of stress as also with the bearing of organizational climate on it. They were introduced to the methods for measuring stress and climate. During this session, they were introduced to ORS (Organizational Role Stress) and MAOC (Motivation Analysis of Organizational-Climate) developed by (Pareek1997). Brief descriptions of the two tools are given below.

Description of Organizational Role Stress (ORS)

The O.R.S. scale was used to measure ten role stressors and overall Role Stress. It is a five points scale (0 to 4), containing five items for each role stressor and a total of fifty statements. Thus the total scores on each role stressor ranges from 0 to 20 and on ORS from 0 to 200. The responses are given on the answer sheets. To get the total scores for each Role Stressor, the ratings given are added together horizontally (for five items in respect of each stressor).

About Role Stressors

- *Inter Role Distance (I.R.D.):* This stressor is experienced when there is a conflict between organizational and non-organizational roles.
- *Role Stagnation (R.S.):* It is the stressor that arises when one feels that there is no opportunity for one's career progression. It is a feeling of being stuck in the same role for comparatively long period of time.
- *Role Expectation Conflict (R.E.C.):* This type of stressor is generated by different expectations by different significant persons about the same role and the role occupant's ambivalence as to whom to please.
- *Role Erosion (R.E.):* This type of stressor is the function of role occupant's feeling that some functions, which

should properly belong to his role, are transferred or performed by some other role. This can also happen when the role occupant performs functions but the credit for them goes to some one else.

- *Role Overload (R.O.):* This stressor is experienced when role occupant feels that there are too many expectations from the significant roles. There are two aspects of this stress; the quantitative overload and the qualitative overload.
- *Role Isolation (R.I.):* This stressor is experienced when the role occupant feels that certain roles are psychologically closer to him while others are at a much greater distance. The main criterion of the distance is the frequency and ease of interaction. When linkages are strong then isolation will be low and in absence of strong linkages the role isolation will be high.
- *Personal Inadequacy (P.In.):* This type of stressor arises when the role occupant feels that he does not have the necessary skills and training for effectively performing the functions expected from his role.
- *Self- Role Distance (S.R.D.):* When the role a person occupies goes against his or her self concept then he feels S.R.D. This stressor is essentially a conflict arising out of mismatch between the person and his job.
- *Role Ambiguity (R.A.):* This stress refers to the lack of clarity about the expectation of role that may arise out of lack of information or understanding, it may exist in the relation to activities, responsibilities.
- *Resource Inadequacy (R. In.):* This type of stressor is evident when the role occupant feels that he is not provided with adequate resources for performing the functions expected from him.

The scale is reported to have been widely used Saiyadain (2003). It has sufficient psychometric properties. Construct validity of the test for our group in question ranged from 0.138 to 0.564 significant at 0.01 to 0.001 levels.

Motivation Analysis of Organizational Climate (MAOC): It was designed to study organizational climate with special reference to motives. These are supposed to be changed in course of interaction of individual with organization. The instrument employs twelve dimensions of organizational climate and the six motives described elsewhere. It consists of twelve categories, each of which includes six statements. Each of these categories corresponds to one of the twelve climate dimensions and each of the six statements represents one of the six motives. Respondents work out individually to rank order the six statements within each separate category according to their perception of how much each statement is like in their organization (or unit, branch, division or department within the organization). Ranks are converted into numbers according to procedure given in the manual (Pareek, 1997). These numbers/ scores can range between 12 to 72.Then the respondent refers to the conversion table and writes the corresponding MAOC Index Number, which can range between(0 100The first two highest of these indices are called dominant, the second two highest as back up and the lowest two are taken as dormant climates or motives. The scale is reported to possess.

Procedure: Each participant was asked to read the instructions carefully and silently, while the facilitator read the instructions aloud. When the participants gave their confirmation regarding understanding of the methods to be followed for filling up the questionnaire, they were asked to fill up the questionnaire. The facilitator kept an eye on the participants while they filled up their responses, so that no question was left unresponded or unanswered. The participants were then asked to score their responses themselves and write the same on their answer sheets and keep the same with them. Subsequently after a break of five minutes MAOC was administered and scored by the participants themselves. Procedure adopted in administration and scoring of the ORS were scrupulously followed in this test also. Here, respondents were asked to segregate their dominant, backup and dormant scores to assess the comparative strengths of various motives/ climates.

In the second stage the facilitator checked their scores personally by personally visiting each individuals desk, without collecting their answer sheets. Then the facilitator guided them to find out three dominant scores among the 10 dimensions of ORS segregate their dominant, backup and dormant stressors. The same procedure was followed in identifying dominant, back up and dormant motives.

In the third stage, the facilitator deeply discussed about the 3 main stressors and the two dominant motives for the group. The facilitator adopted the basic quality of empathy, warmth, genuineness, listening, responding without irritating and providing feedback. The facilitator formed eight dyads on each day and carried out-group discussion.

In the fourth stage brain-storming session was sufficient psychometric property and is widely used in HRD workshops. conducted to verify appropriateness of the dominant motives in reducing stress and succeed in the present set up of environmental changes. With group consensus, the facilitator suggested the group to change their motives hindering individual and organizational progress as also their style of coping with stress.

RESULTS

Microanalysis

To show comparative strength of various stressors of individual members of the group, percentages of participants at the three levels of highest, second highest in respect of each stressor are presented in Table below:

Table 1
Level of Stressors

Stressors	*Highest*	*IInd Highest*	*IIIrd Highest*	*Total*
Inter Role Distance	Nil	3%	6%	9%
Role Stagnation	3%	10%	6%	19%
Role Expectation Conflict	20%	16%	6%	42%
Role Erosion	10%	6%	6%	22%
Role Overload	10%	13%	6%	29%
Role Isolation	3%	10%	6%	19%
Personal Inadequacy	6%	6%	6%	18%
Self Role Distance	16%	16%	26%	58%
Role Ambiguity	3%	3%	16%	22%
Resource Inadequacy	26%	10%	10%	46%

- It can be seen that Inter Role distance was found to be the first highest stressor for none, the second highest stressor for 3% and the third highest for 6%.
- Role Stagnation was found to be the highest stressor for 3%, the second highest for 10% and the third highest for 6%.
- Role Expectation Conflict was found to be the highest stressor for 20%, the second highest for 16% and the third highest for 6%.
- Role Erosion was found to be the first highest stressor for 10%, the second highest for 6% and the third highest for 6%.
- Role Overload was found to be the highest stressor for 10%, the second highest for 13% and the third highest for 6%.
- Role Isolation was found to be the highest stressor for 3%, the second highest for 10% and the third highest for 6%.
- Role Ambiguity was found to be the highest stressor for 3%, the second highest for 3% and the third highest for 16%.
- Resource Inadequacy was found to be the first highest stressor for 26%, the second highest for 10% and the third highest stressor for 10%.
- Personal Inadequacy was found to be the highest stressor for 6%, the second highest for 6% and the third highest for 6%.
- Self Role Distance was found to be the highest stressor for 16%, the second highest for 16% and the third highest for 26%.

Based on this Micro Analysis it can be said that:

1. Self Role Distance was the dominant stressor for 58% m embers of the group.
2. Resource Inadequacy was the second dominant stressor affecting 46% members of the group.

3. Role Expectation Conflict was the third dominant stressor affecting 42% members of the group.

Macro Analysis

To analyse overall impact of various stressors on the group as a whole, macro analysis was carried out through calculation of Means and S.Ds in respect of all the ten stressors.

Table 2
Macro Analysis of Stressors

Stressors	*Mean*	*S.D*
Inter Role Distance	7.00	2.75
Role Stagnation	8.83	4.32
Role Expectation Conflict	9.56	4.48
Role Erosion	8.63	4.70
Role Overload	8.76	3.75
Role Isolation	9.36	3.07
Personal Inadequacy	8.96	3.17
Self Role Distance	10.86	3.63
Role Ambiguity	8.80	2.96
Resource Inadequacy	10.06	5.16

It can be noticed from the table that the value of mean in regard to the Self Role Distance was the highest (10.86), it could be stated to be the dominant role stressor for the group. The stressor of Resource Inadequacy closely followed it with the mean value of 10.06, it could be stated to be the second dominant stressor. The third highest mean was of Role Expectation Conflict 9.56.

Comparative Strengths of Motives

In order to see the comparative strengths of various dimensions of the organisational climate, Means and S.Ds of climate indices of the six motives were calculated.

It can be noticed from the table that value of mean in respect to Dependency climate was the highest (55.76). It was closely followed by Control motive with mean value of 55.66.There appears to be no significant difference between the two means. Based on these values of means, Dependency and Control can be taken as the dominant motives for the group. Extension and Expert Influence ranked third and the fourth (52.70 and 47.53) may be taken as the backup motives. Achievement and Affiliation motives being lowest 44.93 and 37.76 were significantly lower to Dependency and Control.These were taken as dormant motives for the group.

Table 3
Strength of Motives

Motive	*Mean*	*Motive*	*S.D.*
Achievement	44.93	Achievement	15.20
Expert Influence	47.53	Expert Influence	13.35
Extension	52.70	Extension	16.03
Control	55.66	Control	13.24
Dependency	55.76	Dependency	12.44
Affiliation	37.76	Affiliation	10.48

Analysis of Authenticity of Responses Through Survey Feedback

For checking the authenticity of responses given by the participants on organisational role stressors every individual (one by one) was given an opportunity to report his three dominant stressors amongst the ten role stressors and also the dominant motives experienced by the individuals pertaining to the organisational climate. All the participants were asked to define their stressor and how it related to their work and what reason do they attribute for the escalation of the stressors and the motives experienced by them during the performance of their roles and duties.

MATTERS OF CONCERN: DISCUSSION

Self-Role Distance

Both through micro and macro analysis Self Role Distance appeared to be the dominant stressor for the entire group. The reason for the escalation of this role stressor could be attributed to the fact that these doctors all being a part of modern urban life during their education period and now posted in remote rural areas is against their expectation which is more conflicting and stressful. The other reason could be attributed to the fact of the existing political interference and nepotism, which is constantly occurring in various forms at various levels.

Resource Inadequacy

As regards to this role stressor, which again reported to be the second dominant stressor both through micro and macro analysis. The reason for the escalation of this could be attributable to the non-availability of the resources that are very basic and important for the doctors in performing their role effectively. A predominant number of doctors felt that the equipments that they had to use were mostly outdated and lacked sophistication. It was also reported that they did not had a systematic supply and logistic system, which led to shortage of essential supplies. The situation was further more confounded by an indifferent quality of support staff.

Role Expectation Conflict

This ranked the third dominant stressor both through micro and macro analysis. The reason for the escalation could be traced and stated as the combination of previous two dominant stressors, which could be acting as mediating stressors to give rise to this stressor. As stated previously the doctors are in a constant conflicting situation so as to satisfy their superiors, self, poor patients or significant others. They are in a flux so as to meet the expectation of self and significant others. Apart, from this they are left with no resources in hand to utilise their full potential and expertise.

Dependency-Control

These motives characterise the dominant climate for the group which signifies that the members of the group need to be dependent on their superiors for majority of issues and they have to strictly follow the guidelines, set by the higher authorities. The doctor's need to be very cautious with their relationship with their superiors as it plays a significant, influencing factor for critical decisions concerned to the junior officers. Hence they are having a high sense of being dependent and controlled.

CONCLUSIONS AND SUGGESTIONS

The study was conducted on a limited sample, but the results give an insight for application of the model on other such groups with suitable modifications. On the basis of the results following conclusions are drawn:

- Self Role Distance that is the dominant stressor needs to be reduced as it is acting to be the complimentary element giving rise to other stressful factors on rise as reported by the individuals. Hence, regular stress audit needs to be undertaken and attempts needs to reduce it.
- The responses of the individuals clearly exhibit that the organisation needs to develop more resources and create more resources, as they are the primary requirements for the fulfilment of their roles.
- Much needs to be done regarding the Role Expectation Conflict, which is the result of various factors where the individuals are in a constant conflict as to whom to please.
- Higher emphasis accorded to Control and Dependency should be reduced as it leads to more autocratic organisation, which lacks the desired level of contribution on the part of the individuals.
- Achievement was found to be the dormant motive, Expert Influence was found to be backup motives and hence both need to be dominant. As these motives instil the feeling of confidence, growth, motivation and satisfaction that create more stress free, committed individuals.
- HRD interventions towards diagnosing organisational climate and their relationship with organisational role stress and stressors need to be constantly analysed.
- Organisation's needs to be proactive and needs to fulfil the demands pertaining to resources, as they tend to be very critical particularly for these role incumbents.
- Achievement motive needs to be emphasised as it is going to build better morale, increase performance, efficiency and develop a healthy work environment emphasising growth motive which leads the organisation to the roads of success.

REFERENCES

Canon (1932), The Wisdom of the Body, New York, Norton.

Colin Mckenzie (2002), *New Zealand Management Journal,* Volume 49, Issue 2.

David. F. Elloy & Catherine Smith (2003), *Cross Cultural Management,* Vol. 10, Issue 1.

Pandey, Anirudh (2003), *Revisiting the Concept of Stress Rail Transport Journal,* Issue.

Pandey Anirudh & Taruna (2005), *Coping with Neo-Stress, Rail Transport Journal,* Vol. XIV, No. III, Issue.

Pandey Anirudh & Taruna (2006), *Appraising Organisational Climate for Managing Organisational Stress,* Vol. 46, Issue 4.

Pandey Anirudh (1997), "Stress without Distress", *Ascent, Times of India,* Lko, Aug. 18.

Parek U. (2004), "Understanding Organizational Behaviour", Tata Mc Graw Hills.

Pestonjee D.M. (1992), "Coping with Stress", *The Indian Experience,* Sage, New Delhi.

Pestonjee D.M. (1997). Pestonjee, D.M. Pareek, Udai (1997), "Studies in Organizational Role Stress", Rawat Publication, Jaipur.

Pestonjee D.M. (1999), Coping with Stress: The Indian Experience, Sage, New Delhi (2nd Edition).

Saiyadain, M.S. (2003), "Organizational Behaviour", Tata McGraw Hills, New Delhi.

Selye (1956), "The Stress of Life", New York, Tata McGraw Hills.

19

WHY DOES THE PRIMARY HEALTH SYSTEM FAIL?

M.M. Verma

INTRODUCTION

As per census 2001, India is a country of 102.70 crores of people, out of whom majority (around 73%) lives is rural areas. There is a terrific misbalance between the availability of natural and capital resources vis-á-vis the required amount of these resources for allround growth and development of this population. Therefore, this enormity of population leads to sustenance of poverty and ill–health, which results into the falling standards of living for quite substantial proportion of people. (Verma,1991). This sort of situation is unacceptable as it defeats our national developmental goals. Hence, the need for population control.

To achieve this avowed objective (as well as execution of the various national health programs), a vast health infrastructure in the shape of CHCs (30 bedded hospital on each 80–120 thousand population), PHCs (on each 20-30 thousand population), and SCs(on each 3-5 thousand population) has been created. In September 2004, a network of 3,222 CHCs, 23, 109 PHCs, and 1, 42,655 Sub–centers had been functioning in the rural and semi–urban areas of the country (GOI, 2006, 456).

A Community Health Centre (also known as Block PHC) is staffed with a Medical Specialist, a child specialist, a gynaecologist a surgeon and a lady Doctor along with around 25 other paramedical and support staff. A Primary Health Centre (PHC) is staffed with a Medical Officer (In charge), a pharmacist, a staff Nurse, Block Extension Educator/Health Educator, Lab Technician, one male and one female Health Worker and 4-5 other support staff. At the sub-centre (SC) level, a team of health workers (one male and one female) is stationed at the village it self. The overall administrative responsibility of running these centers rests with the MO (IC) of the PHC/CHC.

The female health worker is in charge of the sub–center. She has to serve the intensive care zone of the sub– center, while the male health worker has to cover the peripheral areas (also however, they are required to collaborate and coordinate in the implementation of all the national health programmes including MCH and UIP in order to reach all the households falling in their area. However, inspite of massive efforts in the form of budgetary support and infrastructure development, the performance of (different) family welfare programmers have not been commensurate with the objectives (GOI, 1992; 331). Various factors (Misra *et. al.*, 1982; Shah, 1989; IIHMR, 1990; Gupta *at al;* 1991; 1992; Verma, 1991; Bose, 2000; Verma & Purwar, 2000) have been responsible for the failure of the health system in achieving the goals set under HFA-2000. Some of these may be enlisted as, quantitative and qualitative inadequacies in the available infrastructure and manpower, unmet training needs, managerial weaknesses, lack of and wastage of resources, lack of strategic planning and commitment at the grassroots level, corruption and laxity is the system, and multipurpose health workers still perceiving themselves as uni-purpose workers. The failure of the system has resulted in the resetting of targets under the NPP-2000 (Yojana, 2000). Consequently, the goal of achieving total fertility rate (TFR) of 2.1, which was scheduled to be achieved by the year 2000, has now been fixed for the years 2010.

This paper attempts at analyzing the interaction amongst various variables, which results in the failure of the health system in achieving the set goals, despite the huge investments made by the government over the past decades.

THE INADEQUACIES OF BASIC INFRASTRUCTURE & MANPOWER

For efficient management of the health services delivery system, it is essential that the basic infrastructure is in tact and adequate. However, as NPP-2000 document reports, deficiencies and inadequacies in health infrastructure and manpower are alarming. In view of the set goals, 3776 CHCs, 4212 PHCs and 23190 sub-centers (SCs) are additionally required. The Eighth Plan (1992-97) document mentions: the backlog of SCs, PHCs and CHCs in many states is staggering and the resources required to meet the targets are unachievable in near future. A sum of Rs.6431 crores is additionally required to meet this requirement (*Yojana*, 2000; 70).

In the same way, there is an additional requirement of 27,501 ANMs; 64860 male health workers 42,24 LHVs; 5126 male health Assistants, 2475 medical officers (PHC level); and 12,804 other medical specialists. An additional investment of Rs. 2300 crores plus Rs. 10.00 crores for their training is required to fill up this gap (Yojana, 2000; 70). The Eighth Plan document may often be quoted in this connection, which says: 'Lack of buildings, shortage of manpower and inadequate provision of drugs, supplies and equipments constitute major impediments to full operationalization of the rural primary health care delivery system' (GOI, 1992; 322).

The manpower is the primary health system also has qualitative inadequacies in view of their job requirements, which results in the overall inefficiency of the system a whole. Medical Officers (In charge) of PHC/CHC bitterly lack in the administrative and managerial stills, health supervisors lack in supervisory skills, and the health workers who are the key functionaries at the sub-center level, lack in commitment, sense of purpose, communication skills, motivational skills (Misra *et. al.*, 1982; IIHMR, 1990; Gupta *et. al.*, 1991,1992; Verma and Purwar, 2000). Being the frontline performers at the sub–center level located in the far flung rural areas of the country, the overall success or failure of all the national health programs including the population control program, would ultimately depend upon the overall job involvement and performance of male and female health workers (MPHWs). Hence, if we need to improve the effectiveness of health system in the delivery of health services at the grassroots level, we have to understand, intervene and improve upon the dynamics of the identified variables (Verma and Purwar, 2000) in a positive manner.

WHY THE HEALTH CARE SYSTEM FAILS?

The success of the Multipurpose Health Workers (MPHWs) in the delving of health information and services has been found to be dependent on their acceptability and credibility among the client population, which would be influenced by the content of client-worker interaction, his/her frequency of visits, the quality with respect to delivery of services and follow up and the nature of client population Advertisement and media support may also have positive impact on the client system (Patel, 1968,Yadav,1973, and NIHFW,1985). The worker-client interaction (Rao, 1977) upon which the credibility and acceptability of the workers greatly depends, is influenced by two sets of variables:

(A) Personalistic characteristics, and (B) role clarity of health workers.

The personalistic characteristics of the health workers, which incorporate his/her personality traits, biographical characteristics, values and attitudes, locus of control, interpersonal orientation, his/her attribution style for failures and social achievement motivation, would form the basis of his/her willingness and capacity to interact with client population. The workers motivational skills and their overall job involvement are influenced by the supervisory styles and the supervisory effectiveness of their superiors. The higher the role clarity of health workers, the lower their role stress and anxiety and the greater their job involvement. However, the role clarity of health workers depends, to a great extent, on leadership (supervisory), behavior, which includes such variables as, trust and support, goal emphasis, interaction facilitation, psychological influence, hierarchical influence, and leadership role clarification and consideration behaviors.

As already mentioned, the health workers are placed at the lowest rungs of PHC hierarchy. There is set a of supervisors above them and the roles conveyed by them to the workers at different points of time could crate a lot of ambiguity and confusion which may result in role conflict later on, if these supervisors lack in role consideration behavior towards these workers. There is little professional communication between the M.O (IC) and the health workers. So the roles remain mostly unclarified which result in a wide gap between the expected and perceived roles (Gupta *et.al;* 1991; Verma and Purwar; 2000). Besides, their immediate supervisors (MPHS) who are expected to clarify roles to them from time to time are themselves not clear about their own job duties (Bhatnagar, 1982,Gupta *et. al.* 1991). They go mostly to the sub-centers as inspectors and come back without performing any supervisory roles. The programmes, except family planning and malaria, are being given little attention by these grass-root workers. It forms an important reason for their lower level of acceptance among the client system as confirmed by our study of two primary health centers in central U.P.

The frequency of visit to the sub-center is very much affected by the level of job motivation and job involvement, accessibility of the place of visit and the infrastructure support, such as, availability of roads and transportation, sub-center building, good school for children, etc. Since in most of the rural areas either these facilities do not exist or they are in a poor condition, the health workers mostly prefer to live in the nearby cities/towns and are not able to reach their workplace regularly and timely. In addition, there is a slackness in supervision and management control (Gupta, *et. al;* 1991). Hence, many workers do not visit these villages altogether. Consequently, people in many villages are not even aware that there is some health worker appointed for their area. In such a situation, the population gets hostile towards the workers and the health and family welfare programmes (Misra, *et. al,* 1982).

Health workers' overall objective is to deliver the health and family welfare services to the community they serve. The quality of these services and follow up rendered by MPHWs would basically depend on medical support from PHC and their job Knowledge while the presence of role stress and anxiety among the workers would adversely affect service delivery and follow-up to the client population.

The job knowledge of health workers, apart from leadership (supervisory) behavior develops through training imparted by the MFW training centers, experience on the job, their free, frank and meaningful interaction with the peer group and with the client groups. As stated earlier, though the health workers have been designated as multipurpose health workers, the MPHW training imparted to them has been quite inadequate (IIHMR; 1990, Gupta *et. al.,* 1991, 1992) and has failed to generate in them enough intuition to take up multiple job responsibilities and enhance their job knowledge and skills. Besides, MPHWs in many states still continue to draw their salaries from their parent departments such as, malaria, family planning, etc, and they continue to perceive themselves as unipurpose workers instead of multipurpose workers (Gupta *et. al.,* 1991,1992). The medical support provided by the PHCs has also been found to be inadequate in view of the untimely supply of required medicines and contraceptives, and frequent absence of medical officers from the primary health centers and the community health centres.

Health workers' level of job involvement, apart from their personalistic characteristics and role clarification and consideration behavior of their immediate supervisors, would be fairly influenced by organizational culture, which refers to overall climate prevailing in the organization. It has been observed (Gupta, *et. al;* 1991, 1992; Verma and Purwar, 2000) that there is a wide gap between the policies and actual practices with respect to selections, transfers, postings and promotions, etc. in the health care system. The evaluation and monitoring system in the health organization has also been found to be weak, ineffective and not intact. A climate of power games and politics, resulting in malpractices, interference, pressures and corruption prevails in the system. Because of the resultant erosion in the power of legal authority, a culture has evolved where good performance is seldom rewarded and irresponsibility, corruption and indiscipline are rarely penalized (Mishra et.al, 1982). In such a climate, the new incumbent in the system loses his/her intrinsic motivation to work and soon joins the mainstream of 'on work culture' (Mishra *et. al.,* 1982; Shah,1989; Gupta *et. al.*, 1991).

On the other hand, many in the client system exhibit hostile behavior towards the health workers and the family planning programme (Srivastava, 1989) because of their ignorance, suspicions, and the fear of side-effects from the use of F.P. devices. It also happens due to unfavorable cultural values, beliefs, biases and the religious sentiments of the people. In dealing with such a situation, advertisement and media support becomes crucial as it can help in removing these psycho–social hurdles by educating and convincing the general publics regarding how the adoption of small family norm may be helpful in improving their quality of life. Thus, by introducing positive changes in the nature of client population, media may be helpful in enhancing the acceptability of health personnel and their services in the client system (Mehru, 1968, Yadav,1973, and NIHFW,1985).

CONCLUDING REMARKS

Hence, it can be suggested that for an improvement in the performance of the primary health care system, only those having an intrinsic motivation to mix with and serve the common man, having rapport building capabilities, those who are not loud, hostile, arrogant, and not having negative attitudes toward F.P., should be appointed as MPHWs and health supervisor. The prevailing situation calls for adoption of certain alternate approaches to the recruitment and development of various categories of health personnel employed at the CHC/PHC/SC levels so that a more efficient reliable, task oriented and committed work force may be created. They should be governed by a system of modern and scientific management. All the employees, right from the MO(IC) to the grassroots level health workers, need to undergo new packages of training (Verma, 2001), so that their overall efficiencies and competencies may be improved in order to achieve better performance. The gaps prevailing in the PHC system terms of insufficiency of buildings, human resources, provision of adequate and timely supplies of various sorts, like drugs, contraceptives, and equipments, etc. constitute major hurdles to the full operationalisation of the rural health system. Hence, there is dire need to remove the bottlenecks. Unless we take immediate measures is this direction, success of the primary health care system in achievement of the objectives of the national population policy-2000 may not be possible.

REFERENCES

Bhatnagar, S.C.(1982), "Improving the Effectiveness of a Multipurpose PHC Worker", *Journal of Family Welfare,* Vol. 23, No. 3.

Bose, Ashish (2000), "Population Stabilization in India: Progress and Pitfalls", *Yojana,* Vol. 44 (8) August, p.15-18.

Government of India (1992), "The Eighth Five Year Plan (1992-97)", Vol. II, Planning Commission of India, New Delhi.

India (2006), A Reference Annual, Publications Division, Ministry of Information and Broadcasting, New Delhi.

Gupta, R.B., S.D Gupta & M.M. Verma (1991), "Utility and Existing Situation of Male Multipurpose Health Workers in Rajasthan: An Evaluation", *Indian Institute of Health Management Research,* Jaipur.

Gupta, R.B., M.M. Verma, and B. Jayakrishnan (1992), "Baseline Survey in Himachal Pradesh Under IPP VI &VII", Volume 4 , *Indian Institute of Health Management Research,* Jaipur.

IIHMR (1990), "Training Needs Assessment of Health Functionaries in DANIDA Project Districts in M.P.", Unpublished Report, *Indian Institute of Health Management Research,* Jaipur.

Mehru, Zahina (1968), "Evaluation of Mass Media in Subhash Nager: Five Years of Research in F.P.", *Demographic Training and Research Center,* Bombay (mimeo).

Misra, B.D., Ali Asharaf, Simmons and Simmons (1982), "Organization for Change: A System Analysis of Family Planning in Rural India", Radiant Publishers, New Delhi.

NIHFW (1985), "Evaluation of Media Reach and Effectiveness: A Collaborative Study", *National Institute of Health and Family Welfare,* Technical Report No. 9, New Delhi.

Patel, V.M.(1968), "A Study of Effectiveness of Radio as a Medium of Communication", *Journal of Family Welfare,* Vol. 14, No. 3, (March).

Rao, T.V. (1977), "A Study of Family Planning Worker-Client Transactions, Health and Population Unit", IIM, Ahmadabad.

Shah, M.H. (1989), "Factors Responsible for Low Performance of Family Planning Programme", in Zena, B. & R.N. Pati (eds). "Health and Family Welfare Services in India", Ashish Publishing House, New Delhi.

Srivastava, H.C. (1989), "Exploratory Study of the Non-Acceptors of Family Planning: An Anthropological Investigation in Two Village of U.P.", *International Institute for Population Sciences,* Mumbai.

Verma, M.M. (1991), "Poverty and Ill–Health: Hurdles to Rural Development", *Journal of Health Management,* Vol. 5, Nos. 3&4, p.17-20. IIHMR, Jaipur.

Verma, M.M. (2001), "Developing Health Manpower in India: A Social Work Perspective", Paper Presented at the International Conference on Health and Mental Health at Tampere, Finland on July 1-5, 2001; Accepted for publication in the *Journal of Health Services,* Haworth Press, New York.

Verma, M.M. and P.C. Purwar (2000), "Effectiveness of Health Workers in the Execution of Family Welfare Programme: Application of the Sales Management Model", *Manpower Journal,* Vol. XXXVI, No. 3, July-Sept., 2000, p. 65-82.

Yadav, J.S. (1973), "Impact of Mass Media on Family Planning Programme in India", UNESCO Family Planning Project, *Indian Institute of Mass Communication,* New Delhi (mimeographed).

——— (2000), *Yojana* Vol. 44, No. 8, (August).

20

PROBLEMS IN SOCIAL REHABILITATION OF DISABLED

S.P. Pandey & A.K. Singh

Physically and mentally challenged persons are most marginalized and suffer from social deviance, stigma and social exclusion and oppression. As it is estimated that 600 million persons with disabilities are all over the world, while in India about 70 million disabled live. The prevalence of disability is increasing as globalization, liberalization and modern life style have promoted accidents rate causing impairments and disabilities. Though, efforts on the part of government agencies and non government agencies have been made to rehabilitate disabled, however in absence of a national policy on disabled, only a small proportion of disabled has got benefits from rehabilitation services and programmes. The majority of them are living in rural areas where awareness about government programmes and services is very low and thus they are deprived of such benefit. Moreover, poverty, illiteracy, malnutrition, poor health, drug abuse and alcoholism, diseases etc. are causing disabilities and impairments. About half of the disabilities ad impairments are presentable therefore strategies and approaches to address them effectively and also to rehabilitate physically and mentally challenged persons are needed to our focused attention. With the change of time, there has been paradigm shifting towards addressing the problem of disability. There is more focus on empowerment and rehabilitation of physically and mentally challenged persons rather than welfare orientation. A physical handicap refers to human Herman limitations irrespective of whether disability is attributable to disease, injury or inheritance. Physical disability will lead to a limitation of physical function, whether locomotors, sensory or effective special organism medical definition of physical impairment is adopted and subsequently extended to include sensory, and cognitive forms, in contrast to a definition of disability in socio-political terms, as the outcome of an oppressive relationship between people with impairments and the rest of society (Fincelstein, 1980). Present paper is based on a major study conducted in 2002-03 by Pt. Govind Ballabh Pant Insitute of Studies in Rural Development, Lucknow. Paper attempts to examin the problems of social rehabilitation of disabled.

Twentieth Century social theory typically followed medical judgments in identifying disabled people as those individuals with, physical, sensory and cognitive impairments as less than whole, and hence unable to fulfill valued social roles and obligations. This in capacity left them dependent on the productive able bodied . These and other negative associations meant that disability was perceived as a personal tragedy This encompasses an individual and largely medicalized approach; first disability is regarded as a problem at the individual (body mind) level; second, it is equated with individual functional limitations or other defects: and third, medical knowledge and practice determines treatment option. The various problems confronting the physically handicapped individual in each specific sphere are considered in terms of physical, psychological, social, education and vocational. Every crippling disability results in either a limitation of a loss of locomotor abilities. Interestingly, every major physical disability causes, among other things some sort of psychological disturbance, which may run the gamut from slight imperiously to anxiety, escapism, extreme depression and over aggression. This psychological disturbance may be caused by disability itself. Disability also affects individual's social standing and mental life. Thus, Disabled Person becomes a marginalized person. Disabilities also affect adversely the learning process and enhancing competencies and skills for educational development as well as economic empowerment.

The problematic affects of disability from a social view point are analyzed in terms of health and sickness. Sigma, social, deviance social oppression and social exclusion are associated with disability and impairment. Therefore, disabled persons are viewed as unfortunate because they are unable to enjoy. The social and material benefits of contemporary society. These also include the opportunities for marriage, educational development social interaction, employment etc.

Now-a-days community based rehabilitation projects are being successfully implemented in the disability sector. Moreover, change of mind set regarding disabled persons and also for enhancing the competencies of disabled to harness the abilities of physically and mentally challenged persons. Interestingly, role of NGO's, community based organizations and international agencies have been found praise worthy in the recent past. The paradigm shifts in planning, policy and programmes of rehabilitation have forced more on socio-economic empowerment of disabled and harnessing their abilities. Moreover, disabilities can be prevented to the greater extent with implantation of strategies, programmes and policies for social change, adopting safe techniques of mechanical movement, awareness generation, and control of chronic diseases, malnutrition, and poverty alleviation. Thus, a number of problems are emerging which affect the process of rehabilitation of disabled.

MAGNITUDE OF PROBLEM

There is no systematic, scientific and precise information available on the prevalence degree and kind of disability. The estimate of WHO indicates that about 10 per cent of world's 600 million disabled are in India. NSSO survey revealed that 1.9 per cent of the total population of India i.e. 16.1 million had physical or sensory disabilities in 1991, which included visual, speech, hearing and locomotor disabilities.

DISABILITY AND DEVELOPMENT

Disability has become a focused attention in the recent times with the rise in political activism and voluntarism at the international and national level and also increasing debate about the development of 'alternative' service programmes, particularly, community based rehabilitation, Early advocates of the social model defined impairment as a biomedical issues and concentrated instead on disability, as a social, economic, political and cultural phenomenon. Some commentators have opined that impairment is integral to the experience of disability and therefore, must not be omitted from social analysis of disability. Thus, approaching impairment is biomedical and an individualistic term is peculiar to western philosophical and cultural traditions .Most social research in poorer countries has concentrated on responses to impairment in small scale, rural based groups where religious beliefs may exert a stronger impact than they do on those living in urban environments .Cross national data on the prevalence of 'impairments' and 'disabilities' must be enabled with additional caution, because the collection and processing procedures vary significantly, with some countries relying on professional diagnoses and others on lay responses. The prevalence of impairment amongst the world's population is lower than that of 'disability. Among the 55 nations impairment rates varied seen 0.2% to around 6% .While these surveys demonstrate that most of the world's disabled population lives in the poor nations of the majority world, the incidence of both reported impairment and 'disability' is generally higher in wealthier nations .The wealthy countries have better health and support services hence there is a greater survival rate among people's born with impairments. Secondly, the higher life expectancy and hence larger proportion of people over 50 years old. Thirdly, there are some conditions, such as dyslexia, at are regarded as 'disabling' in minority world countries but which present few problems to some one living in rural areas and are therefore not perceived or reported .Urban areas generally have more medical rehabilitation and support services, as well as greater risk of injury through pollution, traffic and work accidents, and perhaps more possibilities for earning a living by begging or by other livelihoods. It is to be noted that poverty, inadequate sanitation, poor diet and poor housing conditions are causing impairments and disabilities. However, one half of the world's impairment is preventable by introduction of improved policies to confront poverty and malnutrition, to improve sanitation, drinking water and employment conditions and to reduce accidents. Preventive measures are a top priority since in India, to the prevalence of conditions such as polio and blindness is at least four times higher among people who are below the poverty line compared with those who are above it. Poverty and the lack of an adequate health and social care in infrastructure are not the only factors producing impairment in the majority world. The causes of impairment extend to specific cultural practices, natural disasters and the consequences of economic development. Civil wars, ethic conflicts and insurgencies also cause growth of impairments and disabilities.

With the globalization process, developments in communication technologies and information networks and also world wide economic, political and cultural linkages have resulted in generation of consciousness regarding rehabilitation of disabled. There is general agreement that industrialization, urbanization, liberal utilitarianism and medicalization, along with cultural understandings of able bodied normally, particularly as disseminated through western media have influenced the social construction of disability. This led to the systematic exclusion of disabled people from the mainstream of everyday life.

Importantly, community based rehabilitation projects and programs have been focused attention in the recent past. The concept of CBR was contained and championed by WHO with the aim of making 'disability and 'rehabilitation' services available to grass root communities in a cost effective way. Interestingly, medical and related services, along with education were often organized and provided by missionaries and associated charities from the colonial power. The idea was that disadvantage and dependent groups such as disabled and other poor people should be supported by charitable fund raising and private donations. There have been some significant changes in the organization of CBR. This is associated with the changing role of international non-governmental organizations (NGO's) and the increasing priority placed on the involvement of disabled people at all levels and in all contexts by important sponsors of CBR programmes. Whereas NGO's involved in rehabilitation used to be dependent almost exclusively on their own resources for funding. A number of donor agencies are responsible for policy shifts in disability sector while more emphasis has been laid on community development and the promotion of equal rights to disabled. Importantly, there is glowering recognition that disabled people, families and key representatives of local communities must be meaningfully involved at every level and at every stage in the planning and implementation of CBR projects and strategies.

Rehabilitation process deals mainly developing skills in terms of social, mental, physical and promoting to achieve sustainable livelihood. Thus, rehabilitation process involved enabling disabled for their easy and smooth movement, communication and performing daily routine work. Moreover, process of rehabilitation requires services of different types viz.

Physio Therapy,

Occupational Therapy,

Speech Therapy,

Psycho Therapy & Special Devices etc.

Thus, rehabilitation of disabled deals with manpower development with coordinated efforts of community, NGO's and other CBO's.

WELFARE OF DISABLED

The Ministry of Social Justice and Empowerment is the nodal Ministry for the disability sector even though rehabilitation of persons with disability is a multi-sectoral process involving a package of services and activities. In India, efforts to rehabilitate physically and mentally challenged are marked with policy shifts from the regime of treating them in isolation and exclusion and towards empowering them to participate effectively in the development process as well as in the mainstream of national life. International organizations and agencies are equally conscious regarding rehabilitation of physically and mentally challenged. The year 1981 was declared as the International Year of Disabled Persons while in 1982 UN adopted World Program of Action Concerning Disabled Persons. The decade of 1982-1992 was declared as 'UN Decade of Disabled Persons'. While the years 1993-2002 were declared as the Asian and Pacific Decade of Disabled Persons. India has also taken and made considerable progress in all the categories of action for disabled. The most important factor has been a shift in emphasis in policies towards disabled from a welfares and charity approach to that of equalization of rights and opportunities. Importantly, the role of NGO's in disability sector has been found praise worthy while emerging trends and efforts have had a direct impact on the policy makers, persons with disabilities and organizations engage in rehabilitation of disabled persons.

Persons with disabilities (Equal Opportunities, Protection of Rights and Full Participation) Act was enacted in 1995. The Act aims at the elimination of discrimination and the creation of an inclusion society which provides opportunities for development of people with disabilities to their fullest potential. The Act prescribes a 3 per cent reservation in identified posts in all government and public sector offices. Importantly, in order to empower disabled to cope with the challenge of being economically independent and to develop the necessary entrepreneurship and initiative, the national Handicapped Finance and Development Corporation has been set up to support self employment projects for disabled. Moreover, the National Trust for Welfare of Persons with Autism, Cerebral palsy, Mental Retardation and Multiple Disables Act has been passed recently which is expected to be instrumental in providing supports and protection to vulnerable sections of disabled population.

As it has been already mentioned that credit for policy shift in disability sector goes to Rehabilitation Council of India, set up in 1993 under a central legislation enacted in 1992. The main purpose of the RCI Act was to regulate and standardize the programmes of training professionals in the disability sector on the lines of professional bodies such as the Medical Council of India and the Bar Council of India. The RCI has ensured the socio-economic empowerment of disabled. As early as 1974 the government had launched the scheme of Integrated Education for Disabled Children. But there were only 700 teachers to attend to some 45000 children. Even with all the schemes, not more than 2 per cent of the children with disability could be covered. Importantly, the National Handicapped Council an apex advisory body in the disability sector found in 1983 that one of the main reasons for the schemes for the rehabilitations of disabled not making much headway was a lack of trained manpower. In 1984, the conference of State Social Welfare Ministers decided to form a body to regulate and standardize the training programmes. Justice Baharul Islam Committee has also recommended the setting up of a statutory body and the RCI Act of 1992 was enacted. The Act was amended in 2000 to make the RCI more broad based, covering important components such as promotion research in rehabilitation and special education and maintenance of uniformly in the definitions of various disabilities. Thus, the RCI has ranging objectives. These include regulating, training policies and programmes, bringing about standardization of training courses for professionals in this field, prescribing minimum standards of education and training, reorganization institutions offering different courses, deciding on the grant of recognition to degree, diploma and certificate courses offered by foreign universities and institutions on a reciprocal basis, promoting research in rehabilitation a Central Rehabilitation Register for professionals, collecting information on a regular basis on education and training from institutions in India and abroad and encouraging continuing education in collaboration with organizations working in this field.

It is to be noted that when the RCI (Rehabilitation Council of India) was set up there were just 20 training institutions in this sector. Now there are 160 institutions recognized by the

RCI, out of them 29, considered the best, have been accorded incredible status. These institutions are training more than 200 batches in programmes at different levels from certificate programmes to master degree programmes. As many as 21,877 professionals/personnel with recognized qualifications in the area of rehabilitation and special education are now registered with RCI. It has developed and approved 87 training programmes to meet the manpower requirements of the 16 categories of professionals allocated to it. Importantly, a national bridge course was started to upgrade the skills of those working in this field. Started in 1998, the course has covered 12,665 special teachers and rehabilitation workers. The bridge course is conducted by 163 institutions in 23 states. Even, RCI has launched a BED (special Education) course in the distance education made through Bhoj (open) University, M.P. in August, 2001. Similarly, a foundation course for in service teachers has been launched in the District Primary Education Programme (DPEP) of the Ministry of Human Resource Development. RCI has also initialed a proposal to set up a national university for rehabilitation sciences. RCI has formulated a scheme to provide vocational education to the disabled. Moreover, it has launched national programmes of orientation of medical officers working in PHC's towards disability management. Under this programme, 433 master trainers and 12000 medical officers have been trained since December 2002.

In consonance with the policy of providing a complete package of welfare services to the physically and mentally challenged persons and in order to effectively deal with the multi-dimensional problems of the disabled population, the following National Institutions have been set up in each major area of disability:

1. National Institute for the Visually Handicapped, Dehradoon;
2. National Institute for the Orthopaedically Handicapped, Calcutta;
3. Ali Yavar Jung National Institute for the Visually Handicapped, Mumbai;

4. National Institute for the Mentally Handicapped, Sikandrabad;
5. National Institute for Rehabilitation Training and Research, Cuttack;
6. Institute for the Physically Handicapped, New Delhi;

The Artificial Limbs Manufacturing Corporation of India (ALIMCO) as a registered body was established in 1972 with the aim of providing appliances to the physically handicapped population of the country. ALIMCO has set up four auxiliary production centers to augment its manufacturing capacity of wheel chairs and tricycles. Aids and appliances are provided to disabled persons in India. The Corporation has increased its turnover of Rs. 38.87 Crore in 2001-2002 as against Rs. 32.70 Crore in the year 2000-2001 thus registering an increase of 19 per cent over the previous year. The turn over during 2002-2003 upto December 2002 is Rs. 33.60 crore against Rs. 30.08 crore of the corresponding period of the previous year.

The objective of employment of the Handicapped is to help persons with disabilities in getting gainful employment either through special cells in normal Employment Exchanges or Special Employment Exchanges for persons with disabilities; the scheme is implemented through the Labour Department of State Governments/UTs. At present, there are 39 Special cells and 51 Special Employment Exchanges in the country. Percentage of sanctioned strength of disabled in identified posts was reported to be 15.11, 12.91, 28.44 and 38.40 respectively in class A, B, C and D.

In India, disabled were reported to be 43.79 million, highest in U.P. followed by Bihar, Andhra Pradesh and M.P. Out of total disabled; hardly 3.6 per cent were covered under central assistance. Even, on an average Rs. 49 were spent per beneficiary which shows meagre amount.

About 8000 Institutions are engaged in welfare and rehabilitation. Out of these Institutions, hardly 100 institutions are run by government. About 80% institutions (NGO's) are located in 8 states. Andhra Pradesh, Gujarat, Karnataka, Kerala, Maharastra, Tamil Nadu, Uttar Pradesh, West Bengal and Delhi. During 1988-99, Indian NGO's received $500 million for welfare and rehabilitation of disabled. Several international organizations such as SEEDA (Sweden) DANIDA (Denmark), NORAD (Norway), USAID (USA), Britain Council (UK), ACTION AID (UK), OXFAM (UK), German Leprosy Relief Association (Germany), Royal Common Wealth Society for Blind (Holland) etc. are known agencies. Indian NGO's engaged in disability sector include Anuraag, RKM, Aaroh, Caritas, Indian Red Cross Society, Chetna etc. In the state of Uttar Pradesh, a separate Directorate of Disabled Welfare was set up in 1995. While in each district there is a District Disabled Welfare Officer who is looking after disabled. Under the disabled pension scheme Rs. 125.00 per month is provided for poor acute disabled. In this scheme 1.40 lakh disabled have been benefited while scholarships for educational development have benefited to 20.235 students. Disabled are also provided assistance for economic rehabilitation i.e. for shop (Rs. 20.000 with Rs. 5000 subsidy). Importantly, marriage incentives are provided to disabled up to Rs. 14000 for both the disabled person and Rs. 11000 for single disabled person. There are 12 schools and 10 training centers for rehabilitation of disabled. About 10 institutions are also providing bridge course to master workers and teachers. There are 25 institutions with the residential capacity of 475 students to impart education to disabled children.

In order to examine the presumes of disabled, a study was conducted in U.P. by Pt. G.B. Pant Institute of studies in Rural Development. The present paper is based on the said study.

PROBLEMS IN SOCIAL REHABILITATION

The Problems of the disabled are not only those caused by their disability but also those of adjustment in a world whose apathetic or hostile attitude towards them magnifies their troubles and threatens their very existence as human beings. A disabled man, like e very other man, is a 'social being' and is, therefore, no different from his able bodied brethren. It is an irony, however, that he is not accepted by society as he is, for it invariably focuses its attention on his disabilities rather than on his abilities. Significantly, physique is one of the important criteria upon which social distinctions are based. The adverse effects of society's lack of sympathy are varied.

The most harmful outcome of this attitude is the exclusion of the disabled from social intercourse. Therefore, the change of social attitude towards disabled is the prime objective of social planning for rehabilitation of disabled.

Disabled face a number of problems in terms of limited job opportunities and limited job prospects. Moreover, due to poverty, the disabled are unable to get facilities for medical treatment and other business opportunities.

Physically handicapped persons face more problems for physical movement as compared to other type of disability. Out of 300, 144 (48.00%) disabled cannot easily travel while it was reported much higher in case of physically handicapped (67.62%). Hardly 22% disabled properly can travel unlimited-distance Table 1.

Table 1
Disability Wise Problems of Physical Movement

Problem	*Type of Disabled*				
	Blind	*Deaf & Dumb*	*Physically Handicapped*	*Mental Retarded*	*Total*
On Bed	2(4.00)	-	6(5.72)	2(4.00)	10(3.33)
Can't Walk	20(40.00)	-	5(4.76)	8(16.00)	33(11.00)
Can Walk to Limited Yards	19(38.00)	28(29.47)	71(67.62)	26(52.00)	144(48.00)
Can Travel to Unlimited Distance	9(18.00)	67(70.53)	23(21.90)	14(28.00)	113(37.67)
'N'	50	95	105	50	300

Figures in brackets indicate percentage.

During field survey it was found that (86.67%) respondents of assisted centres don't need support for doing routine work while rest disabled need assistance in performing of their daily routine work. About 82% disabled of non assisted centres also revealed that they do not need support in performance of daily routine work Table 2.

Information collected regarding problems faced by the disabled in marital life, only (26.25%) disabled from assisted centres accepted that they don't face any problems regarding their marital life while the majority of the disabled face problems in their marital life. Due to disability they are remained unmarried while the married disabled cannot enjoy marital life. Details are in Table 3.

Table 2
Problems Being Faced in Daily Routine Work

Problem of Daily Routine	Districts							
	Allahabad		Kanpur		Varanasi		Total	
	Assisted Centre	Non-Assisted Centre	Assisted Centre	Non-Assisted Centre	Assistd Centre	Non-Assisted Centre	Assisted Centre	Non-Assisted Centre
Can do Daily Routine	5(6.25)	1(5.00)	7(8.75)	-	4(5.00)	-	16(6.67)	1(1.67)
Can't do Daily Routine	3(3.75)	1(5.00)	3(3.75)	1(5.00)	2(2.50)	1(5.00)	8(3.33)	3(5.00)
Need Support for doing Daily Routine Work	3(3.75)	2(10.00)	2(2.50)	2(10.00)	3(3.75)	3(15.00)	8(3.33)	7(11.67)
Don't Need Support for Doing Routine Work	69(86.25)	16(80.00)	68(85.00)	17(85.00)	71(88.75)	16(80.00)	208(86.67)	49(81.66)
'N'	80	20	80	20	80	20	240	60

Figures in brackets indicate percentage

Table 3
Problems Being Faced By Disabled in Marital Life

Problem of Daily Routine	Districts							
	Allahabad		Kanpur		Varanasi		Total	
	Assisted Centre	Non-Assisted Centre	Assisted Centre	Non-Assisted Centre	Assistd Centre	Non-Assisted Centre	Assisted Centre	Non-Assisted Centre
Unmarried Due to Disabled	14(17.50)	4(20.00)	17(21.25)	5(25.00)	18(22.50)	6(30.00)	49(20.42)	15(25.00)
Can't Support Spouse	22(27.50)	3(15.00)	20(25.00)	3(15.00)	19(23.75)	4(20.00)	61(25.42)	10(16.67)
Strained Relation With Spouse	17(21.25)	3(15.00)	18(22.50)	2(10.00)	20(25.00)	3(15.00)	55(22.91)	8(13.33)
Can't More With Spouse	4(5.00)	1(5.00)	3(3.75)	3(15.00)	5(6.25)	1(5.00)	12(5.00)	5(8.33)
No Problems	23(28.75)	9(45.00)	22(27.50)	7(35.00)	18(22.50)	6(30.00)	63(26.25)	22(36.67)
'N'	80	20	80	20	80	20	240	60

Figures in brackets indicate percentage

About 21% disabled feels that they are unmarried due to their disability while 24% respondents accepted that they cannot support their spouse. Moreover, 21% disabled revealed that their strained marital relations are due to disability. The problems related to marital life are more acute in case of physically challenged persons as compared to other type of disability. Dtails are given in Table 4.

Table 4
Disability Wise Problems In Marital Life

Problem	Type of Disabled				
	Blind	*Deaf & Dumb*	*Physically Handicapped*	*Mental Retarded*	*Total*
Unmarried Due to Disabled	6(12.00)	5(5.26)	28(26.67)	25(50.00)	64(21.33)
Can't Support Spouse	16(32.00)	18(18.95)	32(30.48)	5(10.00)	71(23.67)
Strained Relation With Spouse	18(36.00)	12(12.63)	23(21.90)	10(20.00)	63(21.00)
Can't Move with Spouse	10(20.00)	-	2(1.90)	5(10.00)	17(5.67)
No Problems	-	60(63.16)	20(19.05)	5(10.00)	85(28.33)
'N'	50	95	105	50	300

Figures in brackets indicate percentage.

Other problems are related to daily routine work, participation in festivals and social ceremonies and living economically independent life. The disabled hesitate in participation of social and festival occasions due to inferiority and physical insecurity. While physically handicapped cannot smoothly operate their own business or run the economic activities for their sustenance. Other Problems of disabled are given in Table 5.

Disabled individual is not so much concerned about the attitude of the people at large as about the attitudes of those that are intimately associated with him. His family friends, neighbours, employers and colleagues all are associated with him, therefore their attitudes towards disabled person is very important. Acceptance of the crippled child, both in the physical and mental sense, goes a long way towards the adjustment of his problems. The most usual parental response is that of over indulgence. This leads to emotional

Table 5
Other Problems Being Faced By Disabled

Problem of Daily Routine	*Districts*							
	Allahabad		*Kanpur*		*Varanasi*		*Total*	
	Assisted Centre	*Non-Assisted Centre*	*Assisted Centre*	*Non-Assisted Centre*	*Assistd Centre*	*Non-Assisted Centre*	*Assisted Centre*	*Non-Assisted Centre*
Daily Routine Work	13(16.25)	3(15.00)	16(20.00)	2(10.00)	17(21.25)	1(5.00)	46(19.17)	6(10.00)
Festivals and Social Ceremonies	13(16.25)	1(5.00)	17(21.25)	3(16.25)	18(22.50)	1(5.00)	48(20.00)	5(8.33)
Making Economically Independent	12(15.00)	1(5.00)	19(23.75)	3(16.25)	21(26.25)	2(10.00)	52(21.67)	6(10.00)
No Problem	42(52.50)	15(75.00)	28(35.00)	12(60.00)	24(30.00)	16(80.00)	94(39.16)	43(71.67)
'N'	80	20	80	20	80	20	240	60

Figures in brackets indicate percentage

Table 6
Attitude of Neighbors Towards Disabled

Attitudes	*Districts*							
	Allahabad		*Kanpur*		*Varanasi*		*Total*	
	Assisted Centre	*Non-Assisted Centre*	*Assisted Centre*	*Non-Assisted Centre*	*Assistd Centre*	*Non-Assisted Centre*	*Assisted Centre*	*Non-Assisted Centre*
Neighbors Went to Keep Away	13(16.25)	3(15.00)	15(18.75)	4(20.00)	17(21.25)	2(10.00)	45(18.75)	9(15.00)
Consider No Untouchable	12(15.00)	4(20.00)	10(12.50)	5(25.00)	8(10.00)	3(15.00)	30(12.50)	12(20.00)
Neighbors Went to Mix Up	30(37.50)	7(35.00)	35(43.75)	6(30.00)	32(40.00)	8(40.00)	97(40.42)	21(35.00)
Neighbors are Helpful	25(31.25)	6(30.00)	20(25.00)	5(25.00)	23(28.75)	7(35.00)	68(28.33)	18(30.00)
'N'	80	20	80	20	80	20	240	60

Figures in brackets indicate percentage

maladjustment. As the basic needs of a child or an adult are love, security independence and adventure, very few crippled children are able to satisfy them. Every child wants affection from his parents. He must be assured that he is needed. However, sometimes the crippled child creates disharmony in the family. The parents have to overcome his feeling of wounded vanity, to conquer an often better disappointment one to re-adjust his ambitions. The crippled child is the focus in the family on which from all sides strong emotions clash.

Though the majority of the respondents reported that attitude of neighbours towards them is helpful and they want to mix up with them while a significant proportion of disabled revealed that neighbours want to keep away (18.75%) and consider them untouchables (12.50%). The problem of untouchables is more acute in cause of disabled of non assisted centres than the disabled from assisted Centres. Details are given in Table 6.

The problems and negative attitudes of neighbours have been reported more acute in case of mentally retarded (54.00%) and physically handicapped persons (9.52%). Thus, the disability wise attitudes of neighbours, has been found to be varying. Details are given in Table 7.

Table 7
Disability Wise Attitude of Neighbors Towards Disabled

Attitudes	*Type of Disabled*				
	Blind	*Deaf & Dumb*	*Physically Handicapped*	*Mental Retarded*	*Total*
Neighbors want to keep away	8(16.00)	9(9.47)	10(9.52)	27(54.00)	54(18.00)
Consider as Untouchable	1(2.00)	1(1.05)	36(34.29)	4(8.00)	42(14.00)
Neighbors want to Mix Up	28(56.00)	37(38.95)	47(44.76)	6(12.00)	118(39.33)
Neighbors are Helpful	13(26.00)	48(50.53)	12(11.43)	13(26.00)	86(28.67)
'N'	50	95	105	50	300

Figures in brackets indicate percentage

Behaviour of neighbours towards disabled is given in Tables 8 and 9.

Table 8
Behavior of Neighbors Towards Disabled

Behaviors	Districts							
	Allahabad		Kanpur		Varanasi		Total	
	Assisted Centre	Non-Assisted Centre	Assisted Centre	Non-Assisted Centre	Assistd Centre	Non-Assisted Centre	Assisted Centre	Non-Assisted Centre
Neighbors Mix Up	40(50.00)	8(40.00)	30(37.50)	6(30.00)	36(45.00)	7(35.00)	106(44.17)	21(35.00)
Neighbors Don't Mix Up	10(12.50)	2(10.00)	12(15.00)	1(5.00)	10(12.50)	2(10.00)	32(13.33)	5(8.33)
Neighbor See Disgracefully	8(10.00)	2(10.00)	10(12.50)	3(15.00)	9(11.25)	4(20.00)	27(11.25)	9(15.00)
Neighbors Try to Solve Problems	10(12.50)	4(20.00)	16(20.00)	6(30.00)	15(18.75)	6(30.00)	41(17.08)	16(26.67)
Neighbors Encourage at Common Place	12(15.00)	4(20.00)	12(15.00)	4(20.00)	10(12.50)	1(5.00)	34(14.17)	9(15.00)
'N'	80	20	80	20	80	20	240	60

Figures in brackets indicate percentage.

Table 9
Disability Wise Behavior of Neighbors Towards Disabled

Behaviors	*Type of Disabled*				
	Blind	*Deaf & Dumb*	*Physically Handicapped*	*Mental Retarded*	*Total*
Neighbors Mix Up	28(56.00)	39(41.05)	51(48.57)	9(18.00)	127(42.33)
Neighbors Don't Mix Up	5(10.00)	3(3.16)	12(11.43)	17(34.00)	37(12.33)
Neighbor Seen Disgracefully	7(14.00)	5(5.26)	10(9.52)	14(28.00)	36(12.00)
Neighbors Try to Solve Problems Help	8(16.00)	30(31.58)	13(12.38)	6(12.00)	57(19.00)
Neighbors Encourage at Common Place	2(4.00)	18(18.95)	19(18.10)	4(8.00)	43(14.34)
Total	50	95	105	50	300

Figures in brackets indicate percentage.

Most of the disabled of assisted centres reported that neighbours are helpful to them and want to mix up with them. However, a higher proportion of respondents also revealed that neighbours are disgraceful (11.25%). Importantly, the problems of disabled as behavior of neighbours are more acute in case of mentally retarded and least in case of Deaf and Dumb. Moreover, in most of the case neighbours are helpful to the disabled.

Social attitudes towards disabled are shown in Tables 10 and 11.

The main problems are related to disgraceful behaviour, dishonour, marriage settlement and non-cooperation. Importantly, majority of the disabled reported that due to disability their social relations are limited (71.67%). About 8% are facing the problem of inferiority complex while about 12% of disabled are feeling insecurity due to disability. The inferiority complex has been found more acute in case of blind (16%) and least in case of physically handicapped (5.7%). Disability has can be limited social relations while problem of social adjustment is more acute in case of Deaf and Dumb.

Though social behaviour towards disabled has been reported to be positive and helpful to disabled however, they still feel that disability has caused problems in marriage

Table 10
Social Attitude Towards Disabled

Attitudes	Districts							
	Allahabad		Kanpur		Varanasi		Total	
	Assisted Centre	Non-Assisted Centre	Assisted Centre	Non-Assisted Centre	Assistd Centre	Non-Assisted Centre	Assisted Centre	Non-Assisted Centre
People Want to Mix	25(31.25)	8(40.00)	29(36.25)	7(35.00)	28(35.00)	9(45.00)	82(34.17)	24(40.00)
People Don't Want to Mix	7(8.75)	3(15.00)	6(7.50)	2(10.00)	8(10.00)	1(5.00)	21(8.76)	6(10.00)
People Don't Cooperate	6(7.50)	2(10.00)	4(5.00)	1(5.00)	7(8.75)	3(15.00)	17(7.08)	6(10.00)
People see Disgracefully	13(16.25)	2(10.00)	15(18.75)	6(30.00)	16(20.00)	3(15.00)	44(18.33)	11(18.34)
Problems Arise in Marriage Settlement	18(22.50)	3(15.00)	14(17.50)	3(15.00)	12(15.00)	2(10.00)	44(18.33)	8(13.33)
Problems of Dishonor	11(13.75)	2(10.00)	12(15.00)	1(5.00)	9(11.25)	2(10.00)	32(13.33)	5(8.33)
'N'	80	20	80	20	80	20	240	60

Figures in brackets indicate percentage.

settlement. This problem is more acute in case of blind (22%) and least in case of physically handicapped (14.29 %). The problem of dishonour has been reported higher in case of physically handicapped. Details are given in Table 12.

Table 11
Disability Wise Social Problems of Disabled

Social Problems	*Type of Disabled*				
	Blind	*Deaf & Dumb*	*Physically Handicapped*	*Mental Retarded*	*Total*
Limited Relations	33(66.00)	60(63.16)	82(78.10)	40(80.00)	215(71.67)
Problems of Social Adjustment	2(4.00)	11(11.58)	7(6.67)	5(10.00)	25(8.33)
Insecurity Feeling	7(14.00)	18(18.95)	10(9.52)	2(4.00)	37(12.33)
Inferiority Complex	8(16.00)	6(6:31)	6(5.71)	3(6.00)	23(7.67)
'N'	50	95	105	50	300

Figures in brackets indicate percentage.

Table 12
Social Behaviour Towards Disabled

Behavior	*Type of Disabled*				
	Blind	*Deaf & Dumb*	*Physically Handicapped*	*Mental Retarded*	*Total*
People Want to Mix	20(40.00)	36(37.89)	42(40.00)	8(16.00)	106(35.33)
People Don't Want to Mix	2(4.00)	5(5.26)	8(7.62)	12(24.00)	27(9.00)
People Don't Cooperate	7(14.00)	6(6.32)	4(3.81)	6(12.00)	23(7.68)
People see Disgracefully	3(6.00)	23(24.22)	18(17.14)	11(22.00)	55(18.33)
Problems Arise in Marriage Settlement	11(22.00)	18(18.95)	15(14.29)	8(16.00)	52(17.33)
Problems of Dishonor	7(14.00)	7(7.36)	18(17.14)	5(10.00)	37(12.33)
'N'	50	95	105	50	300

Figures in brackets indicate percentage.

The personal problems of disabled are shown in Table 13. The main problems are related to social relations, social adjustment and insecurity. However, the disability has caused limited social relations of disabled. The other problems are related to social status and fear. Though, the disabled reported that they gained sympathy of people due to their disability, however, a few revealed that their social status has inclined due to this disability. Details are given in Table 14.

Table 13
Personal Problems Being Faced By Disabled

Problem	Districts							
	Allahabad		*Kanpur*		*Varanasi*		*Total*	
	Assisted Centre	*Non-Assisted Centre*	*Assisted Centre*	*Non-Assisted Centre*	*Assistd Centre*	*Non-Assisted Centre*	*Assisted Centre*	*Non-Assisted Centre*
Limited Relations	53(66.25)	16(80.00)	60(75.00)	14(70.00)	55(68.75)	17(85.00)	168(70.00)	47(78.33)
Problems of Social Adjustment	6(7.50)	1(5.00)	7(8.75)	2(10.00)	8(10.00)	1(5.00)	21(8.75)	4(6.67)
Insecurity Feelings	10(12.50)	2(10.00)	11(13.75)	1(5.00)	12(15.00)	1(5.00)	33(13.75)	4(6.67)
Inferiority Complex	11(13.75)	1(5.00)	2(2.50)	3(15.00)	5(6.25)	1(5.00)	18(7.50)	5(8.33)
'N'	80	20	80	20	80	20	240	60

Figures in brackets indicate percentage.

Table 14
Social Problems Being Faced By Disabled

Social Problems	*Districts*							
	Allahabad		*Kanpur*		*Varanasi*		*Total*	
	Assisted Centre	Non-Assisted Centre	Assisted Centre	Non-Assisted Centre	Assistd Centre	Non-Assisted Centre	Assisted Centre	Non-Assisted Centre
Social Status Declined Due to Disability	4(5.00)	1(5.00)	6(7.50)	-	3(3.75)	1(5.00)	13(5.42)	2(3.33)
Social Status Slightly Affected Due to Disability	15(18.75)	1(5.00)	14(17.50)	1(5.00)	17(21.25)	2(10.00)	46(19.17)	4(6.67)
Sympathy Gained Due to Disability	40(50.00)	15(75.00)	38(47.50)	17(85.00)	36(45.00)	13(65.00)	114(47.50)	45(75.00)
Indifference Social/Psychological Attitude	19(23.75)	3(15.00)	21(26.25)	2(10.00)	22(27.50)	4(20.00)	62(25.83)	9(15.00)
Fear	2(2.50)	-	1(1.25)	-	2(2.50)	-	5(2.08)	-
'N'	80	20	80	20	80	20	240	60

Figures in brackets indicate percentage.

The proportion of disabled who reported that their social status has declined due to their disability has been reported higher in case of blind (12%) while. Moreover, about 22% blinds reported that disability has affected their social status. Details are given in Table 15.

Table 15
Social Status Due to Disability

Social Status	*Type of Disabled*				
	Blind	*Deaf & Dumb*	*Physically Handicapped*	*Mental Retarded*	*Total*
Social Status Declined Due to Disability	6 (12.00)	4 (4.21)	3(2.86)	2(4.00)	15(5.00)
Social Status Affected Due to Disability	11(22.00)	9 (9.47)	19 (18.10)	11(22.00)	50(16.67)
Sympathy Gained Due to Disability	28 (56.00)	54 (56.84)	55 (52.38)	22(44.00)	159(53.00)
Indifference Social/ Psychological Attitude	5 (10.00)	27 (28.42)	28 (26.66)	11(22.00)	71(23.67)
Fear	-	1(1.06)	-	4(8.00)	5(1.66)
'N'	50	95	105	50	300

Figures in brackets indicate percentage.

The relationship between a physical disability and mental deficiency has long been a subject of controversy and has been engaging the attention of many an educationists and many a psychologist from time to time. Special education for disabled has been demanded by the Psychologists and educationalists. In some cases, special schools such as hospital schools, home teaching, day and boarding special schools, and special arrangements in ordinary schools etc. have been implemented. Importantly, the solution of disability lies in promotion of vocational education since disabled may earn their sustenance to some extent and their dependency on others may be reduced to the greater extent. Vocational training and rehabilitation is the need of hour to tackle the problems of disability. The main problems of education are shown in Tables 16 and 17.

The disabled have limited educational and vocational educational opportunities, choices and their education is also

Table 16
Problems of Educational Development

Problem of Educational Development	*Districts*							
	Allahabad		*Kanpur*		*Varanasi*		*Total*	
	Assisted Centre	*Non-Assisted Centre*	*Assisted Centre*	*Non-Assisted Centre*	*Assistd Centre*	*Non-Assisted Centre*	*Assisted Centre*	*Non-Assisted Centre*
Suspended Education Due to Disability	15(18.75)	3(15.00)	17(21.25)	2(10.00)	17(21.25)	3(15.00)	49(20.42)	8(13.33)
Limited Choice	13(16.25)	2(10.00)	15(18.75)	1(5.00)	14(17.50)	1(5.00)	42(17.50)	4(6.67)
No Further Study	12(15.00)	3(15.00)	13(16.25)	4(20.00)	11(13.75)	5(25.00)	36(15.00)	12(20.00)
Parent Not Willing	18(22.50)	5(25.00)	15(18.75)	4(20.00)	16(20.00)	5(25.00)	49(20.42)	14(23.33)
Be Lated Education	14(17.50)	4(20.00)	12(15.00)	5(25.00)	15(18.75)	3(15.00)	41(17.08)	12(20.00)
Educational Backwardness	5(6.25)	2(10.00)	6(7.50)	3(15.00)	4(5.00)	1(5.00)	15(6.25)	6(10.00)
Physically Encumbrances	3(3.75)	1(5.00)	2(2.50)	1(5.00)	3(3.75)	2(10.00)	8(3.33)	4(6.67)
'N'	80	20	80	20	80	20	240	60

Figures in brackets indicate percentage.

Table 17
Disability Problems of Disabled in Educational Development

Problems of Education	*Type of Disabled*				
	Blind	*Deaf & Dumb*	*Physically Handicapped*	*Mental Retarded*	*Total*
Suspended Education Due to Disability	15(30.00)	12(12.63)	13(12.38)	17(34.00)	57(19.00)
Limited Choice	8(16.00)	4(4.21)	22(20.95)	12(24.00)	46(15.33)
No Further Study	3(6.00)	26(27.37)	17(16.19)	2(4.00)	48(16.00)
Parents Not Willing	7(14.00)	24(25.26)	23(21.90)	9(18.00)	63(21.00)
Be Lated Education	9(18.00)	19(20.00)	22(20.95)	3(6.00)	53(17.67)
Educational Backwardness	3(6.00)	10(10.53)	8(7.62)	-	21(7.00)
Physically Encumbrances	5(10.00)	-	-	7(14.00)	12(4.00)
Total	50	95	105	50	300

Figures in brackets indicate percentage.

late due to disability. Moreover, they face inferiority complex in educational development and face a number of problems related to educational development and vocational training.

21

NEED FOR REHABILITATION OF DISABLED

S.P. Pandey & O.P. Singh

Disability has been an issue in focus through out the plan period. In India too, efforts to rehabilitate, physically and mentally challenged persons, through specially designed educational and vocational strategies have a chequered history. But the Policy shifts in tackling the problems of disability and rehabilitation of disabled have focused on new approach with multi pronged strategies. However, disabled face a number of problems. Moreover, the institutions engaged in rehabilitation of disabled also face problems and challenges in enabling disabled, harnessing their abilities. The Paper has attempted to review the situation of disability in India, Government efforts in tackling the disabilities and the problems of disabled in their rehabilitation. The paper is based on a major study conducted in Varanasi, Allahabad and Kanpur in UP during 2003-2004 by Pt. G B Pant Institute of Studies in Rural Development, Lucknow.

As it has been already mentioned that parents of disabled were surveyed to analyse their needs for rehabilitation of their wards. Besides, disabled were also enquired about their needs for social and vocational rehabilitation. In this part of the report such needs for rehabilitation have been analyzed. More than one fourth respondents reported that financial assistance is required for self employment. Similar proportion of disabled reported the need of financial assistance for arranging marriage of disabled and their wards. About 19% respondents demanded for financial assistance from government for undergoing medical treatment. Details of need of financial assistance are given in Table 1 below.

Table 1
Need of Financial Assistance

Needs from Govt.	*Assisted Centre*	*Non Assisted Centre*	*Total*
Financial Assistant for Self Employment of the Disabled	180(26.44)	26(25.74)	206(26.34)
Financial Assistant for Marriage and Children's Marriage of the Disabled	176(25.84)	22(21.78)	198(25.32)
Financial Assistant from Govt. for the Medical Treatment and Appliances	120(17.62)	26(25.75)	146(18.67)
Disability Pension Plan	116(17.03)	16(15.84)	132(16.88)
Provided loaning for the Disables form Banks as a Subsidy	89(13.07)	11(10.89)	100(12.79)
'N'	681	101	782

Figures in brackets indicate percentage.

The financial assistance is required more in case of disabled from non-assisted centres than the respondents of assisted centres. About half of the disabled were of the opinion that appliances should be distributed free of cost to the disabled. Similarly, 42% respondents demanded that appliances should be available locally for their use. Need of appliances is given in Table 2.

Table 2
Need of Appliances

Needs from Govt.	*Assisted Centre*	*Non Assisted Centre*	*Total*
Free Distribution	120(50.00)	25(41.67)	145(48.33)
Modern and New Technologies	20(8.33)	10(16.66)	30(10.00)
Availability of all Type of Appliances in the Same Area/Market	100(41.67)	25(41.67)	125(41.67)
'N'	240	60	300

Figures in brackets indicate percentage.

Again, the respondents were asked about the distribution of appliances. About half of the disabled from assisted centres

Table 3
Distribution of Appliances

Need	*Districts*							
	Allahabad		*Kanpur*		*Varanasi*		*Total*	
	Assisted Centre	*Non-Assisted Centre*	*Assisted Centre*	*Non-Assisted Centre*	*Assistd Centre*	*Non-Assisted Centre*	*Assisted Centre*	*Non-Assisted Centre*
FreeDistribution	26(32.50)	6(30.00)	21(26.25)	5(25.00)	23(28.75)	4(20.00)	70(29.17)	15(25.00)
FinancialAssistance for Purchases	40(50.00)	8(40.00)	43(53.75)	7(35.00)	39(48.75)	8(40.00)	122(50.83)	23(38.33)
Should beGifted byInstitution/ NGO's	14(17.50)	6(30.00)	16(20.00)	8(40.00)	18(22.50)	8(40.00)	48(20.00)	22(36.67)
'N'	80	20	80	20	80	20	240	60

Figures in brackets indicate percentage.

were of the view that financial assistance should be granted for purchase of appliances. While (29.17%) respondents demanded for free appliances. Against it, (36.67%) respondents from non-assisted centres were of the view that appliances showed be gifted by NGO's or institutions Details are in Table 3.

During the survey it was found that (42.33%) respondents reported that services for medical aid should be extended while one fourth respondents were of the view that resource should be mobilized for extending medical aid to disabled. About half of the respondents of non-assisted centre demanded financial supported from government for medical treatment. Need for medical intervention is shown in Table 4.

Table 4
Need for Medical Intervention According to Households

Needs from Govt.	*Assisted Centre*	*Non Assisted Centre*	*Total*
Resource Mobilization	68(28.33)	5(8.33)	73(24.33)
Extension of Services to Medical Aid	120(50.00)	7(11.67)	127(42.33)
Financial Support from Government for Medical	25(10.42)	30(50.00)	55(18.34)
Proper Medical Treatments from the Hospital	12(5.00)	10(16.67)	22(7.33)
Free Medical Facilities	15(6.25)	8(13.33)	23(7.67)
'N'	240	60	300

Figures in brackets indicate percentage.

Again, about 40% disabled were of the view that financial support should be extended from government for medical aid which 29% disabled of assisted centres and (26.67%) disabled from non-assisted centres demanded accessibility to credit. Details are in Table 5.

About 36% respondents demanded for entrepreneurship development programmes and 24.67% respondents were of the view that job oriented and gainful trainings should be started. Again, one fourth households also demanded technical education and trainings. The need for vocational training is shown in Table 6.

Table 5
Need for Medical Intervention According to Disabled

Medical Intervention	Districts							
	Allahabad		Kanpur		Varanasi		Total	
	Assisted Centre	Non-Assisted Centre	Assisted Centre	Non-Assisted Centre	Assistd Centre	Non-Assisted Centre	Assisted Centre	Non-Assisted Centre
Resource Mobilization	12(15.00)	3(15.00)	10(12.50)	2(10.00)	13(16.25)	4(20.00)	35(14.58)	9(15.00)
Extension of Services to Medical Aid	13(16.25)	4(20.00)	14(17.50)	3(15.00)	11(13.75)	4(20.00)	38(15.83)	11(18.33)
Financial Support from Govt.	31(38.75)	7(35.00)	35(43.75)	9(45.00)	32(40.00)	8(40.00)	98(40.83)	24(40.00)
Accessibility to Credit	24(30.00)	6(30.00)	21(26.25)	6(30.00)	24(30.00)	4(20.00)	69(20.76)	16(26.67)
'N'	80	20	80	20	80	20	240	60

Figures in brackets indicate percentage.

Table 6
Need of Trainings According to Households

Needs from Govt.	*Assisted Centre*	*Non Assisted Centre*	*Total*
Job Oriented and Gainful Training	60(25.00)	14(23.33)	74(24.67)
Vocational Training	38(15.84)	9(15.00)	47(15.67)
Engineering/Technical Training	53(22.08)	19(31.67)	72(24.00)
E.D.P.S.	89(37.08)	18(30.00)	107(35.66)
Total	240	60	300

Figures in brackets indicate percentage.

It was found that (63.33%) disabled from assisted centres were of the opinion that vocational trainings should be organized. Against it, (51.67%) respondents from non-assisted centres were of the view that vocational trainings should be organized. Thus, the majority of the respondents (households and disabled) were of the view that vocational and job oriented programs should be launched for rehabilitation of disabled. Details are given in Table 7.

It is interesting to note that (49.67%) parents of disabled accepted that NGO's can play a crucial role in prevention of disability as well as rehabilitation of disabled. While (20.67%) respondents felt the need of community mobilization for this cause. Importantly, school teachers have different and challenging role in educational development of disabled. For this purpose school teacher needs orientation and training skills. Details are given in Table 8.

Importantly, community mobilization and its participation in mitigation of disability and rehabilitation of disabled are needed. Therefore, the disabled felt the need of community mobilization (45.42%) in case of assisted centres and (40.00%) in case of non-assisted centres. Again, community may play an important role in change of social attitude and mind set of the parents of disabled. Moreover, creation of social and conducive environment is need of hour for changing mind set and social rehabilitation of disabled. Details of the need of educational development according to disabled are given in Table 9.

The social behaviour and attitudinal change may be ensured through the enhancing role of community based organizations and NGO's. Such organizations may play a vital role in

Table 7
Need for Training According to Disabled

Training	Districts							
	Allahabad		Kanpur		Varanasi		Total	
	Assisted Centre	Non-Assisted Centre	Assisted Centre	Non-Assisted Centre	Assistd Centre	Non-Assisted Centre	Assisted Centre	Non-Assisted Centre
EDP's	10(12.50)	2(10.00)	8(10.00)	1(5.00)	6(7.50)	3(15.00)	24(10.00)	6(10.00)
Vocational Training	53(66.25)	10(50.00)	50(62.50)	9(45.00)	49(61.25)	12(60.00)	152(63.33)	31(51.67)
Job Oriented Training	17(21.25)	8(40.00)	22(27.50)	10(50.00)	25(31.25)	5(25.00)	64(26.67)	23(38.33)
Total	80	20	80	20	80	20	240	60

Figures in brackets indicate percentage.

Table 8
Need of Educational Development According to Households

Needs from Govt.	*Assisted Centre*	*Non Assisted Centre*	*Total*
Community Mobilization	55(22.92)	7(11.67)	62(20.67)
NGO's Role in Educational Development	118(49.17)	31(51.67)	149(49.67)
PRI's Role in Educational Development	30(12.50)	8(13.33)	38(12.66)
School Teacher's Role in Educational Development	37(15.42)	14(23.33)	51(17.00)
'N'	240	60	300

Figures in brackets indicate percentage.

community mobilization, counseling of disabled, mobilization community to mix up with disabled and overall the psychological change. Details are in Table 10.

The disabled also were of the view that they need graceful social behavior, positive and constructive social attitude. Moreover, social mobilization is needed for social rehabilitation of disabled. Details are given in Table 11.

The prospective role of NGO's, PRI's, SHG's, and school teachers has been exposed by the disabled as well as their parents Table 12.

The above analysis simply demonstrates that social rehabilitation of disabled may be ensured through active and enhanced role of community based organization and NGO's. While financial assistance is required for medical aid, purchase of appliances and extending services for enhancing skills and technical knowledge. Moreover, easy access to credit and promotion of professional education are required for social rehabilitation of disabled.

The main observations are given to understand the problems and need for social rehabilitation.

1. Disabled are most marginalized. About 70 million people are disabled in India. Globalization, liberalization and modernization have resulted in growing disability and raised the problems of rehabilitation of disabled.

Table 9
Need of Educational Development According to Disabled

Training	Districts							
	Allahabad		*Kanpur*		*Varanasi*		*Total*	
	Assisted Centre	*Non-Assisted Centre*	*Assisted Centre*	*Non-Assisted Centre*	*Assistd Centre*	*Non-Assisted Centre*	*Assisted Centre*	*Non-Assisted Centre*
Creation of Social and Conducive Environment	20(25.00)	6(30.00)	16(20.00)	6(30.00)	15(18.75)	5(25.00)	51(21.25)	17(28.33)
Community Mobilization	30(37.50)	7(35.00)	36(45.00)	8(40.00)	43(53.75)	9(45.00)	109(45.42)	24(40.00)
NGO's Role in Educational Development	10(12.50)	4(20.00)	8(10.00)	3(15.00)	810.00)	3(15.00)	26(10.83)	10(16.67)
Role of Community Based Organization	20(25.00)	3(15.00)	20(25.00)	3(15.00)	14(17.50)	3(15.00)	54(22.50)	9(15.00)
'N'	80	20	80	20	80	20	240	60

Figures in brackets indicate percentage.

Table 10
Need of Social Behaviour and Attitudinal Change According to Households

Needs from Govt.	*Assisted Centre*	*Non Assisted Centre*	*Total*
Mobilization	40(16.67)	8(13.34)	48(16.00)
Counseling	39(16.25)	6(10.00)	45(15.00)
Consider to Mix Up	53(22.08)	12(20.00)	65(21.67)
Helpful Nature of Neighbours	68(28.33)	17(28.33)	85(28.33)
Change the Psychological Attitude	40(16.67)	17(28.33)	57(19.00)
'N'	240	60	300

Figures in brackets indicate percentage.

2. There has been a range of international initiatives that has helped shape the approach to addressing persons with disability. The international conferences and legal enactments made the provision for harnessing the disabled and their rehabilitation.
3. There has been a shift in emphasis in policies towards disabled persons from a welfare and charity approach to that of equalization of rights and opportunities.
4. Ministry of Social Justice and Empowerment, Government of India is the Nodal Ministry for the disability sector even though rehabilitation of persons with disabilities is multi sectoral process involving a package of services.
5. Present study is based on empirical data collected from field survey in assisted and non-assisted centres of Kanpur, Varanasi and Allahabad of U.P. covering 300 disabled and 300 households as parents.
6. The process of rehabilitation is comprised of three; (i) Physical; (ii) Socio-Psychological and (iii) Vocational. Community based rehabilitation is the best approach for rehabilitation of disabled.
7. There is no systematic and scientific database available on the disability, rough estimates suggests that about 70 million people are disabled in India. Disability is more pronounced in rural areas and among males. In the state of U.P., more than 1.39 crore persons were found physically and mentally challenged.

Table 11
Need of Social Behavior Attitudinal Change According to Disabled

Need	*Districts*							
	Allahabad		*Kanpur*		*Varanasi*		*Total*	
	Assisted Centre	*Non-Assisted Centre*	*Assisted Centre*	*Non-Assisted Centre*	*Assistd Centre*	*Non-Assisted Centre*	*Assisted Centre*	*Non-Assisted Centre*
Community Awareness	36(13.33)	12(15.38)	40(14.55)	10(12.66)	41(15.19)	8(10.83)	117(14.36)	30(12.88)
Social Mobilization	56(20.74)	14(17.95)	54(21.08)	15(18.99)	60(22.22)	14(18.42)	174(21.35)	43(18.46)
Counseling and Guidance	26(9.63)	10(12.82)	22(8.00)	11(13.92)	30(11.11)	12(15.79)	78(9.57)	33(14.16)
Healthy Interaction	30(11.11)	11(14.10)	29(10.55)	12(15.19)	27(10.00)	14(18.42)	86(10.55)	37(15.88)
Graceful Behaviour	62(22.96)	16(20.52)	65(23.64)	15(18.99)	60(22.22)	15(19.74)	187(22.94)	46(19.74)
Positive and Constructive Attitude	60(22.22)	15(19.23)	61(22.18)	16(20.25)	52(19.26)	13(17.11)	173(21.23)	44(18.88)
Total	270	78	275	79	270	76	815	233

Figures in brackets indicate percentage.

Table 12
Prospective Role of
Community Based Organizations in Rehabilitation of Disabled

Organizations	*Good (Effective)*	*Average*	*Not-at-all*	*Total*
NGO's/V.O.	275(91.67)	20(6.67)	5(1.66)	300
PRI's Local Bodies	160(53.34)	100(33.33)	40(13.33)	300
SHG's	155(51.67)	125(41.67)	20(6.66)	300
Opinion Leaders	86(28.67)	80(26.67)	134(44.66)	300
Youth Clubs	50(16.67)	100(33.33)	150(50.00)	300
School Teachers	265(88.33)	25(8.33)	10(3.34)	300
Total	165(55.00)	75(25.00)	60(20.00)	300

Figures in brackets indicate percentage.

8. Disability has become a focused attention in the recent times with rise in political activism and voluntarism at the international level and also increasing debate about the development of alternative service programmes and particularly community based rehabilitation.
9. Rehabilitation Council of India is doing yeoman service in the field of disability. It has wide ranging objectives. These include regulating, training policies and programmes, bringing about standardization of training courses for professionalism in this field, prescribing minimum standards of education and training, recognition institution offering different courses, deciding on the gamut of recognition to degree, diplomas and certificate courses offered by foreign universities and institutions, promoting research in rehabilitation, collecting date related to disabilities and rehabilitation of disabled etc.
10. About 8000 institution are engaged in welfare and rehabilitation of disabled in India. Most of them are NGO's, Trusts and private institutions. Even without financial support some NGO's and Trusts are engaged in rehabilitation of disabled.
11. The socio-economic characteristics of the surveyed families and disabled show that disability is common in all the sects, castes, economic status and age groups.

They are a few families where there are more than one disabled persons. However, disability is more pronounced in disadvantages classes and economically poor class.

12. Disability has been defeated to some extent due to process of rehabilitation. Despite the disability, most of the disabled are enjoying social and domestic life however; they face a number of problems in their life.
13. The disabled persons have been benefited by the programmes of rehabilitation and services extended by the assisted centres and Institutions. However, a number of disabled are not able to have access to these services.
14. The assisted centres are providing education, vocational and medical aid to the disabled persons. However, the services and rehabilitation of the surveyed institutions and centres have been found confined to education and vocational services. Again, only a few centres are providing medical aid.
15. The disabled are facing so many problems in their life. The problems are mainly related to physical, psychological and social. Again, family attitudes, social attitudes and behaviours towards disabled persons have been found to be negative in the sense that disability has marginalized the physically and mentally challenged and also caused tension, fear and social insecurity among disabled.
16. The disabled as well as their parents were of the view that government should provide financial assistance for purchase of appliances, aids and medical treatment. Moreover, government may provide subsidies to the manufacturers of appliances and surgical aids so that the poor disabled may purchase such appliances and aids.
17. The disabled also felt that credit facility should be extended to them for launching of economic enterprises and self employment ventures.

18. Educational development is the need of hour and educational institutions need orientation and training for extending services to the disabled as well as launching of special educational programmes.

POLICY RECOMMENDATIONS

1. The Ministry of Social Justice and Empowerment, Government of India should make special efforts for ensuring closer contacts between the special employments exchanges for the physically handicapped, vocational rehabilitation centres, industrial training institutes, polytechnics, Management Associations and special institutions for education and vocational training for disabled. This can be achieved by organizing workshops or by making the Director of the Employment Exchange, or Management Associations on ex-officio member of training institutions. This will help in making existing training programmes more jobs oriented and trainees might get employment in the open market.
2. Certain number of seats for rural disabled may be reserved for disabled in some of the educational institutions, Industrial training Institutions Polytechnics etc. Thus, migration of rural disabled to urban centres for their vocational training may be checked and they will get equal opportunities.
3. Welfare institutions, associations, trusts, NGO's etc. may also be supported for upgrading their training centres and convert them into Industrial Training Institutions. Some such organizations may be provided financial support to work as Nodal Agency and building their institutional capabilities so that disabled are more benefited.
4. The scope of scholarship should be widened and rate of scholarship should be higher for those who go for higher education in special institutions for the disabled.

5. Educational institutions should be encouraged and provided funds for arranging special education for disabled. These institutions also need orientation and training for providing such services.
6. A National Policy for the empowerment, development and welfare of disabled may be formulated by clearly defining the goals of the programmes, the measures required to meet these goals, the priorities to be laid in programme formulation, planning, review and coordination of the services and legislative and administrative support required to achieve these goals.
7. The Ministry of Social Justice and Empowerment, Government of India and other welfare organizations and associations should give wider publicity through mass media to various welfare and rehabilitation schemes for the disabled for their education and training, etc.
8. More concrete efforts should be taken to check road accidents victims through networking with road side training centres and hospitals; there should be effective check on Polio, Tuberculosis, Leprosy, infection in Bones etc.
9. The reserved posts for disabled should be strictly monitored so that the concerned department may not be in position to give employment to non-disabled persons.
10. Voluntary organizations should be provided financial support for mobilizing community to change of social attitude, involvement in rehabilitation services and generation of awareness regarding prevention of disabilities and rehabilitation programmes. There should be more volunteer groups to take up the enormous task of changing attitudes in society towards persons with disability. Volunteering is an opportunity for people with disabilities to become able, empowerment and integrated into the mainstream.
11. Multi-sectoral approach is needed to tackle disability. A new look in strategies and approaches for

involvement of NGO's in various aspects of rehabilitation of persons with disabilities and in human resource employment, vocational education, educational services and employment is needed. Only well established, reputed and committed NGO's should be involved in rehabilitation of disabled. Such organizations should be regularly monitored and evaluated of these activities.

12. Disabled should be provided financial support or subsidies for undergoing medical treatment, particularly for surgery, they should also be assisted in terms of accessibility to credit facilities for purchasing of appliances, aids and starting economic enterprises.

22

EQUIPPING DAIS FOR A HEALTHIER TOMORROW

Rameshwwari Pandya

INTRODUCTION

The information of health service planning in India was laid by the Bhore Committee report in 1946, which had prioritized the needs of women and children. India was the first country to launch a National Family Planning Programme in 1951 and the Reproductive and Child Health Programme (RCH) was launched in 1997. The major objective of this RCH programme was to improve the health status of the most neglected sections of the Indian population, women and girls of socially disadvantaged groups, particularly those living in remote, rural settlement.

Reproductive health implies, that people are able to have a satisfying sex life and that they have the capability to reproduce and the freedom to decide when and how often to do so. It also includes sexual health, the purpose of which is the enhancement of life and personal relations and not merely counseling and care related to reproduction and sexually transmitted diseases (World Health Organization, 1994). Reproductive health is a crucial part of general health. It is not only a key element of health during adolescence and adult hood, but also sets the stage of health beyond reproductive years for both women and men has its effects. Women's health status varies widely both within and among countries because of factors such as local disease prevalence, health related behaviors, and women's educational attainment, exposure to health information, influence on decision making and access to health care, poverty, environmental degradation, civil conflict and migration also influence women's health.

Whereas agriculture and animal husbandry get priority, sanitation and personal cleanliness are neglected. There is no proper health care facilities. The health of rural woman is often impaired due to frequent child births, ignorance and superstition in which she has to live and work. Most often, they go without medicine and doctor's consultancy, but go to the local 'vaid' and get herbal mixtures to cure themselves from diseases and illness. In the absence of any health centre and trained doctors, they are deprived of the basic medical facilities and in consequence remain ignorance and unhealthy. For pregnant women, the only hope is the untrained village midwife, who backed by her long experience is bold enough to meet any emergency. The Indian Primary Health Care (PHC) system has an extensive nationwide network with more than 20,000 primary health centres staffed by doctors and over 1,00,000 sub-centres staffed by female and male health workers. 1,31,000 village level sub-centres has been set up to provide primary health care including maternal care and family planning services. Unfortunately, the PHC system has primarily focused its attention on family planning, and to some extent, on immunization. All the other components of primary health care have been neglected. Women are only recognized by the health system in the context of maternal and child health (MCH). Their general health and reproductive health needs are ignored.

The fundamental issues concerning women and their health are nutrition, sanitation, infections, overwork, work hazards, stresses, mental tensions, pregnancy, child birth and sexual harassment. Women face high risk of malnutrition, retardation in growth and development, disease, disability and even death at three critical stages in their lives–infancy, early childhood and reproductive phase. India is one of the few countries where there are fewer women than men: only 93 women for every

100 men. In 1901 the sex-ratio was 972 women per thousand men. In 1991 it was declined to 927 per thousand men. The main reason of this declining sex-ratio is high mortality rate among females in all age groups. It is noteworthy that in India about 15 million girls are born per year but almost one fourth die before 15 years of age, despite being considered biologically stronger than boys. Mortality indicators show that upto the age of 35 years more females than males die at every age level.

Table 1
Death Rates

Year	*(0-4 Years)*		*(All ages)*	
	Male	*Female*	*Male*	*Female*
1970	51.7	55.1	15.8	15.6
1985	36.6	40.4	11.8	11.8
1990	24.8	27.9	9.7	9.6
1991	25.6	27.5	10.0	9.7
1992	24.9	28.2	10.0	10.2

Source: Sample Registration Service, Fertility and Mortality Indicators for respective years, Registrar General and Census Commission, India New Delhi.

The Table 2 offers the state wise estimates of Maternal Mortality Rate. The maternal mortality rate in India is unacceptably high. The maternal mortality rate is a measure not only of poverty but also of priority society gives to a problem that is of life and death concern to women. According to National Family Health Survey 1992-93, about 1,25,000 women die in India each year due to causes related to pregnancy and child birth.

The survival of mothers and babies is closely correlated with the care and attention received at the time of delivery. Gynaecological and reproductive morbidity among women is high in India. At the time of delivery, no more than 20 per cent of all women have some contact with medical or paramedical personnel. Deliveries are largely conducted by untrained personnel and in unhygienic conditions, both of which contribute significantly to poor maternal health. All deliveries must be managed by trained birth attendants. Normal deliveries can be managed at home or at the institution but in all cases infection must be prevented by ensuring clean delivery practices. Because complications can develop without warning, it is critical to put in the plan effectively to ensure timey referral and management of emergency complications. Death from haemorrhage, for example, can occur within two hours of the onset of bleeding. Establishing effective referral systems for life threatening complications is therefore, critical for saving women's lives. Communities should be involved in organizing timely transportation for women needed care to the referral facilities.

Table 2
Maternal Mortality Rate

Sl. No.	*State*	*Maternal Deaths per 100,000 Births*
1.	Kerala	87
2.	Maharashtra	336
3.	Punjab	369
4.	Tamil Nadu	376
5.	Gujarat	389
6.	West Bengal	389
7.	Andhra Pradesh	436
8.	Haryana	436
9.	Himachal Pradesh	456
10.	Bihar	470
11.	Assam	554
12.	Rajasthan	550
13.	Uttar Pradesh	624
14.	Madhya Pradesh	711
15.	Orissa	738
16.	India	453

Source: NFHS, 1992-1993 and Indirect estimates of MMR from League Table.

Two decade ago, in 1981, no more than 15% of all rural births were performed in an institution and as many as two thirds were delivered by untrained workers and others. And in such states in Bihar, Jammu and Kashmir, Madhya Pradesh, Orissa, Rajasthan and Uttar Pradesh more than three out of four births are delivered by an untrained attendant. And what is disturbing is the evidence than over the 1991 to 2005 period, the picture has hardly changed. The proportion of births conducted institutionally increased from 8 to 15 per cent in rural areas and from 32 to 47 per cent in urban. The proportion of births delivered by untrained attendants fell from 81% in 1971 to 68% in 1987 in rural areas and from 43% to 39% in urban areas. Even so, there are rural areas of the country where 9 out of 10 births are delivered by an untrained attendant. (Khan et al. 1986 for U.P., Kanitkar and Sinha 1989 for Bihar, Rajasthan and Gujarat). In such circumstances, the role of the estimated 5 lakh traditional birth attendance in India–about 1 per 1000 population–becomes especially important (Singh and Paul 1988, Planning Commission 1985). However, the vast majority of births in India takes place at home The National family health survey shows that in 1992-93 only 25.6 per cent of all births and 16.1 per cent of all rural births were conducted in institutions and as many as 65% were delivered by traditional birth attendants.

An immediate priority therefore, is to ensure safe home delivery by trained birth attendants. Traditional birth attendants must be trained to recognize danger signs and ensure timely referral to the hospitals. Collaboration between the health sector and the traditional birth attendants is an important way of bridging two very different cultures concerning reproductive health, but this link has not yet been effectively implemented. The little evidence which is available suggests that trained attendants do in fact have significantly better health care knowledge and can better recognize high risk conditions, suggesting the importance of training of traditional birth attendants. As a part of the safe motherhood initiative, first level

VILLAGE

Village Health Guide	Sub Centre (SC) (For every 5000 population) with ANM/Multi purpose female worker (MPW-F) Multi purpose Male worker (MPW-M) Primary Health Centre (PHC) (For every 30,000 population) with Medical Officer and His Team of Para Medical Staff	Traditional Birth Attendant (TBA) (Dai)	Aanganwadi worker (for every 700 persons in Tribal Areas and Every 1000 persons in Non-Tribal Areas)

referral units (FRUs) with specialists and equipment are now being established to treat complicated pregnancies and obstetrician emergency in selected states and districts. Innovative approaches needed to attract specialists to work at these rural units and expand their reach so that peripheral level institutions can be upgraded to provide specialist care.

Hence understanding need and importance of training Dais, was recognized. This area of research attracted the attention as the review of studies reveal that women are victimized more than men in the matter of poor health.

Reason for Taking up Dai Project with ONGC-Baroda

At the stage of initial conceptualization of the project, it came to the knowledge of the project worker the ONGC was funding some projects and Centre for Adult and Continuing Education was taking up these projects which were:

- Literacy awareness programme.
- Health and Nutrition awareness.
- Dai Training programme.
- Child care.
- HIV/AIDS awareness programme.

The project worker decided to take up Dai Training programme as it seemed more challenging a task to work with women's health.

- Since last few years UBS/UCDS agency have also expressed needs in terms of training paramedical under the community development programmes.
- Health is one of the aspect under the community development which is carried out by this department. Health means covering each and every dimensions that is children, mothers and family. The students who work as community volunteers find children and mothers health to be considered most neglected.
- Even the Department of Home Science Extension and Communication, M. S. University, Baroda is working for community development since past many years and has been focusing on health aspect widely.

- Dai Training is an important training through which women or dais trained will successfully deliver child and help low per centage of death of child and mother.
- Teaching aids are the most effective means of communicating and the use of teaching aids for village or community people makes it very much effective and easy in passing on a message.
- Thus to make the experiment successful, teaching modules helped in dai training classes as a means of communication.
- Thus as a researcher of Extension and Communication and understanding the need for trained Dais in villages for controlling death rates of women and child this project was undertaken.

Objectives

1. To study the need for trained Dai.
2. To study the Job chart/performance of duties by Dai in various Nursing homes and hospitals private and government, small and big and those in urban and rural setting.
3. To identify the concepts and generalization or content to be promoted through Dai training programme.
4. To study the Government approved syllabus for Dai Training and update it.
5. To develop teaching modules for promotion of Dai Training.
6. To promote awareness regarding personal hygiene, reproductive health and family life education amongst the women of village Dabka.
7. To train the women of village Dabka for "Dai Training" through the use of various communication strategies and materials.

METHODOLOGY

Research Design

At the stage of initial conceptualization of the project, it came to the knowledge of the project worker that ONGC, Baroda is funding some projects. One of the five projects was on "Dai Training". All the villages identified by ONGC were surveyed for this specific purpose with other team members. It was decided to take up village Dabka.

Firstly, the project worker contacted the Sarpanch of the village, Ms. Kailashben Jadav. The project worker, sarpanch and the team members visited the village to make the women aware about the Project.

Several initial visits across two months were made to the village to enable the investigator to get familiar with the setting and build rapport with the women. During this period, the purpose of the study was reiterated. While meeting women in the village the style of asking questions was informal and conversational. The sequential steps followed in data collection were as follows:

- Initial visits were made by the two research investigators on a number of occasions in order to get acquainted with the local people.
- Simultaneously, there were informal introductions of the two investigators to the local doctor and Traditional Birth Attendant (Dai).

Figure 1 shows the complete plan of the Project.

Figure 1
Plan of the Project

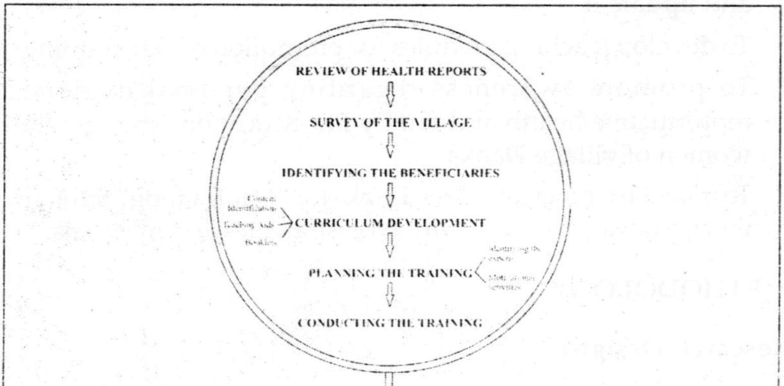

Sample

Analysis of data obtained through structured schedule. Out of 89 households which were surveyed only 23 women were selected. The criteria for selecting the women was as follows. Age range of 20-45 years and was ready to attend the 21 days training. A list of women was prepared after building a good rapport with them. All the women were selected from the same area. A dialogue with them showed that main concern was that training would increase their prestige in the community. At the start of the training, 17 women enrolled but later that number increased to 23. The most promising feature is that three daughter-in-laws of old Dais came forward to undergo training to carry on their traditional occupation.

Inauguration of the Project

A formal inauguration of the Project was done on 8th December 1998 in the village Dabka were all the women from Dabka village were invited. The Vice-Chancellor of The Maharaja Sayajirao University, Dr. Anil Kane, The Regional Direction ONGC, WBRC Shri N. Lal, DGM-Drilling Shri Gupta, Manager Public Relations Mrs. Narayani Mhail, Hon. Director of the Centre for Continuing Adult Education and Community Services Dr. Kalpana Parlikar and the staff from the Faculty of Home Science along with important village leaders were the invited guests. The function started with a prayer, followed by speech of chief guests and introduction of the Project was given. An exhibition was also arranged in which different charts, posters, flash cards were displayed. The PTC college ground of Dabka was the venue of the inauguration function.

Curriculum Development

Before planning the actual training programme for the Dais several informal sessions were held to understand the level of knowledge of Dais, their beliefs concerning pregnancy and delivery practices. This was done to have two-way process of acknowledging the traditional knowledge and giving new modern knowledge. The curriculum which is followed by District Health Office was followed.

Teaching Aids

For better retention of knowledge different teaching aids like flash cards, posters, charts and booklets with bold illustrations were planned and made as it would help the research worker in teaching the important concepts. Teaching materials were also collected from other agencies which are working in the area of Women's Reproductive Health like.

1. Baroda Citizen Council
2. S.S.G. Hospital, Baroda
3. CHETNA (Ahmedabad)
4. Tribhovandas Foundation (Anand)

Planning the Training

Identifying the Experts

The effort to collaborate with government PHC was planned but it had to be abandoned due to lack of support from District Health Office. The next alternative was to utilize local resource persons and private doctors from Baroda City who were well-versed in rural obstetrics. We also took help of Dais who have access to the women in the community. We were initially reluctant to choose the option because the Dais are very old and have physical limitations. Nevertheless, we thought if given a situation we could utilize, the Dais as the key persons and also as master trainers. The different experts from Baroda were taken to Dabka village to impart training.

Motivational Activities

Different motivational activities were planned by the project worker to ensure good attendance throughout the training. The motivational activities on various topics like Food, Health, Legal education etc. Activities which were planned and carried out were as follows:

1. Slide show	-	Care during pregnancy, Deficiency diseases, Healthy and unhealthy living conditions, supplementary income generating activities.
2. Film Strips	-	Why small family ? Immunisation schedule for your child. Food we eat.......

3.	Video Films	-	Meena Hasi Kali Kem Mari ?
4.	Illustrative Story	-	Importance of education, Small family happy family
5.	Food Demonstration	-	Khajoor Roll, Chocolate Burfi, Palak Pooda, Nan Khatai, etc.

Table 3
The Daily Plan of Work during the Project was Approximately Distributed in the Following Manner

Activity	*Time (Minutes)*
Casual talking	15
Motivational activities	50
or	
Expert Talk and Discussion	60
Attendance and instructions for the next class	15
Total	Nearly 1.½ hrs.

Training of Dais

The objective of the programme is to impart correct information on pregnancy and delivery in a very simple manner so that Dais, who are mostly illiterate, can understand the basis of why they have to change certain practices. First they were exposed to the basics of human anatomy and physiology and modern concepts of obstetrics and gynaecology. The next step was to train them the diagnosis of problematic pregnancy. As majority of the Dais were illiterate the training was participative and conducted according to their capacity. Different topics were covered by the experts during the training. The Dais were not only given the facts, but also given ample opportunities for discussion and clear their doubts and share their experiences. Several practical sessions on How to wear the gloves ?, Process of Sterilization were conducted so that, hands on experiences are given. They were taught the use of ready kit for delivery, how to do per vaginal and per speculum examination.

A field visit was arranged to give enriching learning experience. During the training in S.S.G. Hospital they were taught about scientific medicine, and micro organisms by looking through microscope, Functioning of Auto-clave Room. Practical tips of how to handle emergency during pregnancy, visit to labour room and modern operation theatre. This helped them understand the rationale behind the practice of sterilization. The practical traiing as well as the visit to the gynaecology ward of S.S.G. Hospital was crucial as it improved their knowledge and gave them confidence.

Validictory Function

A Validictory Function was organized on 30th March 1999 for all the Dais who had successfully completed the training programme, after the training programme was over. Dr. Kalpana Paralikar was the chief guest and Dr. Mukesh Bhatt and Ms. Kailash Ben Jadav were the special invitees for the function. The venue of the programme was PTC college Dabka. The dais had not received any salary or honorarium for getting the training so along with the certificate, Ready Made Delivery Kit and a Steel Box along with cash of Rs. 75/- as a token money was given to all the 23 Dais in a public function which was attended by the village women and students of P.G. Diploma in extension from the Faculty of Home Science, Baroda.

RESULT AND DISCUSSION

Description of the Study Setting

The present section describes the study setting and the demographic and socio-economic characteristics of the population and sample. The locale of the study was Dabka village, Padra Taluka of Baroda.

DABKA: Where Training Was Done

Dabka is a village situated about 38 km away in Padra Taluka of Baroda District. It has a population of nearly 15,000 people. An alarming 40 per cent of the population live in poverty. The project worker along with other team members surveyed all the villages adapted by ONGC namely Vadu, Mufpur, Karkhadi, Chokari, and Dabka in Padra Taluka.

Village Dabka was selected because of various reasons which were:

- No Government PHC in the village.
- Lady Sarpanch in the village.

- The women were motivated to learn about women's reproductive health.
- Women belonging to the age group of 18-45 years were available for the project.

Health facilities in the area are limited. The few health services that exist focus on family planning and maternal and child health. Pressure to meet contraceptive targets set by the National Family Planning Programme has resulted in poor quality of services. Government assistant nurse-midwives (ANMs) are not properly trained for reproductive tract infections (RTIs). In this area, there are hardly any women doctors. While women's general health is neglected, her reproductive health is even more deplorable. Poverty, women's low status and ignorance contribute to women suffering from a variety of reproductive health problems and high prevalence of reproductive morbidity among women. The above conditions prompted us to conduct an Action Research on Dai Training.

Background of Dais

The Social Status of women is low, female literacy is only 30%. Generally, women's workload in this area is very heavy. Many have to rise at 4-5 a.m. and work throughout the day till 7-8 p.m. The usual work includes farm work, which is backbreaking especially during the harvesting season and household work, which includes collecting firewood, cooking, washing and caring for the children. Due to heavy burden of work and relatively poor diet, most women are malnourished. In this area the total fertility rate is high. Almost 44.5 per cent of birth takes place at home and are attended by traditional birth attendants. Four of them were trained by the Government but the training was negligible. Antenatal care (ANC) is generally very poor and only restricted to tetanus immunization and iron supplementation through government PHC system.

The highlights of demographic and socio-economic characteristics of all the women who attended the Dai training programme are as follows:

- Majority of the women (56%) belonged to the age of 40-50 years.

- Little less than half of them were educated till primary rest of them were illiterate but could read and write their names.
- Majority of the women (69%) were living in nuclear family have 5 or less than 5 members in the family.
- Majority of them had less than 4 children.
- All the women were Hindu by religion and had Gujarati as their mother tongue.
- Majority of the women (67%) of the women reported that they had two or more than two family members working in the family.
- For little less than fifty per cent of the women had monthly income between Rs. 1000 to 1500 per month.
- Majority of the women were engaged in unskilled jobs such as domestic help and farm labour.
- More than 40% of them were living in Kutcha homes but had electricity in their homes but no water connection, so they were using community water tap.
- Treatment of minor illness (80%) of them used home remedies and few only (4%) reported that they go to Bhoova for treatment. All 100% said they go to hospital to seek medical help in case of serious illness.

The Dais in Action

After training, the Dais were given the basic Delivery Kit for attending deliveries, so that they could conduct delivery hygienically and safety. The Dais are to conduct antenatal examinations, identify and refer high-risk cases to the Referral Hospital.

The Dais are also able to examine women internally, diagnose pregnancy and related symptoms. This is no easy task as Dias encounter many barriers to learning, since all of them are not equally fast learners. They have difficulty with the lessons. In most cases, village women are not willing to be examined internally even by the Dai. Dais do make occasional mistake in treatment. But by and large they know the way to safe delivery. The Dai training provided them with a whole new experience. Their roles have expanded from that of a mere attendant and scavenger to a community health worker who provides a range of services to women and children. This would bring new meaning to their lives. Because of the new skills and additional roles given to the Dais, the villagers would give them more respect and recognition. An old woman in the village commented that the Dais have become the first contact for health care of pregnant women. This recognition from the community would significantly enhance the self esteem of the Dais. As a result of this Action project, which was a new experience, the dying tradition of Dai, is being revived Younger women, particularly daughter-in-laws of the Dais who earlier did not see any prospect in this field came for training.

Problems Faced During the Project

1. The place where the training was planned and started initially as it was a open verandah, so young boys and men used to come and gather around the place which was disturbing, so women showed hesitation in coming to attend the training. So the place was shifted to interior of village in one of the village leaders house.
2. When only talk or lecture session were arranged the attendance used to be very thin, to make the sessions more interesting use of more teaching aids were planned and incorporated.
3. Distance was always one of the main constraints as the village Dabka is 38-40 km away from Vadodara and there is no direct link in terms of transport facility.
4. Initially project worker decided to work with all the women of the entire village who were from 18-45 years age. Due to the social stigma attached to this profession only women from Harijan Vas came forward for the training.
5. The topic "Dai Training" is very personal to women's health, so it was very difficult to convince the women to learn about it and so it took little longer time.

6. A major problem during the training programme was irregular attendance. This was checked by planning and using variety of motivational activities and food demonstrations. The motivational activities were selected with dual purpose of providing recreation and education.

CONCLUSION AND SUGGESTIONS

Women patients are usually brought to the hospital when it is an emergency. Poverty makes the situation worse and women and children are the hard hit. Today 80% of health care is in private hands which provide for quality health care for those who have the purchasing power According to the Human Development Balance Sheet of South Asia, 1997, in India there is only one doctor for every 12,500 people, 135 million people are denied access to primary health care. The Report added that 88% of all pregnant women aged between 15 and 45 suffer from anaemia. Research studies have shown a definite link between low socio-economic status and lack of knowledge and utilization of preventive health services. This is the reason that although we have family welfare, safe motherhood and child survival programmes, yet maternal mortality rate continues to be embarrassingly high. As women are unlikely to seek health personnel in time, health personnel must seek them. Women need health care at the door step. More attention to a woman's health needs can prevent the serious problems which undermine her position and capacities. Women are the providers of health care, yet they have little or no control over the priorities of health services, environment or research. The emphasis here should be on direct participation.

Drawbacks of the Rural Health Care System

1. Lack of proper health services due to problem of distances, transportation and communication facilities.
2. Lack of and shortage of supplies of medicines.
3. Non-availability of medical and para medical staff.
4. Doctor and medical staff overburdened with administrative work of completing paper work.

5. Lack of refresher courses of training for 'Dais' who play a very' important role in women's health care.

What Will Work? Suggestions

1. The undergraduate curriculum in the medical colleges for teaching maternal and child health should be reviewed and modified suitably particularly to deal with health problems of women and children in the rural areas.
2. From time to time refresher training on following topics:
   - Health education
   - Preventive health care like ante-natal care, immunization of children, promoting use of preventive equipment like gloves and mask.
   - Referral to large hospitals.
3. Improving women's nutrition through "Shakti Packets".
4. The real challenge before us is to tackle the careless attitude which most women have towards their health needs and nutrition. Too often, especially in rural areas, females eat last and least. This neglect of health needs of women leads to serious problems and in further undermining their position and their capacities, so, there is a need that this practice must be discouraged by convincing them that the women's health is as important as that of other family members.
5. Maternal mortality is a very severe problem, it can be checked to some extent by providing such Dai training at different places under such Action Project.
6. Post Graduate and Undergraduate students can take up assignment and projects for developing Information Education and Communication (IEC) materials related to "Dai training" as people specially in rural areas do not know the complications which can arise during home delivery.
7. Suitable incentives should be offered to make the training acceptable to the Dais.
8. Para-professional and semi-professional workers from the community should be trained to provide simple promoting,

preventive and curative health services needed by the community. Young persons, elementary school teachers, educated and willing house-wives should form part of the pool and these services should be planned to cover the entire country.

9. Conducting Research on :
   (i) Effectiveness of Training of different para medica staff in terms of duration of training.
   (ii) Problems of Dais and other para medical staff in the rural areas.
   (iii) Studies are also required to assess how the trained Dais are performing their roles.
   (iv) Study of logistics and management problems of "Training Programmes".
   (v) More methodological studies are required to evaluate the usefulness of the "Training programmes".
   (vi) Studies into attitudes, beliefs and practice of traditional birth attendants (Dais) should be made to improve upon the training programme now designed for them and to obtain their greater participation in maternity and family planning services.
   (vii) To assess the access of village women to the traditional and modern Reproductive Health Services.

The institutions of higher learning have a very useful and practical role to play. They have genuine contributions to make both in the spheres of policy making and implementation. The university system should undertake evaluation, research and documentation of projects related to women's health. The university system can be more focused in environment building and motivation. The local level bodies, such as Panchayati Raj institutions, political leaders, women's activities and religious leaders should be meaningfully involve in advocacy, motivation and programme implementation. Women are an active part of our work force making up for more than half of world's population. They bear the burden of "paid work" as a part of the work force and "unpaid work" in the house. It is sad to see that development has not benefitted men and women equally. This means that customs, habits and other social traits of the community are to be considered.

The combined demands with the fact that Health of women is a necessary commitment to social development of the country calls for a focused visionary approach to women's health. The attainment and acceleration of our national goals in terms of economic development, strengthening of social infrastructure gender equality, health and education of women is a must.

REFERENCES

Bang R. A., Bang A. *et. al.,* (1989), "High Prevalence of Gynaecological Diseases in Rural Indian Women: Lancet-1 (8629), 85-88.

Baroda, M.S. University of Baroda. WOHTRAC and WSRC. "Workshop Report on Qualitative Research Approaches and Women- Centred Health Care" Baroda : Centre for Operation Research and Training, 1997.

Bhadauria, Mridula (1999), Some Issues of Women's Health. *Social Welfare* Vol. 46, No. 1. April.

Bhadauria, Mridula (1997), Women in India: Some Issues, APH Publishing Corporation, New Delhi.

Black M. (1993), The Health and status of Women-girls and Women, New York UNICEF.

Burisch (1983), Mathias and Edith Marx, Humanising Development Training. Development and Cooperation No. 6, Nov.-Dec.

CHETNA (1993), "A Decade of Health Education", Ahmedabad; Chetna .

CHETNA (1995), "A Workshop on Women and Occupational Health", June 1-3, Ahmedabad, Sardar Patel Institute of Public Administration; Chetna.

CHETNA (1993), "Wah!-Women and Health Training Programme, India", Ahmedabad, Chetna.

CHETNA (1990), "Women's Health Mela: An Innovative Training Approach for Women", 5-7 April 1990. Ahmedabad; Chetna.

Dhanu, A. (2000), Networking for Adolescent Reproductive Health. CHETNA News, Jan.-March.

EPW Research Foundation Poverty Levels in India : Norms, Estimates and Trends, *Economic and Political Weekly,* 28 (34): 748-68. 1993.

Evaluation of Traditional Birth Attendant Training Scheme in India: A Collaboration study New Delhi: National Institute of Health and Family Welfare, 1983.

Florence M. Tadiar, G.R. Malayang and A Baldemore (1998), Her Story. The International Council on Management of Population program, Philippines Oct.

Friedmann, J. (1996), Rethinking Poverty; Empowerment and Citizen's Rights. *International Social Science Journa*l Vol. XLVIII, (2): 161-172.

Gopalan, S. (1995), Fourth World Conference on Women-Country Report, Department of Women and Child Development, Ministry of Human Resource Management.

Khan, M.E. *et. al.,* (1985), "Health Practices in Uttar Pradesh", A Study of Discrimination Against Women. (Working paper no. 45). Baroda: Operation Research Group, p. 44. 1985.

Khan, M.E. et. al., (1990), " Nutrition and Health Practices among the Rural Women-A Case Study of Uttar Pradesh India", (Working paper No. 3), p. 26.

Mahajan P. Mani and Siby K., Josep (1996), "Human Resource Utilization", Musing on an Alternative Development. Pardigm Kurukshetra, Dec., p - 11.

Mittal, D.N. (1993), Women and Education Development Process: University News, 31(3), Sep., p. 3-4.

Ninth Five-Year Plan (1997-2002), Vol. II, Govt. of India, Planning Commission, New Delhi, p. 8-9.

Prasad C. (1994), Training for Agricultural Development: A Basic Functional Area, *Journal of Rural Reconstruction,* 27(1). 1994.

Rodin, J. and Ickovics, J.R. (1990), Women's Health : Review and Research Agenda as we Approach the 21st Century, *American Psychologist,* 45, 1018-34. 1990.

Srinivasan, S. and Prasad P.D. (2000), Reproductive and Child Health Programs and Women's Health-Problems and Prospects, *Social Welfare,* Vol. 47, No. 1.

INDEX

A

Abortion, 98, 112
Abul Kalam, APJ, Former Pres of India, 109
Academy of Medicines, 40
Adil Shah II, 206
Adiyan Women, 119
Age and Sex, 80, 81, 142
Agricultural Technology, 184
AIDS, 147, 148, 150, 154, 157, 158, 167, 169, 170, 172
  Awareness Campaigns, 162
  Cases, 173
  Epidemic, 147
  Infection, 159
  Research, 147
  Socio-Economic Impact of-, 169
  Virus, 149
ALIMCO (Artificial Limb Manufacturing Corp of India), 285
Alleviation of Poverty, 47
Ancient Medicines, 145
Andhra Pradesh, 6, 89
Andhra Pradesh—Tamil Nadu, 88
Anganwadis Centres, 143
ASEAN Countries, 153
ASHRAM Schools, 186
Asian and Pacific Divide of Disabled Persons, 282
Atharvaveda, 195
Attappady Hill Area Dev. Society, 112
Autonomous Development Councils, (ADCs), 103
Ayurveda, 219
Ayurvedic System, 235

B

Balika Samridhi Yojna, 102
Bangladesh, 163, 164
Bar Council of India, 283
Belgium—US, 87
Bhore Committee Report, 319
Bihar—UP, 322
Bihar—Uttar Pradesh, 89, 90
Birth Control, 6, 38
Blindness, 6
BPL (Below Poverty Line), 11, 12
Bride Price, 118
Buddhists, 71
Burma, 159

C

Call Centre Industry, 245

Cancer, 244

Charak, 219

CHCs, (Community Health Centres), 267, 269, 273

Child

- Development Schemes, 94
- Marriage Restraint Act, 55
- Sex Ratio (CSR), 57-59, 64, 67, 70, 76, 79

China, 56, 73, 85, 87, 88, 93, 163

China—Turkey, 92

Chitraka, 235

Christian Missionaries, 60

Commercial Sex Workers (CSWs), 148, 159, 166, 172

Common Minimum Programme, 8

Communicable Diseases, 6

Communication

- Strategies, 29
- Technologies, 280

Community,

- Based Organization Role, 308
- Jain, 71
- Sikh, 70

Cost of Effective Techniques, 5

Cottage Industries, 188

Counseling of Disabled, 310

Criminal Law, 55

Crude Birth Rate (CBR), 86, 87, 88, 280, 281

- Program, 281

Crude Rates, 115

Custodial Rape Cases, 55

D

Dai (s), 319-337

- In Action, 332
- Project, 324
- Teaching Aids, 328
- Training, 325, 329
- Training Program, 331

Dakshin Kannada, 184

Darjeelin, 165, 167

Dependency Clinmate, 262

Devadasi, 75

Developing Countries, 29, 48, 49, 63, 84, 85, 87

Development

- Communication, 29-32, 35, 37, 41-44
- Program, 115
- Strategies, 5

Directive Principles, 54

Disability, 279

Dowry, 79

- Deaths, 55
- Prohibition Act, 55

DPEP (District Primary Education Program), 284

Drug

- Addicted Areas, 167
- Smuggling, 159

E

EAG States (Empowered Action Group States), 4, 6-10, 15, 16
- Bihar, 3
- Chhatisgrh, 3
- Jharkhand, 3
- Madhya Pradesh, 3, 4
- Orissa, 3
- Rajasthan, 3, 4
- Uttar Pradesh, 3, 4
- Uttaranchal, 3

Economic
- Development, 4, 33, 84
- Growth, 4, 5, 173
- Growth and Development, 48
- Structure, 5
- System, 121

Economy, 112, 188, 189

Education, 5, 16, 39, 47, 48, 113, 115, 188
- And Economy, 142
- Female, 118
- Medical, 4
- Sexual Health, 95

Educational
- And Vocational Strategies, 303
- Disturbances, 246

Empowered Action Group (EAG), 3-5

Environmental
- Awareness, 3
- Health Conditions, 12
- Pollution, 49

Epidemic, 147, 159

Equalization Grants, 10

F

Factories Act, 55

Family Planning, 98, 103, 320
- Communication Policy, 31
- Methods, 98
- Programs, 85, 89-92, 94

Family Welfare Program, 30, 32

Female
- Child Mortality Rates, 56
- Empowerment, 113
- Fertility, 71
- Foeticides, 60
- Health worker, 268
- Infanticide, 67, 75
- Literacy, 118
- Mortality, 57

Female-Male Ration (FMR), 54, 56

Fertility, 75, 77, 78, 84-94
- Control, 93
- Decline in India, 88
- Global, 87
- In India, 88
- State-wise, 88

Finance Commission (12th), 10

Food Security, 11

G

GB Pant Institute, 277, 303
Gender
And Development, (GAD), 48
Discrimination, 63
Disparities, 54
Germany, 87
Girl Child, 66, 67, 70, 72, 82, 103
Global Child Sex Ratio, 58, 59
Globalization, 280, 310
And Liberalization, 276
Goa, 89, 158, 159
Golden Triangle
Drug Trail, 159, 167
Zone, 173
Gram Panchayat, 187
Guduchi, 234-242
Gujarat, 59, 72

H

Haryana, 59, 72
Haryana and Punjab, 76
Healing Techniques, 198, 200, 203
Health and Family Planning, 34, 36
Communication, 37
Program, 32, 33
Health and Family Welfare, 42-44
Agencies, 40
Development, 44
Workers, 39
Health
And Indian Women, 50
Care Industry, 19, 20, 23
Communication Structure, 36
Communication, 28
Indicators, 3
Infrastructure, 267
Projects, 6
Scenario Planning in India, 319
Sector Reforms, 7
Workers, 271
Healthcare, 47, 50
Healthcare System, 270
Heart Diseases, 244
Hill Area Development Program, 130
Himachal Pradesh, 59
Hindu Succession Act, 55
HIV, 148-150, 156, 157, 172
Cases in India, 158
Infection, 148, 153, 159, 161, 166, 172
Positive Cases, 176
HIV/AID, 51, 97, 100, 102-104, 145, 147-153, 157, 159, 160, 162, 166, 168, 169, 170, 172-174, 180, 181
Global Scenario, 150-151
South East Asia—Malawi, 151
Awareness Project, 324
High Prevalence States (HPS), 172, 173
Andhra Pradesh, 172

Karnataka, 172
Manipur, 173
Nagaland, 173
Tamil Nadu, 172
Impact of-, 172
Indian Scenario, 152
Infection, 163, 164
HIV/STI, Prevention Project, 162
Hospital Market, 20
Hypertension, 244

I

ICDS (Integrated Child Development Services), 58
IDUs (Injecting Drug Users), 149, 159, 161, 167, 173
Immoral Traffic (Prevention) Act, 55
Indecent Representation of Women (Prohibition) Act, 55
India and
China, 88
South African Economic Summit, 150
India's
Bermuda Triangle, 79
Bermuda Triangle, Punjab-Haryana-Gujarat, 79
Family Planning Program, 78
Fertility Decline, 78
India—China, 85
Indian
Customs, 75
Child Marriage, 75
Dowry, 75
Sati, 75
Widow Marriage, 75
Mass Media, 37
NGOs Engaged in Disabled Sector, 286
Penal Code, 55
System of Medicine, 6
Women, 50, 53, 75
Infant
Mortality, 51, 76, 116
Mortality Rate (IMR), 112
Infection Diseases, 147
Information Technology, 19
Infrastructure Development, 4
Internal/International Migration, 66
International
Organizations, 286
Year of Disabled Persons, 282
Irula, 130-132
Irula Tribe Female Population, 142
Italy, 87
ITDP (Integrated Tribal Dev. Plan), 184, 185

J

Jawar Rojgar Yojna (JRY), 130
Jod Gomat Dargarh, 208
Juvenile Sex Ration (JSR), 54, 59, 61
District-wise Rural Urban Variations, 62
States/Union Territories, 61

K

Kasturba Gandhi Shiksha Scheme, 102
Kerala, 60, 89, 90
  Model of Development, 116
  Population, 110
  Scheduled Tribes, 111
  Scheduled Tribe Population-, 110
  Socio-Economic Development, 89
  Status of Women in-, 109
  Tribal Communities, 111
  Tribal Women in-, 112
  Tribes of-, 110
  Women, 112, 113, 115
Kerala—Tamil Nadu, 90
Kishori Shakti Yojna, 102
Koragas, 189, 190
Kota, 130-132
Kota Tribe Female Population, 142

L

LAMPS, 188
Land Alienation, 189
Leprosy, 6
Less Developed Countries, (LDCs), 91, 92
Liberalization, 310
LIC (Low Income Countries), 16
Life Expectancy, 50, 279
Literacy, 184
  And Education, 54
  Rate, 72, 114
Low Fertility Rates, 115
Low Income States (LIS), 9

M

Madhumeha (Diabetes), 234-238
Madhya Pradesh, 6, 7, 10, 11
Madhya Pradesh and Rajasthan, 7
Madhya Pradesh—Haryana, 89
Magical and Religious Beliefs, 145
Maharashtra, 6, 60
Maharashtra—Nagaland, 153
Manipur, 159
MAOC (Motivational Analysis or Organizational Stress), 257, 259
Marginal Workers, 134
Marriage-cum-Pregnancy Counseling, 104
Marshal Plan in Europe, 47
Mass Communication, 43, 44
  Process, 37
Mass Media, 40, 41, 43, 44
Maternal
  And Child Health (MCH), 320
  Morality, 50
  Mortality Rate, 321, 322
  Mortality Rate, State-Wise, 322
Maternity Benefits Act, 56
MDGs (Millennium Development Goals,), 9

Media, 31
Electronic, 36, 43
Mass Media Tecnology, 31
Print, 36, 43
Traditional, 31
Medical
Care, 35
Judgments, 277
Termination of Pregnancies Act, 55
Migrant Labour, 166
Ministry of
Health and Family Welfare, 3, 6, 36
Information and Broadcasting, 36
Social Justice and Empowerment, 284, 316, 317
Mizoram, 60, 167
Modernization, 47, 310
MRS (Medicare Relief Society), 12
MS University, Baroda, 324
Multipurpose Health Workers, (MPHWS), 270, 272, 273
Muslim Population Growth Rate, 72

N

Nagaland, 159, 167
National
Family Planning Program, 319
Handicapped Council, 283
Institutes for Handicapped, 284-285
Policy on Empowerment of Women, 115
Rural Health Mission (NRHM), 8, 12, 15
Trust for Welfare of Persons, 282
Nepal, 166, 167
Nepal and Bhutan, 163
New Philosophy of Health, 146
NFHS (National Family Health Survey), 11
NGO (Non-Governmental Organizations), 7, 39, 40, 51, 52, 82, 91, 95, 103-105, 174, 184-186, 188, 191, 192, 278, 281, 282, 306, 308, 310, 314, 318
NHP (National Health Policy), 4
Nilgiris Hills (Tamil Nadu), 121, 122, 142
Primitive Tribes, 121, 122
North Bengal, 162, 163, 167
North East States, Bihar, WB, 163
NPP (National Population Policy), 38
NSDP (National Slum Development Program), 14
Nuclear and Joint Families, 122, 123

O

ONGC, 324, 325, 326
Organizational
Climates, 255
Rate Stress (ORS), 257, 259
Stressors, 246
Orissa and Tamil Nadu, 6

P

Pakistan, 73
Panchayats, 39, 40
  Role of-, 190, 191
Panchayat Raj Institutions (PRIs), 38, 310
Paniya, 130, 131, 132
Para Medical Personnel, 35
Para Medicals, 35
Patrineal Kinship System, 79
Persons Living With HIV AIDS, (PLWHA), 174-181
Persons with Disables—Act, 282
Physical Disables and Mental Deficiency, 300
Physically Handicapped, 277
Planning, 4, 7, 34, 48, 191, 278
  Commission, 184
  Developmental, 5
  Socio-Economic Development-, 91
  Strategies, 32
Policy
  Planners, 30
  Recommendations, 316-318
Policy Highlights of Urban Health States, 11
  Of Madhya Pradesh, 11
  Of Rajasthan, 11
  Uttar Pradesh, 13
Political Empowerment, 113
Population, 66, 67, 84-86
  Control, 40, 267
  Female, 67, 126
  Growth, 39, 84, 85, 91
  Growth Rate, 72
  Indian, 28, 319
  Irula, 124
  Policies, 93
  Scheduled Tribes, 110, 111, 114, 183
  Structure, 60
  Tribal, 112
  Urban, 89
Poverty
  Alleviation, 5
    In India, 52
    Strategies, 47, 52
  Rural, 3
  Urban, 3, 11, 15, 16
    Policy Highlights, 14
Pre-Marital Sex, 95, 99
Prevention and Rehabilitation, 35
Primary Health Centres (PHC), 3, 12, 143, 196, 267-269, 271, 272, 320, 328, 330
  System, 320, 331
Primitive Tribal Groups (PTG), 183, 186, 187
  In Karnataka, 183
  Literacy Status, 185
Punjab, 59, 72
  And Gujarat, 78
  And Haryana, 67
Punjab—Uttar Prades, 81

R

Rajasthan, 6, 7, 10, 11

Regional Disparities, 73

Rehabilitation, 276, 279, 281, 282, 303

 Council of India (RCI), 282-284, 314

 Need for Financial Assistance, 304

 Need for Medical Intervention, 204

 Of Disabled, 303-318

 Of Physically an Mentally Disabled, 277

 Policy and Progammes of-, 278

 Problems, 310, 312-316

 Services, 276

 Social, 310

Reproductive and Child Health Program (RCH), 319

 Services, 104

Reproductive Health, 96, 97, 101, 319

Reserve Forests, 165

Rituals, 208, 211

River

 Bhima, 210

 Tungbhadra, 205

Role Stressors, 257-258

Rural Healthcare System, 334

S

SAARC Countries, 153

Saint Doodpher Dargah, 197

SAP (Strategic Action Plan), 7

Saraswati, Sriman Narasimha, 210

Sati, 55

Scheduled Areas, 121

 Administration and Control, 121

Scheduled

 Castes/Tribes, 75

 Tribe Population in India, 121

 Tribes Females, 115

Sectors, Economic and Social, 34

Self-Employed Women Association (SEWA), 52

Self-Help Groups (SHGs), 310

Senior Citizens, 12

Sex

 And Age, 66

 Determination

  Clinics, 60

  Techniques, 79

  Tests, 75, 78

 Ratio in India, 66

 Structure, 67

 Trade, 165

Sexism, 75

Sexual

 And Reproductive Health (SRH), 95

 Health Education, 95

 Health, 96, 97, 101

Sexually Transmitted Diseases (STDs), 95, 100, 161, 166, 172

 Clinics, 157

Shifting Cultivation, 187, 190
Shirisha Plant, Role, 219
Shrine,
Karbibasajja Shrine, 205
Sri Kshetra, 210
Sikhs and Jains, 71
Sikkim, 165
Siliguri, 163, 164
Social
Change, 42
Isolation, 32
Justice, 118
Social
Rehabilitation, 286
Sector, 6
Disease Control, 6
Family Planning Program, 6
Nutrition, 6
Primary Education, 6
Social Welfare Program, 29
Society (ies), 33-35, 42, 48, 50, 52, 53, 66, 67, 73, 109, 145, 147, 195, 234
Indian, 28, 29, 36, 53, 67, 78, 79, 81, 82
Multi-Dimensional, 67
Patriarchal, 79
Socio-Economic
Development, 33, 34, 75, 77, 92
Divide, 7
Plans, 39
Software Technology Park, 245
South Asian Countries, 56
Spain, 87
SPAN (Sub Plan of Action on Nutrition), 15
SSN (Social Safety Net), 6
State Population Policy, 11
Stress, 244, 246, 247, 248
Coping Strategies, 248-249
Organizational, 254, 255
Stroke, 244
Swajal Project, 7
Swasthya Mela, 6

T

Tamil Nadu, 89, 121
And Andhra Pradesh, 153
And Maharashtra, 158
Terrorism, 158
Total Fertility Rate (TFR), 86, 87, 93, 268
Tourism, 165
Traditional
Healers, 197, 203, 204
Of Badami (Bijapur), 202
Of Melapur, 203
Of Yelavatti, 200
Healing Centres, 195
Hindu Family, 67
Water Resources, 132
Tribal
Cooperative Marketing Dev. Federation of India, 188
Development, 183

Development Scheme, 186
Female Labourers, 116
Groups, 112, 183, 184, 187, 189, 191
Displacement of-, 191
Societies, 118
Women, 112, 113
Empowerment Project, 188
of Kerala, 118
Tribes, 118,
Adiyan, 118
Colanaiken, 118
Educational Status, 128
Irulas, 122, 123, 133, 134, 136-138, 142, 143
Jenukuruba, 184
Kattunaiken, 118
Koraga, 118, 184
Kotas, 12, 126-128, 133, 134, 136-138142, 143
Kurumba, 118
Literacy Status, 128
Irula, 128
Kota, 128
Paniya, 128
Toda, 128
Marital Status, 127
Occupational Status, 134
Of India, 118
Of Kerala, 113
Paniyas, 122, 124, 126, 128, 133, 134, 136-138, 142, 143
Primitive, 110, 142, 184
Social Conditions, 129
Todas, 122, 124, 134, 136-138, 142, 143
Tribes-wise Asset Values, 139
Tripura, 60

U

UHPs (Urban Health Programmes), 4
UN (United Nations), 6, 84, 85, 282
Decade of Disabled Persons, 282
Development Program, 7
Development Studies, 88
Program on HIV/AIDS, 150
Sanctions, 59
UNICEF, 81
UPA Government, 8
Urban
Population, 14
Slum Health Projects, 4
US, 47, 73
Uttar Pradesh, 6, 7, 10, 11, 72, 271
Uttar Pradesh, Bihar—Rajathan, 9
Uttar Pradessh, Madhya Pradesh and Rajathan, 15
VAMBAY (Valmiki Ambedkar Awas Yojna), 14

V

Vocational Training, 308
Voluntary Counseling and Testing Centres, (VCTC), 174

W

Water Crisis, 11

Wayanad (Kerala), 109, 112, 113

  Agricultural Labour, 116

  Plural Society, 119

WHO (World Health Organization), 6, 145, 146, 150, 278, 280

Women

  Constitutional Provisions for-, 55

  Emancipation of-, 116

  Empowerment, 11, 109

  In Development Process, 48

  In Development, (WID), 48

  Related Legislations, 55

  Socio-Economic Status of-, 50

Women's

  Educational Attainments, 320

  Health in India, 47

  Health Status, 319

  Health, 49, 50

World

  Bank, 6, 66

  Economic Forum, 113

  Health Assessment, 145

  Population, 84, 85, 87

  War II, 47